The Trouble With Words

A Commonplace Book

***

Maxine Ruvinsky

The Trouble With Words: A Commonplace Book

Cover Design: Lulu Conchita Galway
Printed in Canada

TABLE OF CONTENTS

Chapter 1

Discovering the Commonplace Book

I'd been doing it for decades before I discovered there's a name for the practice. It's a hard habit to break, since it grows only more compelling with time and repetition. It's still relevant, though, and still favoured by those enamoured of the printed word. It's called keeping a commonplace book.

The practice consists of copying passages from your reading into personal notebooks, sometimes along with your written responses. Devotees of the word have been doing it for centuries, and they're doing it still. What I had always imagined was a personal quirk, turns out to be a time-honoured tradition and even, among writers, a sort of method.

I was still commonplacing when I retired from my university teaching post and came home to Montreal, still copying out favourite excerpts and responding copiously with words of my own. But now I had a name for the practice, and now I knew I was not alone in the near-obsession. Now I understood the history behind the commonplacing habit. I was emboldened.

Still enamoured of the printed word, still awash in a sprawling love of language, I was fuelled by a newly naïve optimism (is there any other kind?). I felt armed with a name and a sort-of-a-plan for what to do with all that linguistic energy: I would write my own commonplace book.

***

I left home in 1999 to teach at a small B.C. university's just-founded School of Journalism. I wanted to practise and profess free expression, to make for my aspiring students a difference that would count. I believe I did. After years of teaching, my idealism was chastened, not by the students (always the best part of the job), but by the ever-shifting politics. Whoever said that the venality of academic politics comes from the low stakes involved spoke the truth. I never stopped writing, though, and if my idealism is subdued, at least now it has teeth.

It wasn't until the spring of 2015 that serendipity kicked in and I chanced upon the term "commonplace book." In the months of rapt investigation that followed, I learned that an obsession with books and note-taking long precedes me. And while the term "commonplacing" remains unfamiliar to most, the practice is in fact widely shared. And so it has been for centuries, by book lovers and especially by writers (some famous, others not so much).

The only difference between commonplace books kept by readers and those kept by writers seems to be that readers just copy into their notebooks the bits they find they like and want to remember. Writers, on the other hand, use commonplacing as prompt (they respond with their own writing to the excerpts they preserve) and as quarry (they mine their notebooks for work they intend to publish). In fact, I've never known a writer who doesn't engage in some form of commonplacing. That got me to thinking.

Upon the return to Montreal in 2015, I was determined to concentrate on that elusive beast: my own writing. I had by this time published several books with Oxford University Press (the first of these was a grammar book, now in its third edition, a voice-rich, plain-speaking, teach-yourself text that turned out to be a runaway bestseller—who knew?). At home in Montreal, in a somewhat cocky email to the book's supervising editor, I declined (politely, I thought) to write a fourth edition. I noted that I was so happy writing what and how I wanted, that the idea of a fourth edition left me cold.

I note here that I do not mean to disparage the art and practice of scholarship; quite the contrary, I see scholarship as a noble and critically important part of the eternal human quest for knowledge (and perchance wisdom), one not displaced by modern electronic technologies but made even more relevant in the face of these. Researching the history of the commonplace book, I gained even greater respect for scholars. I saw how important their combined efforts are in preserving records that might otherwise be lost to the inquiring minds of successive generations.

My discovery of commonplacing had me buzzing with new ideas—and old ideas too—about current writing habits and those of bygone centuries.

Years before learning about commonplace books, I had been impressed with something Virginia Woolf wrote about what makes great writers great: not that they are without fault or weakness or error (human after all), but that great writers had managed to master their own perspective. I remember thinking: okay, that's it, that is what comes across in memorable writing, in the kind of passages that provoke you to write them down so you can revisit them, and that's what all my lifelong copying and studying and scribbling was about, too: an attempt to master my own perspective, to gain the strength and peace of mind of knowing my own convictions to the very core.

This is finally what gives any writing that has it the force of conviction. The mastered personal perspective is like the ground from which a writer may ascend (and without which a writer is likely to stay stuck, rooted to ground, poised perhaps, but not for take-off).

***

So there I was, with a name and a sort-of-a-plan. First, I would gather my commonplacing quotations and notes on the subject of language in a protofile called The Trouble With Words. I wanted to understand how words make meaning when words in themselves have no stable meanings, and no meanings at all without context. I wanted to figure how language computes. I wanted two other things: to integrate the three major perspectives or voices of my own writing life (journalistic, scholarly, and personal), and to address myself to language lovers of all ages, especially those who have always wanted to write but never quite mustered the courage.

To begin, I wouldn't concern myself with the ritual outline or the standard proposal or the search for an agent. I would write with only the thinnest notion of a theme. I wouldn't even think about trying to publish. I'd just let it rip and see where the writing took me. It would be glorious and freeing and give me in my senior solitude a new lease on life (hey, let the clichés roll). And for a while, it really was that satisfying (not to mention replete with clichés).

I spent the next several years in outright and unabashed reading gluttony, sometimes spending whole days taking notes (not writing, you see) with an encyclopedic passion, responding to the notes I was taking, in childlike abandon, glorying in the disorganized profusion.

I believed then that I would remain completely happy writing for myself and for love in obscurity for the rest of my days. How grand is this, I congratulated myself: no more armies of editors, no more mealy-mouthed reviewers, no more writing by committee, and especially no more defending myself against academic editors whose main purpose, despite their welcome expertise, appeared to be an eerily concerted mission to excise voice wherever they found it. Plus, I further figured, who says I need to publish? Reading is so much easier, so much less exacting, than writing, especially writing for publication—what could go wrong?

Alas, I miscalculated. After several years spent happy as an unfettered child, reading and taking copious notes on volume after volume (including the six months spent on the algebra I suddenly remembered I'd loved in high school so long ago), submitting fully to my various intellectual passions without feeling in the least constrained to make any kind of sales sense—well, dear reader, I didn't see it coming, but yes, the enchantment began to fade.

I was surprised (nonplussed really) to find myself increasingly dispirited and in the grip of a brand-new reader/writer double bind: either I admired the book I was reading and mining with such fervour (for its erudition, its insight, its style, or all of those) that my own urge to write was paralyzed; or I found such fault, such inadequacy, that even my standby book love took a disabling hit. My urge to write was only slightly (that is to say not definitively, not enough comfortably) overpowered by my resistance, however cleverly disguised.

I was stuck.

Though reading instead of writing and then writing about my reading had worked for a nice while, it no longer satisfied my pressing need, for as long as I can remember, for both practices, both reading and writing, and for the stream of words to move between the worlds, the interior one and the one outside my skin.

So I stopped reading and taking notes in what I had always called my "study notebooks" (one of the ways I had of tricking myself into writing was to pretend I was just studying). I retreated into the writing of morning pages, meant for no one but myself, noisy with multi-voiced arguments around the conference table of my mind. But in addition to the stream-of-consciousness, burn-off-the-excess, what-do-I-have-to-do-today, run-on verbiage typical of my journal writing in morning pages, I found myself (somewhat to my horror) writing about writing again, and worse, writing about writing my commonplace book, and worst of all, planning the various ways and means I would enlist to get it done.

At the same time, and in equal measure, as the image of my awareness emerged like a photograph in the (pre-computer) developing trays of the old-style photographic darkroom, so too did my panic increase. My desperation, no longer subterranean, urged a search for reasons to take myself off the hook of another book. Of course part of me knew it was a battle I was bound to lose. After so many years of writing and resisting writing, I had at last learned that once I start mentally strategizing over a book project, there is no escape and no peace until I submit.

It's always been this way with me and writing. As soon as I form the intention to write (for other people, for publication, to banish the thinking safely circling inside me to the cold of the real world outside), I remember: I don't actually *like* to write.

The entire business suddenly seemed like so much avoidance on steroids. I was forced to face the truth: this wasn't just the usual resistance to getting down to work, this was a whole-life fork in the old road (the kind I knew would lead to only more forks in the road, should I manage to gather my courage enough to take the first step and submit to the book that was stalking me without mercy). Toni Morrison was right when she said there comes a time when you finally can't find anywhere the book you're hoping for and looking for, the one you really need to read right now. That's the time you have to admit that the book you seek is the one you must write yourself. For this writer, that time had come. (The sixteenth century's Michel de Montaigne said: "If I knew my own mind I would not make essays. I would make decisions."[1] I can relate to that.)

So I forced myself to begin with no plan in sight. Even then, I wasn't too much bothered by not knowing where the book would take me—after all, I rationalized, how could I know what I was going to say before I'd said it?[2] Deep down, was I secretly hoping the book idea would be brutally rejected outright, such that I could then retreat into a safely virtuous, even tragically wounded, silence?

But silence, tragically wounded or otherwise, has never been my style.

When the going got rough, I forced myself to persevere. I quit my evasive half-measures and my stalling and I took the plunge. I suit-cased the trepidation, wrote a proposal, and met with an agent recommended by a friend. The agent liked the proposal and paid for lunch. He cut to the point without missing a beat: "Why not write a how-to-write-your-own-commonplace-book?" he suggested. "I *know* I can sell *that*."

Bad advice. It screwed me up for several months, as I bravely soldiered on, trying to write for a market instead of from the overflowing heart/mind. In the end, angels rushed in and the truth did out. Long story short: I blew off the agent and embraced the book-to-be, dollar consequences be damned.

I could—I would—embrace a labour of love for all the unsung intellects, for readers and writers young and old and undeclared, for all the devoted members of—if not the Republic of Letters—at least for the minions of the unofficial Reading-and-Writing-Bug Club.

One problem remained: I didn't actually know how to use commonplacing as writing method, how to turn that long stretch of notebooks into a little book of essays on language, a subject so central to humanity that it has fascinated experts and non-experts alike for centuries.

***

After months of agonizing false starts, I came, at least and at last, to know my own mind. The book I envisioned might never find a publisher, but what I could learn from writing it was mine forever. I was confident in my ability to learn and I self-counselled courage: I could teach myself anything. After all, hadn't I taught myself to read music? Hadn't I finished my doctoral course prerequisites by working the night shifts at the Montreal bureau of the Canadian Press? Hadn't I always loved an intellectual challenge and risen to meet it? Three times, yes. So I figured I could indeed learn how to write essays the commonplace way, and having lived to tell the tale, share the learning with all who read and write.

Yes, I decided, on less sober second thought, the idea for a book based on commonplacing notes admirably withstood scrutiny. If I wrote such a book, I could learn how by doing, and because the learning would be fresh and intriguing for me, its relating would likely prove readable and useful. A kind of self-searching honesty (required to write a good book) would be bound to lead to insight that could be shared. This in turn might lead to greater ease in the reading/writing process. It might even invite gifts of wisdom heretofore unimagined in this homestretch of the journey of my life.

And then all those notebooks, which had seemed too daunting to sort out, would now seem instead to await my reinvigorated perusal with metaphorically open arms. It occurred to me that my second readings would have a purpose, a basic format—maybe even a bona fide plan—and who knows but that the whole process might give rise to new ideas for more books after that, and each one would be easier to complete than the one before, and I would finally overcome the struggle inherent in writing!

This is what I call the just-post-conception manic phase of my writing bug (before any wheels have fallen off, but only because there are not yet any wheels attached, nor anything solid to attach them to).

The solution came to me in a series of flashes: I would keep working on the passages from my notebooks that addressed "the trouble with words," and then craft the excerpts and my responses into a series of essays on language. I would discover how to use commonplacing as writing method in the process of using it to write the book.

I call this the phase of enabling calm just before the search for a proper vehicle and the wheels of words must begin.

Even then, the cautious urgings of a second self persisted: "Let's just read a thousand more books and take copious notes, and maybe then we can write."

Just another form, virtuous perhaps, elaborate for sure, but still just another form, of avoidance.

What finally brought me beyond the brink of beginning was remembering that writing, despite the inherent struggle (apparently insuperable), is still the only thing I do, the only practice I maintain, the only activity in which I engage on a daily basis, during which there is no part of me held back or in abeyance, counting off the time, standing just behind me, peering over my shoulder, saying: Uh, excuse me, but shouldn't we really be doing something else?

Provoked by that oh-so-superior-almost-sneering voice, I rebelled, I talked back. Look, I said: all I really need to do is sketch an actual plan, however fledgling, and then execute it. But how exactly?

Answers emerged aplenty as I continued to write, seeking just the right words in exactly the right order, envisioning the form and content that would honour my original vision. I learned that commonplacing by any other name works as prompt and provocation (eliciting reader response), and as method: by means of written response, the reader becomes a writer. In fact, I'd been commonplacing for decades—and even using it as basic writing method—long before I chanced on a name for the centuries-old practice.

Looking back, it's not a stretch to say I learned to write the commonplace way, and that I am in this regard hardly alone, and more, in decidedly good company.

Chapter 2

What's a Commonplace Book? (And Some Reasons to Write Your Own)

If in your reading you have come across memorable passages, you may have marked them somehow, with a pencil in the margin of the text or perhaps only by turning down the corner of the page, intending to return sometime and reflect on the words. This would have left you with a collection of beat-up books, pages dog-eared and pencil-smeared, from which you would have profited little. If you did return later to the noted words, time likely would have dimmed your memory of why you marked the passage in the first place. If, on the other hand, you bothered to copy the passage down in a notebook of your own, and went a little further by adding to the excerpt reflections of your own, you were creating a commonplace book.

Welcome to the unofficial club: you are in some excellent, time-honoured company.

The fact is that writers (and not only writers) have been keeping commonplace books for centuries. Philosophers and scientists, doctors and lawyers, teachers and students, people in business and people in the arts—indeed thinkers of every description throughout time—kept commonplace books. They kept them to remember and revisit the words of their favourite authors, or in the service of mastering a discipline, or to keep track of accounts. Writers kept them, and sometimes published them, in order to mine the collected insights for other works. Some commonplace books served humbler purposes, entirely without literary aspiration. For example, homemakers kept commonplace books for storing practical information in household management, including everything from recipes to ownership records. The famous seventeenth-century philosopher John Locke may have got his idea for a new method of commonplacing from the way his mother Agnes organized her own notebooks.[1]

Commonplace books were often shared within the family and handed down through the generations. The practice of commonplacing was so widely observed that in some cases a second person would continue writing in a notebook someone else had begun, so as not to waste paper, and for purposes of his or her own. While traditional commonplace books included transcribed quotations and reflections (both appreciative and argumentative), they usually contained as well a range of other materials (like jokes and anecdotes, diagrams and calculations, rumours and resolutions), materials never intended for publication.

Since antiquity, the commonplace book has been recognized as an effective rhetorical and educational tool. The ancient practice enjoyed a revival during the European Renaissance as scholars sought to retrieve the fruits of classical learning for their own age. The commonplace book then was a foundation of the educational system. It was used to teach students everything from basic Latin to advanced rhetoric, to train young people for the professions (law, medicine, and later, science), and in the composition of professional texts that synthesized information (such as legal case books, for instance). As a standard tool for organizing and retrieving information, it was as common as today's ubiquitous cell phones and online reference works.

From 1500 on, the commonplace method was the central technique of Western education.[2] Unlike the classical Greeks, leading Renaissance humanists did not worry that transcribing quotations would weaken the capacity to remember; indeed, they expected the practice to strengthen memory. The copying was meant, however, to spark reflection and independent thought, not to substitute for it. And though the thematic headings would change with the times and the field of study, the commonplace book itself remained routine practice among writers and educators as the way to preserve and organize knowledge.

General consensus puts the heyday of the commonplace book in the early modern period of European history (roughly 1500 to 1800), and throughout this period, the practice was widely embraced. These were centuries of radical change: expanding populations, increasing urbanization, challenges to religious authority, and rapid change in the English language itself (with the number of English words doubling between 1500 and 1650, many of them borrowed from Greek and Latin).

All the canonical greats of early modernity, including Montaigne, the so-called father of the personal essay, kept commonplace books. In that span of three centuries, everyone with intellectual ambitions, virtually everyone who was anyone (and many who weren't) kept a commonplace book. The roster of the Renaissance and early modern canon includes names well known by students of the humanities and the sciences alike. Back then, there was no strict demarcation of these disciplines. (C. P. Snow didn't write his famous piece on the "two cultures" until 1959.) The list of famous commonplacers includes virtual icons like the Italian Renaissance artist and polymath Leonardo da Vinci in the fifteenth century, the English philosopher and statesman Francis Bacon in the sixteenth, and the still celebrated mathematician Isaac Newton in the seventeenth.

The tradition was maintained through the eighteenth and nineteenth centuries: famous white males who kept commonplace books include American "founding father" Benjamin Franklin and English naturalist Charles Darwin. Mark Twain did it. So did Thomas Hardy. Jonathan Swift, in his *Letter of Advice to a Young Poet*, insisted on the importance for poets of keeping a commonplace book. American teacher and writer Bronson Alcott called the practice "an informal schooling for authors" that promised "the keys of great authorship."[3] Interest in the commonplace tradition persisted among authors of the nineteenth century. Emerson and Thoreau were taught how to keep a commonplace book at Harvard University. George Eliot, one of the few women writers to make it into the canon, kept a series of commonplace books that she mined for her novels. Through much of the early twentieth century, commonplacing as an intellectual aid remained in widespread use. As late as the mid-twentieth century, the term "commonplace book" was still current in some circles and the method was still was practised by writers (such as America's Ernest Hemingway and England's E. M. Forster). Later in the twentieth century, Canada's own Michael Ondaatje made reference to the commonplace book in his 1992 novel *The English Patient* (the narrator of this story carries with him copy of *The Histories* by Herodotus, which he treats as a commonplace book, adding his own comments and gluing in pages from other books).

Neither was the practice limited to writers. American filmmaker Frank Capra, English actor Alec Guinness, and Spanish painter Pablo Picasso also kept commonplace books. There are doubtless many more whose names don't appear in any Who's Who, people who kept commonplace books in past centuries, and some who still do keep them, perhaps calling their notebooks by other names.

If you regard the commonplace book as a variety of "book learning," its roots go almost as far back as the origins of writing itself, back to classical Greece, when Socrates, who didn't write, and his student Plato, who did, both worried that the new-fangled technology would in the long run injure memory. Aristotle, Plato's student, cast aside worry and wrote volumes, and his influence lasted for centuries on just about every subject that remains a subject, despite that his once solid authority is today more often challenged than marshaled. According to many critics, Aristotle, despite his proto-scientific contributions, was badly mistaken on several fronts.

> "... his errors have had enduring harmful effects. His doctrines of natural inferiority and female inferiority, respectively, justified or helped to justify slavery and the inequality of the sexes until our own time. His great authority also helped to defend tyranny, in the name of 'benevolent' despotism, and his doctrine of ethnic inferiority helped to justify racism. All of these errors—for that is what they are—might have endured without Aristotle. But it would have been harder to justify them."[4]

Throughout its history, the commonplace book served as spur to independent thought; it stood to challenge and even to undermine established authority as much as it did to preserve the knowledge of old. Innovators in every field have always progressed by questioning received knowledge, not by worshipping at its fount. Commonplace books amount to important historical documents; they often reveal more about social attitudes than do official documents or authoritative tomes. The word "history" itself comes from the Greek, historia; it means inquiring into the past through the study of its documents. Without documents, we have only pre-history.

Commonplace books existed before single sheets were bound into codices, before the advent of moveable type or affordable paper, before manuscripts and typewriters, and way long before the coming of the digital age, with its masses of information available for manipulating at a click. Long before computers made almost universally available the opportunity to create and store information, promising a potential democratization of learning barely imaginable before their advent—there was the commonplace book. In fact, we have come so far so quickly in information technology that it's hard to think of published books (or the notebooks that must have preceded them) as technology. Back in the 1940s the word "computer" still referred to a human being performing calculations and the term "automatic computers" was reserved to distinguish machine computers from human ones.

To this day, the commonplace book enjoys periodic revival and attention among some scholars, among book writers and readers, and even among book-loving bloggers. The practice (if not the publication) of the commonplace book persists in today's relentlessly digital landscape. And yet in the gleaming twenty-first century, the commonplace book is little remembered. That seems a pity, because from my perspective, the commonplace book is more than an ancient information technology: it represents a prototypical form of knowledge creation, a way of reading and thinking and writing, with barely discernible seams.

***

Benét's Reader's Encyclopedia gives the commonplace book only a few lines: "a notebook of quotations, ideas, words, and phrases, collected and often classified according to subject matter"; such notebooks "are used for reference, as a storage place for thoughts, or as a collected miscellany of arguments on any given theme."[5] An old dictionary puts it more plainly, blithely incorporating its gender bias: "a book into which a person copies other men's writings or sayings which strike him as worth collecting."[6]

Pretty straightforward if broad, it would seem, but scratch the surface of a definition and you discover divergent interpretations, beginning with an august dictionary's own. The Concise Oxford Dictionary defines the word "commonplace" as an adjective, to mean unoriginal or trite; as a noun, to refer to an everyday saying or pedestrian topic of conversation, or even, without the put-down, as a general truth. Finally, the word refers to a notable passage copied into a commonplace book.[7] This last appears to avoid a disparaging tone, but it also avoids the conundrum of potential meaning inherent in the word "notable." When does a notable passage once regarded as a general truth or universal gem of wisdom become on the one hand a contested fact or a challenged assumption, and on the other, a cliché? Those dead metaphors your teachers advised you against writing must once have lived, and many phrases of old and noble ancestry include countless ones coined by Shakespeare, now common to the modern lexicon, with nary a nod to the Bard.

The interpretation of the term "commonplace" in "commonplace book" is a matter of apparent confusion and contention. According to some, the term refers simply to the practice of keeping the quotations you want to preserve in a common (same) place; others trace the reference to the nature of the quotations—writings and sayings that have become so common, so well-known and accepted as general truths (such as Bible excerpts), that readers are assumed to be familiar with them even if they cannot supply a precise chapter-and-verse reference. Still others believe that the term refers to those who kept commonplace books as people of no particular note, that is, general readers (not experts or specialists), who kept commonplace books for personal reasons without thought to publication. The first two interpretations make no reference to the keeper's social status, and the third evaluates only mildly.

But if you take the word "common" on its own (not as part of "commonplace"), the business of status is clearly delineated (if not explicated). The ambiguity is not a matter of simple differences of agreement or context, but inheres in the word itself. The Oxford dictionary illustrates the word, used as an adjective, with the following phrases: to mean "widespread" (a common mistake, a common soldier, and the common people); to mean "shared" (common knowledge, common land). The third definition is preceded by a tag that indicates its particular reference to social class, thus: "derog. low-class; vulgar; inferior (a common little man)." It's interesting how a sniff of derision stubbornly clings to the tag even in its supposedly non-derogatory meanings within dictionaries. The same holds for many other uses and derivations of the word (for instance, "common errors" but not "common talents," even though the latter, in my teaching experience, is at least as common as the former). This is just what I mean by the phrase "the trouble with words," trouble that begins with any attempt to use words to come to grips with a given term, especially one as removed from contemporary culture as the commonplace book.

Of course, matters of linguistic interpretation are matters ever debatable. Still, even without taking a position on matters of meaning or of relative quality or status, uncertainty prevails with respect to the supposedly simpler task of nailing down the history of the commonplace book. To answer apparently simple questions gets complicated: the when and where of the very first commonplace books and the context of their disappearance; how changes in technology affected the format of a commonplace book and, more broadly, how such books were actually used by people during the years of their prominence from the Renaissance into the nineteenth and even early-twentieth century. None of these issues—tangled strands of a skein—can be taken separately, and yet without trying to separate them, there is no way to begin. (I deal in depth in the next chapter with "the trouble with words"; but for now, having briefly entered the territory of trouble, and in the interests of a next paragraph, I now make an opportune exit.)

According to a majority of cultural historians, the commonplace book had ancient and medieval antecedents, reached a peak in the late Renaissance, was still widely practised in the nineteenth century, and began its decline in the twentieth. Others locate the loss of the commonplacing habit in the nineteenth century instead of the twentieth;[8] still others place it as early as the seventeenth.[9] Some suggest it was the eighteenth-century rise of the novel that presaged the decline of commonplacing.[10] Though its form and influence changed over time (especially with once-new technologies like print), still the commonplace book continued to reflect an older tradition rooted in the substantially oral culture of antiquity and Renaissance humanism.

In a 2005 exhibit at the University of Chicago on the history of the book, readers of the 1500s and 1600s are portrayed as full participants in the production of meaning, not simply passive imbibers of words.[11] The items on display came from a wide range of disciplines: legal and medical texts, educational, literary and religious books, practical manuals and how-to books on everything from cooking and carving to measuring and memorizing.

The way a commonplace book was arranged (usually under subject headings) represented a summary of its major themes and a model for organizing information—a kind of window into the early modern mindset, a time when reading and writing were regarded as two sides of the coin of knowledge creation.

By "appropriating" the words of others in collecting quotations, and by supplementing and re-organizing these extracts for personal use, the keeper of the commonplace book revealed the nature of reading itself as a kind of appropriation—not in the pejorative sense of improper borrowing or use of cultural references from outside the writer's group identity, but appropriation in the sense of learning, of making knowledge one's own. To appropriate can mean "to take possession of, especially without authority" (as the verb is often understood in contemporary usage), but it can also mean "to devote (money, etc.) to special purposes,"—a meaning suggestive of behaviour not necessarily improper and perhaps even laudatory, for example to appropriate government monies and means to save people from starvation.

If definitions differ, interpretations diverge even more, sometimes radically. For example, while the commonplace book was basically a reading journal, the keepers of such journals often included information garnered elsewhere: from lectures or conversations as well as from text, and from an assortment of extraneous materials, such as anecdotes, practical reminders, recipes, jokes, and more. The practice was informal, just as those of us who still use pencils might use them to add reminders to spare paper or a small note pad or even to the inside cover or blank page in a paperback book, the kind you travel with so as not to be left without reading material while you wait for a ride or an appointment.

Some versions stressed the addition of the commonplacer's own annotations, while others, like the ones you see today online, do away entirely with annotations of any sort, (advising neither reflections on the quoted passages nor reflections extraneous to them); these define the practice as one of collecting quotations, not by transcribing them into a handwritten notebook, but rather by "downloading" text: "cutting and pasting" words from one electronic page to another. I remember how amazed my journalism students were when I explained that the terms "cut" and "paste" at the top of their word processing screens referred in "olden" times—*my times*—to a process of actually cutting paragraphs or sentences from one draft on cheap yellow paper to paste them into another, so as to avoid having to retype the whole page. It must have seemed to them crazy labour intensive, even primitive—as indeed it does to me now—this change from typewriter to computer having occurred within the span of my own single writing life.

Obviously, copying electronic text from one place to another is much faster than copying by hand, especially if you dispense with annotations. Such method is, however, antithetical to my perspective and purpose: the commonplace book as an intellectual tool.

Whether you look to past or future, the practice of commonplacing, with respect to changing technologies and social attitudes, is like a dance of cause and effect, the one forever becoming the other in a social synthesis with multiple fault lines. In short, the history of the commonplace book is convoluted: sorting it out entails analyzing changes not just in technologies (from parchment to computer screen) but also in social contexts and in competing interpretations of their meanings. Finally, in terms of purpose and significance, while some dismiss the commonplace book as an outdated "clearinghouse" for information, others deem it an important early method of preserving knowledge, like a prototypical encyclopedia meant for personal use.

Some scholars suggest that the personal diary preceded the commonplace book; others, that the diary itself evolved from the ship's log of sea-going exploration. The diary and the commonplace book are sometimes treated as a single phenomenon. In a passage lauding the commonplace book, a nineteenth-century writer and teacher simply conflated the terms, implying that the one includes the other. He wrote that "if we had a detailed record of works" by noted writers, we would see how large was "their indebtedness to their diary and commonplaces."[12]

I distinguish the commonplace book from the personal diary: the latter is chronological and introspective, doesn't rely on quotations, and deals in fairly intimate ramblings not generally meant for publication, though those of the famous may well come to the attention of publishers. In some ways, the two forms are closely related. While most diaries don't necessarily discuss the diarist's reading, some diaries do, especially if the diarist is a writer. Virginia Woolf extolled the virtues of the commonplace book but never published her own, though some of her nonfiction prose does reflect on her reading and writing.[13] The closest we have to a proper commonplace book are excerpts from her notebooks, edited and published posthumously by her husband, Leonard Woolf, as *A Writer's Diary: Being Extracts from the Diaries of Virginia Woolf.*[14]

Some published commonplace books clearly favour the chosen excerpts over the writer's annotations. W. H. Auden's *A Certain World: A Commonplace Book* is a case in point: the book contains relatively few additions by the author to the writing he chose to reproduce. It reveals almost nothing of how Auden's chosen excerpts relate to his life or even his thinking (though he was not otherwise reticent about the latter). According to one reviewer: "He was becoming a 1930s English high-brow version of Bob Dylan in the early 1960s—the apparent voice of a leftish generation."[15] He didn't need the publicity—Auden was already a famous poet long before he published his commonplace book in 1970. In fact, he had written in the foreword to *A Certain World* of his preference for privacy. He didn't like the idea of editors having access to his personal writing, and perhaps he agreed to publish a commonplace book in part to prevent more searching intrusions into his private papers after his death. In the foreword to *A Certain World*, Auden wrote the following:

> "Biographies of writers, whether written by others or themselves, are always superfluous and usually in bad taste. A writer is a maker, not a man of action. To be sure, some, in a sense all, of his works are transmutations of his personal experiences, but no knowledge of the raw ingredients will explain the peculiar flavour of the verbal dishes he invites the public to taste: his private life is, or should be, of no concern to anybody except himself, his family and his friends."

The commonplace book differs as well from scrapbooks, in which people collect clippings but don't usually add their own written responses. Some scholars regard the scrapbook as a later iteration of the handwritten notebook, once printing technology allowed for the clipping of items from newspapers and other printed matter instead of labouring to transcribe them.

One notable source makes the case for the scrapbook, not as a replacement or remediation of the commonplace book, but as a milestone in itself, a remarkable populist advance. In her book *Writing with Scissors: American Scrapbooks from the Civil War to the Harlem Renaissance*, Ellen Gruber Garvey notes that these scrapbooks did often include written annotations, and she argues that they thus amounted to a special kind of writing. She suggested that by cutting items from newspapers and pasting them into scrapbooks, people got in on the act of history, creating records from a particular viewpoint. She, too, compared these scrapbooks of 150 years ago to today's digital world, calling them "the ancestors of Google and blogging"—democratic means that allowed people to create their own archives.

From my perspective, what's more important than iterations in form, more important than diaries or newspaper clippings or even electronic notebooks, is precisely the evoking and recording of reader response—because the one thing that all precursors, variations, and reiterations of the commonplace book have in common is the practitioner's belief that the quoted material is worth preserving—and worthy too, if the keeper annotates, of reflection and response.

In other words: the annotations are the thing. What distinguishes the commonplace book from other forms is precisely its addition of the writer's own thoughts and responses, a notebook seen not only as knowledge to be recorded and preserved, but also and more importantly, as a record of one's own evolving thought. (To acquire or remember codified knowledge, one has only to consult existing reference works, but the recovery of one's own earlier thinking and memories—one's prior selves—cannot be found in any reference work but one's own.)

All writing vehicles, from handwritten diaries to computer programs, may indeed encourage writing (and especially the sometimes barely perceptible move from reading to writing), but none does so as well or as surely as the commonplace book, despite its low-tech face. A notebook and a pen (or their electronic equivalents) can easily be carried on one's person, available to work with almost anywhere. You don't see people writing in paper notebooks as often you did when I was young, but you still see them "writing" by clicking the keyboards and staring at the screens of their electronic devices, and you see this basically everywhere, from cafés to airports.

Snapshots in the Life and Times of the Commonplace Book

The Dutch Renaissance humanist Desiderius Erasmus is among the first to have taught the commonplace method in his rhetoric textbook *De Copia*. The text stressed the importance of the art of note-taking, an emphasis that was maintained throughout the early modern period, with the commonplace book as the standard method. Like others of his era, Erasmus urged the commonplace method for the acquisition of knowledge, and educated people of the time routinely carried notebooks for the purpose. When *De Copia* was published in 1512 it was widely read, the way a bestselling how-to-write book is today. *De Copia* stressed taking quotations from existing texts not for posterity, but for practical purposes: to use them by rewriting them and incorporating the result into new texts of one's own.

The commonplace method helped people to read in a focused way, both to understand what they read and to improve their writing. To appropriate or borrow from existing works was common practice in the early modern period, when people read in a less sequential way, going from text to text and passage to passage within a single text, not in the order the text was arranged or in the sequence the books were published, but as the spirit urged and purpose required. They were expected to copy down quotations and then use them liberally, to rewrite them, revise them, and rearrange them for their own compositions. "Reading and writing were therefore inseparable activities," wrote Robert Darnton.

> "They belonged to a continuous effort to make sense of things, for the world was full of signs: you could read your way through it; and by keeping an account of your readings, you made a book of your own, one stamped with your personality."[16]

It's not known whether Shakespeare kept commonplace books (like so much that is unknown or unclear about the playwright at the pinnacle of the Renaissance pantheon) —if he did, none survives.[17] But since Shakespeare was largely self-taught, and the commonplace book as an educational tool was uncontested at the time, we can assume he was familiar with the practice. Ben Jonson, considered in his day second only to Shakespeare, did keep a commonplace book and recommended the practice to others. Jonson read widely, and his own commonplace book (*Timber, or Discoveries Made Upon Men and Matter*) was published posthumously in 1641. Jonson was himself classically well-educated and believed that someone who has taught himself, without reference to the writings of others, badly limits his potential. Or precisely:

> "No man is so foolish, but may give another good counsel some times; and no man is so wise, but may easily err, if he will take no other's counsel but his own. But very few men are wise by their own counsel; or learned by their own teaching. For he that was only taught by himself, had a fool to his Master."[18]

Michel de Montaigne's essays originated in his commonplace book. He too had been a well-educated child (with a tutor who spoke to him in Latin and woke him daily with music). In 1571, when he was nearing forty, Montaigne retired to his château in Dordogne, where he spent the next decade writing the first two books of his famous *Essaies*. Some scholars suggest that the way his essays are arranged (under thematic headings like "On Friendship") reflects how Renaissance commonplacers in general organized their extracts under headings of their own devising. The English essayist and philosopher of science Francis Bacon (1561-1626), an early icon of empiricism and scientific reasoning, also recommended keeping a commonplace book, writing this:

> "There can hardly be anything more useful ... than a sound help for the memory; that is a good and learned digest of Common Places ... I hold diligence and labour in the entry of commonplaces to be a matter of great use and support in studying."[19]

Bacon's own essays, first published in 1597, contain aphorisms so well known today that they are routinely cited without attribution, and perhaps without knowledge of their provenance (for example, this one, from his essay Of Boldness: "If the Hill will not come to Mahomet, Mahomet will go to the hill"—the first known appearance of the proverb in print).[20]

John Milton (1608-1674), the famous English poet and author of the epic poem in blank verse *Paradise Lost*, kept a commonplace book. Milton is regarded by many as his country's greatest literary light after Shakespeare. He was opposed to scholasticism and to any kind of tyranny imposed by church or state (he had even met Galileo in Florence when the latter was under house arrest for what were then considered his heretical views). In *Paradise Lost*, Milton wrote this: "The mind is its own place, and in itself can make a heaven of hell, a hell of heaven." And in his famous *Areopagitica*, a plea for free expression, this: "Give me the liberty to know, to utter, and to argue freely according to conscience, above all liberties." And this:

> "For books are not absolutely dead things, but do contain a potency of life in them to be as active as that soul was whose progeny they are; nay, they do preserve as in a vial the purest efficacy and extraction of that living intellect that bred them."[21]

In the early modern period, the physician and philosopher John Locke (1632-1704), whose political writings and activities are still referenced, proposed a "new" method for keeping and organizing a commonplace book. He had been commonplacing since his university days, years before he decided to take the tradition in firm if finicky hand (the method required indexing entries by arranging them alphabetically, with pages divided into five horizontal boxes, one for each vowel following the initial consonants of a word). A version of the new method was appended to his famous "An Essay Concerning Human Understanding," published in 1690. A separate book, *A New Method of a Common-Place Book*, was published in 1706, two years after Locke died. It was much read and discussed and, among scholars, still is.[22] Locke's new method was said to have improved on the three main methods practised by his predecessors ("the systematic or textbook approach, the alphabetical approach, and the sequential or index-based approach"). Locke himself had used these approaches in his commonplace books before he incorporated them into his new method, which was meant to facilitate finding entries and to avoid wasting paper: a no-nonsense way for physicians and natural philosophers to keep track of burgeoning knowledge in their disciplines, rather than to preserve "elegant quotes on a very limited set of classical topics." One scholar sees Locke as critical to "the emergence of the very notion of 'facts.' "[23]

Locke is famous today as a founder of liberalism and one of the most important thinkers of his day, a defender of freedom against feudal traditions, with international influence on later enlightenment thinkers.[24] Modern ideas about consciousness and identity have roots in Locke's theory of mind. But in Locke's own time, his new method was ridiculed by some traditionalists, who dismissed it as a step backward in the arts of learning—much the way today's traditionalists dismiss such online tools as Wikipedia or even the whole generation that's grown up with it.

Scientists and philosophers of the seventeenth and eighteenth centuries, from René Descartes and Isaac Newton to Jean Jacques Rousseau and Voltaire, though they may have differed on means and methods, were all inspired by the hope and ideal of improving humanity's lot. They sought justice and opposed persecution, especially religious persecution. By the eighteenth century, the language of science and philosophy in Europe had changed from Latin to French, allowing the spread of knowledge and ideas previously limited to a much smaller community.

In North America too, these makers of the new inspired people like Franklin and Jefferson, both of whom according to one reviewer were "avid note takers and letter writers to a man"[25]—undeclared members of what historians call the Republic of Letters, a group of itinerant European scholars active in the fifteenth century and through much of the early modern period, who communicated by letters and exemplified this sort of idealism. (I use the word idealism as it is commonly used, to indicate ideals based on positive regard for others, and not to indicate philosophic idealism as opposed to philosophic realism). They pursued knowledge and believed that scholars should stand for justice and against tyranny, that they should try (hold the applause) to make the world a better place.

The work of this idealized republic prefigured the scholarly journals of later eras. As members of the republic wrote letters and acted as advisers to publishers, they made knowledge harder for authorities to censor. They shook worldviews whose questioning was once considered heretical, bringing to broader public awareness such important works as those of Copernicus, the Renaissance mathematician and astronomer who moved the sun to the centre of the universe. They formed new academies that challenged the existing universities of their day and laid the foundations for new disciplines, disciplines that ultimately found homes in the very universities they had earlier challenged. (I add here a word in defence of the much maligned "Google generation": perhaps it presages a new republic of letters, digitally powered.)

Francis Daniel Pastorius (1651-1720) was typical of this Republic of Letters. A German lawyer, poet, and educator, he came to America to join the colony of William Penn (an early Quaker and the founder of the state of Pennsylvania). Pastorius exemplified the passion for making the ideal real (for example, he and three friends wrote a document in 1688 that later became famous, a protest against the slave trade, which they compared to the religious persecution of Quakers). Pastorius knew how to embrace the new along with the old. He kept a commonplace book that he called "Bee-Hive," so-named because he likened the process of commonplacing to the way bees produce honey. His single manuscript, Bee-Hive is now housed at the University of Pennsylvania. Written two centuries after the advent of printing, Pastorius copied out by hand passages that impressed him, arranged them under topical headings, and provided an index: like a handwritten personal encyclopedia. He saw it as a trove of wisdom, valuable beyond measure.

Pastorius is said to have been obsessive about note-taking and to have considered the commonplace method the best way to preserve knowledge. But he was also interested in the latest innovations in medicine and engineering, and so consistently updated his manuscript. His efforts resulted in a large and reliably accessible store of information, what one critic called "a vast handwritten search engine."[26] The way Pastorius used commonplacing to write Bee-Hive—copying down everything he read that he thought was important, ordering the quotations under subject headings, and adding comments of his own—exemplifies the nature of the commonplace book as an information and literary technology, even a proto-encyclopedia.

Although books resembling encyclopedias had existed for centuries, the first books to use the word "encyclopedia" in their titles were written in the sixteenth century. Radically different from the modern encyclopedia, they were written in Latin, and though they arranged information under subject headings and provided indexes, their coverage was idiosyncratic rather than comprehensive. The modern encyclopedia—which comes in concise and multi-volume forms, is written in the vernacular, provides thorough coverage arranged under headings alphabetically ordered, and is printed rather than handwritten—wasn't developed until the eighteenth century, sometime after the appearance of the first dictionaries.

On the other hand, the *idea* of compiling knowledge has been around for at least the last two thousand years. The various forms of the dictionary (knowledge about words) and the encyclopedia (knowledge about knowledge) as basic reference works have changed over the centuries—from handwritten manuscripts to printed books to digital documents—and so has their naming: there are dictionaries that read more like encyclopedias and some that are even called "encyclopedic dictionaries" (like the lovely but hefty faux-leather-covered Webster's I recently bought for $15 in one of my favourite of only a few English bookstores left in Montreal).

I love to peruse such reference works and especially to compare them, but this habit does nothing to restore whatever faith I may ever have enjoyed in the notion of their ultimate authority. (I remember, in the early 1960s, riding an elevator with a man who, noticing the button I sported with the words "Question Authority," asked me whether I had trouble with authority. "More than my fair share," I answered, adding: "The truth is I always wanted a button that said 'Fuck Authority,' but the one I wear is as close as I could get.")

As for encyclopedias in general, their authority is necessarily relative (some are excellent, others hopeless). Even the great ones are of little use if their statements are never questioned. The very word "encyclopedia" has—as have all words—a history, which means their understandings are conceivably open to interpretation, interrogation, investigation. According to one of my favourite authorities (my two-volume Shorter Oxford English Dictionary[27]), the word comes from two Greek words first used in a manuscript by Quintilian meaning "general education." According to Wikipedia, which cites numerous sources including Quintilian (35-100 CE), the online Encyclopedia Britannica, and Robert Darnton's *The Business of Enlightenment: A Publishing History of the Encyclopédie, 1775–1800*, the word comes from the two Greek words *enkyklios* ("circular, recurrent, required regularly, general") and *paideia* ("education, rearing of a child"), the two translated roughly as "complete instruction" or "general education." Also according to Wikipedia, these two Greek words were "reduced to a single word due to an error by copyists of Latin manuscripts." This referenced thus: "According to some accounts, such as the American Heritage Dictionary, copyists of Latin manuscripts took this phrase to be a single Greek word, *enkyklopaidia*."

From this supposed error—two Greek words into one Latin word—comes our English word "encyclopedia." In order to adequately parse the evolution of the word, I would need to have a serious knowledge of ancient Greek and Latin, and way more skill in transcribing across ancient languages and drawing conclusions from their historical context, all of which expertise I regretfully lack. I wonder, though, whether the two original Greek words were translated by the Latin copyists into one not because of simple error but because the two Greek words "meant"—were best translated as—the one Latin word. If this were the case, it would indicate not error but an advance in understanding the nature of translating from one language to another.

Not that all of the preceding matters much (everything you never wanted to know about the books that propose to tell all) in everyday communication or even in matters of meaning. But it does suggest, beyond the dream of knowledge that will stay put long enough for any of us to master any small part of it, the individual's role in the creation and contesting of what we call knowledge and the meanings we impart to it in all its guises. It shows how right Einstein was about imagination being more important than knowledge, not because novels are necessarily a better read than encyclopedias, but because the latter, despite their claims to ultimate authority, require imagination of the very "facts." For statements to come to be established as facts, they have to have been interpreted. And to interpret words and collections of words as facts and knowledge, we have little to aid except for more words (the trouble with words, all over again).

Among dictionaries, Samuel Johnson's *A Dictionary of the English Language*, published in 1755, is certainly one of the most famous. Johnson (aka, Dr. Johnson) was among the most influential men of letters in the London of his day. His dictionary was a veritable feat of scholarship: working solo, he took seven years to complete the book. And it was timely. By the mid-eighteenth century, books were widely available and affordable. Gains in literacy and technological advances in printing and book-making meant that for the first time in history, common people could avail themselves of reading material (not only books but also other printed materials like newspapers and maps). Not the first English dictionary, Johnson's was nevertheless the best of its day. There were dictionaries published as early as the sixteenth century, but they were unlike modern dictionaries. Instead of word definitions, they gave quotations (then called "illustrations") containing the featured words. Johnson's dictionary was the first to actually try to document the English lexicon, and it remained the standard until Noah Webster decided that America needed one of its own and published in 1828 his American Dictionary of the English Language. The Oxford English Dictionary followed later in the nineteenth century. Until then, Johnson's dictionary was considered pre-eminent: he had basically invented the methodology, one rather like that of a commonplace book. According to one reviewer, "Johnson was paying old debts and seeking out wisdom about himself ... as well as compiling perhaps the greatest commonplace book in the history of mankind."[28]

Johnson had planned to draw on the work of previous dictionaries the way legal documents draw on precedents, but he didn't want to get bogged down in unnecessary detail. He wanted the dictionary to be both thorough and readable, and he was after all a writer, given to going on. Instead of just defining or describing words, Johnson added notes on their usage and literary quotations (often from Shakespeare) to illustrate their meanings. Unlike other lexicographers, he also used humour, for instance defining "excise" as "a hateful tax levied upon commodities and adjudged not by the common judges of property but wretches hired by those to whom excise is paid." He defined a lexicographer as "a writer of dictionaries; a harmless drudge that busies himself in tracing the original and detailing the signification of words."[29]

The first edition of the dictionary contained a list of 42,773 words. Johnson, who had no college degree, defended himself in advance against criticism, writing at the end of his preface to the Dictionary: "... it may repress the triumph of malignant criticism to observe, that if our language is not here fully displayed, I have only failed in an attempt which no human powers have hitherto completed."[30] Elsewhere, Johnson had his biting say about potential critics. On the occasion of his ceasing to write for the periodical The Rambler, he addressed his reading public:

> "Time, which puts an end to all human pleasures and sorrows, has likewise concluded the labours of the Rambler. Having supported for two years the anxious employment of a periodical writer, and multiplied my essays to six volumes, I have now determined to desist. What are the reasons of this resolution, it is of little importance to declare, since no justification is necessary when no objection is made ... for I have never been much a favourite of the publick, nor can boast that, in the progress of my undertaking, I have been animated by the rewards of the liberal, the caresses of the great, or the praises of the eminent. I have, however, no intention to gratify pride by submission, or malice by lamentation, nor think it reasonable to complain of neglect from those whose attention I never solicited. If I have not been distinguished by the distributers of literary honours, I have seldom descended to any of the arts by which favour is obtained."[31]

If these be sour grapes, they are the sweetest sour grapes I've ever read.

Several years before Johnson's dictionary, the French philosopher Denis Diderot began publishing the monumental *Encyclopédie, ou Dictionnaire raisonné des sciences, des arts, et des métiers* (Methodical Dictionary of the Sciences, Arts, and Trades). The original plan was to translate the English Cyclopaedia of Ephraim Chambers, but the work, undertaken by Diderot and some 150 other scientists and philosophers, turned out to be a much expanded enterprise, ultimately comprising 35 volumes published between 1751 and 1772. "In spite of its imbalance ... errors, and unacknowledged plagiarism," says *Benét's Reader's Encyclopedia*, "it was a highly successful business venture. At one point there were four thousand subscribers, and the profit is said to have been 300 percent."

One of the earliest forerunners of the encyclopedia in England was *De proprietatibus rerum* ("On the Properties of Things"), a compendium originally compiled in the thirteenth century (c. 1240) by a Parisian scholastic named Bartholomeus Anglicus. Widely consulted in medieval times, the encyclopedia was translated into French (1372) and into English (1397). In later centuries, it was common practice for owners of the encyclopedia to make marginal additions, sometimes inventing new headings and departing from areas of authorized knowledge covered in its pages; in other words, people who owned a copy of the book treated it as they might a commonplace book, adding information gained in their communities and useful to them in everyday life. At the beginning of the seventeenth century, one man is said to have used the book's front flyleaf to copy down information about a medical remedy obtained from neighbours.[32]

The idea of compiling knowledge in comprehensive volumes has been around since there was a word for knowledge, and one of its earliest manifestations, even before proper dictionaries and encyclopedias, was the commonplace book. And that is finally the most interesting thing about such reference works in the history of knowledge: they are, and are expected to be, as hyper-authoritative as possible in the attempt to preserve knowledge; yet in order to remain accurate and thorough, they require continual updating, to correct and revise, to explain new and emerging facts and ideas.

With each addition and each revision, however, comes the possibility of simple error and, more difficult to suss out or correct, misinterpretation. That is *why*, as Einstein said, imagination is more important than knowledge and that is *what* makes scholarship and discourse and everyday conversation the compelling uses of words they are, what takes the word beyond the tedium of repetition even unto the creation of new words. (Anyone who has witnessed the acquisition of language by children can attest to how gloriously this acquisition reflects not just their innate linguistic brilliance and powers of invention, but even more importantly, their capacity for understanding meanings whose transcription into as-yet-unlearned words would no doubt confound their grasp.)

In any case, between about 1750 and 1815, the combined weight of authority in all its forms had begun to lose some of its shine, and by the early nineteenth century, faith in reason itself was beginning to crumble. (I note here that faith in reason is still after all faith, and reason an exercise in same.)

Among early nineteenth-century commonplace books (called *zibaldone* in Italy, the term translates roughly as "miscellany") was a famous one written by Giacomo Leopardi, today considered among Italy's greatest poets. One American critic has called Leopardi's commonplace book "the least known masterpiece of European literature."[33] The book was published in 1898, more than 60 years after Leopardi died (in 1837). The poet had been commonplacing from a young age, and in his short life, had read countless volumes and mastered several disciplines and languages. His *zibaldone*, which he kept separately from his poetry notebooks, is a massive work, some two thousand pages long. It's said it took a small army of experts to translate the book for an English audience. In this tome, Leopardi expressed at length his views on art and life. To call the book melancholic would be putting it mildly: Leopardi's thoughts amounted to a thoroughly gloomy summing up, according to which human life is without meaning, all striving is futile, and misery is the common human lot. (Margaret Atwood said somewhere that people without hope don't write novels, and Leopardi didn't.)

Hot on the heels of reason's threatened demise, came various forms of resurgence in faith, not in religion or knowledge per se, but in the power of words. A century after John Locke had sought to standardize the commonplace method for practical purposes, his countryman, the famous English poet Samuel Taylor Coleridge (1772-1834), came along to question the value of organizational schemes as such. Many of Coleridge's contemporaries in the English Romantic movement joined in rejecting Locke's or anyone else's penchant for strict organization, but they still kept commonplace books. Coleridge's notebooks, however, were shamelessly disorganized; his entries lucky to be sorted even by date of transcription. He jettisoned the use of general headings and other niceties of the kind proposed by Locke and Locke's forbears. He dispensed with order as unnecessarily constraining and included wide-ranging bits and pieces in his notebooks, appearing to glory in the busy abundance they provided. Some modern critics don't even call them commonplace books, referring to them instead simply as notebooks.

Others insist Coleridge should be reinstated as someone who not only practised the commonplace tradition but also transformed it, in a kind of evolutionary leap, one that exemplifies how the Romantics in general (much influenced by then-current philosophies of idealism and transcendentalism) viewed the history of knowledge.[34] In his notebooks and in his writing style, Coleridge favoured a loose structure and an emphasis on the workings of the individual mind over a devotion to received knowledge. It's clear that he used material he'd collected in his notebooks for his prose pieces, but how he used this material is open to debate. Some call it plagiarism. Others defend the poet against this charge.

As debates go, this one is not as straightforward as it might appear. Britain didn't grant ownership rights to writers in a copyright act until 1814. At that time, it was customary not to use quotation marks for commonplaces of old, such as extracts from the Bible or from writers as well-known as Shakespeare (it was expected that readers would know them well enough that the precise source need not be cited). Before the rise of modern authorship and copyright laws, writers were encouraged to incorporate quotations and even illustrations or diagrams from previous texts, often enough without attribution, and in the case of visual content, actually cutting and pasting fragments into new illustrations. Commonplacers in the nineteenth century saw the practice as part of a social network, a way for people to share ideas (as people do today in social media sites and online chat rooms).Among writers, those of the Romantic movement embraced collective effort and collaboration.

One scholar in defence of Coleridge argues that like the early modern humanists, the English Romantics thought of reading and writing as "co-terminous," unlike the English Victorians who followed them, who regarded reading and writing as discrete categories (privileging writers and writing over readers and reading). There is good reason, some argue, to view Coleridge's copying and borrowing (not to say plagiarism) with a more tolerant eye. Coleridge (a co-founder, along with his friend Wordsworth, of the English Romantic movement) kept his notebooks in such disarray that his use of others' words without what we regard today as appropriate attribution was basically unintentional. To wit: "It is quite possible that he did not realize he was copying another author's work."[35]

I found this defence stunning: it's the same way that contemporary journalists caught plagiarizing have from time to time tried to defend themselves by saying in essence the following: "I forgot to put quotation marks around quoted speech when I was taking notes and then when it came time to write the article, I forgot I was quoting, and took the quotation for original writing of my own." Not that I doubt the sincerity of the argument—I've heard it often enough as a journalist and as a teacher of journalism. And it sounds, sure enough, like a caught-in-the-headlights rationalization, barely a lame excuse. Except for that this *is* the way journalists (and academics too) are routinely taught to "write," that is, to rely excessively on and crib copiously from "received" knowledge. In other words, it says something about the way writing is taught and practised, and it underlines the importance of certain elements I regard as indispensable to learning (elements I address in the chapters that follow.)

Of plagiarism, I note that we have continued to treat historic quotations as nineteenth-century writers did all kinds of quotations: we eschew marks and precise attribution for "historical" quotations, reserving these for quotations from modern sources, and reserving the term "plagiarism" for transgressions against them. Plagiarism, seen as the attempt to pass off someone else's writing as one's own, is a still a firing offence and a badge of shame in journalism and other forms of professional writing.

But in addition to saying something about the way writing is taught and practised, the defence against the charge of plagiarism levelled at Coleridge (and the similar one espoused by modern day reporters with their spiral bound notebooks, their digital recorders, and their notebook computers) may speak to other important differences between the nineteenth and twentieth century, such as changing conceptions of "the writer." By 1850, being a writer often meant being a well-paid clerk who held down a designated job in society, a job to which a certain status accrued. The idea of a professional writer as a special kind of person, a kind of latter-day romantic who though he wrote for money yet stood against the status quo as a debunker of social hypocrisies, developed slowly, in contrast to the more classical notion of the writer as a person of means who wrote, even if condescendingly, for the good of all (perhaps especially the good of all within his or her social class). The rise of the (by necessity self-promoting) career writer (as an imaginative freelancer or a writer of novels, whether as an instant success or a long suffering little-known) belongs to the twentieth century. In an interesting essay, Tim Parks exempts poets from this characterization. He wrote that if people read only poetry, copyright itself would disappear because poetry is the one thing people would still write, even if they never got paid. Rather a romantic notion, but maybe true all the same.[36]

Perhaps the original Romantics played fast and loose with quotations because they hadn't yet begun to think of "writing" as something separate from reading, or as something particularly special in human endeavour or history. Perhaps, too, changing ideas of the commonplace book as it evolved over time have more to do with changing conceptions of the individual (as a discrete if not isolated entity) than with changes in format or technological means or even style as such. Changing views of individuality from era to era—the apparent demoting or privileging of the individual—may in turn have more to do with the changing realities of earning a living than with anything theorized or assumed as an element of "literary culture."

In any case, even though the importance of the old-style Latin learning so prized by Renaissance scholars was waning by the early eighteenth century, the commonplace book was still going strong. It had functioned throughout the early modern period as a kind of textbook, supplying material for study (for example, to teach students how to form an argument in books like John Walker's 1785 *Rhetorical Grammar* and William Milns's 1794 *The Well-Bred Scholar*) as well as for modelling. The practice of modelling (known also as "imitation pedagogy") encouraged learning to write through the imitation of older works; it flourished in the primarily oral classical era and throughout the Renaissance.

Ironically, while classical scholars worried about the potential for writing to injure the power of memory, later scholars feared that perpetual quoting diminished the powers of invention and of the mind itself. Yet such texts were meant to stress received knowledge not solely for its own sake but for the sake of creating original compositions: the books were meant to help students move from compiling quotations to writing original essays. The processes of reading and writing were seen as closely intertwined and mutually nourishing, with skill in one honing skill in the other. But towards the end of the early modern period, the practice of modelling, as the study of rhetoric generally, began to fall into decline. By 1800 many schools no longer taught either.

The eighteenth century had seen the French and American revolutions; meanwhile, the Industrial Revolution had fundamentally changed the way people lived, and the economic means whereby they lived. By the nineteenth century, with enlightenment thinking called into question, reason was on the defensive. As one contemporary writer has put it: "Reason, on close examination, had become the representing of representations."[37] Once the banner of an age of enlightenment, reason had become Coleridge's serpent devouring its own tail.

Still, many nineteenth-century writers continued to use commonplace books. How they used their books might differ, but the basic options were much the same then as they remain today: you impose order early, or you organize as you go, or you vacillate between the two modes. For example, Mark Twain in America and Thomas Hardy in England were contemporaries, but Twain kept his commonplace notes disorganized, reflecting Coleridge's preference, while Hardy, a Victorian influenced by the Romantics, followed the more formal practice of the traditional method.

The rise of technology in the nineteenth century (with the advent of such as photographs and typewriters, the telegraph and the phonograph) encouraged the preservation of information in forms (such as scrapbooking) that didn't require the work of transcribing. Other changes of the century brought conceptual reversals stunning enough to threaten the social order. Still, notable thinkers favoured the commonplace book. These included Ralph Waldo Emerson, the essayist and poet who led the transcendentalist movement, and the ever irreverent Twain in a now de-colonized America; and in England, seminal figures like Charles Darwin, the naturalist whose theory of evolution threatened the human animal's presumed right to planetary dominance, and the writer George Eliot (Mary Anne Evans), who in her novels and journalism helped to shake her century's complacence in matters of social class.

George Eliot's commonplace books are a good example of how nineteenth-century writers used them as research method. Eliot was concerned with issues of class and with the poor and beleaguered working classes in particular. A contemporary of Karl Marx, Eliot mined her commonplace books for historical details, for character, and for plot development. And unlike the Romantics, who messed with quotations from other writers and frequently altered them without notice or other fanfare, Eliot tended to quote faithfully and concerned herself with accurate sourcing. In her commonplace books, she always noted the author she was extracting from, and she kept her commonplace books separate from notebooks for her novels in order to guard against inadvertent plagiarism. When she put epigraphs in her novels, they would come at the beginning of chapters, clearly separate from her own narrative.

Eliot became one of the leading writers of her generation, producing poetry, journalism and translations in addition to her novels. In her most famous work, the novel *Middlemarch, A Study of Provincial Life* (based on a fictitious town, set in the years 1829 to 1832, and featuring a large cast of characters), she addressed controversial themes such as the status of women and the institution of marriage, the nature of self-interest and the varieties of hypocrisy, the matter of education and the need for political reform. In *Middlemarch*, she based the character of Casaubon (the much older and miserable man that the book's heroine, Dorothea, is married to) on a real-life sixteenth-century scholar. While she was writing *Middlemarch*, Eliot kept four commonplace books: one was untitled; two were called "Miscellaneous Quotations" and "Interesting Extracts." The last was devoted to the novel and she called it "Quarry for Middlemarch." Eliot complained often of the disorganization of her mind and used her commonplace books to address the problem (and judging by her novels, that worked).[38]

In terms of education, there are indications that even into the twentieth century, some attempts were made in the United States to return the commonplace book to a method within the secondary school curriculum, especially in order to teach writing,[39] but it's unclear when the practice was abandoned. Of the many people I've questioned (including academics and writers), only several knew what a commonplace book was or had ever kept one as a student or been advised to keep one, though I have gathered some anecdotal evidence of exceptions to that general observation, exceptions that suggest commonplacing was still valued and practised by a notable few as recently as forty years ago.[40] The famed Canadian pathologist William Boyd (1885-1979), noted for the "unusually vivid language" in his many successful textbooks, was a commonplacer.

> "The common belief is that the success of Boyd's books was due largely to their lively style, for pathology books are often dull. From his student days, and during the most productive years of his life, Boyd kept a commonplace book in which he wrote in longhand selections from what he had read. The book came to light during research towards a biography of Boyd."[41]

If the nineteenth century brought challenges to faith in reason and in the status quo, the carnage of the twentieth century threatened to upend faith in anything at all. Even before the Second World War, science and empiricism no longer seemed the bastions of explanation and certainty that they once had. In the twentieth century, only the most stalwart or the most uncaring could speak of pursuing knowledge for its own pure sake, without reference to the political horrors unleashed by two worldwide conflicts, the second of which was predicted in the aftermath of the first never to occur.

In literature, the response to the atrocities of the twentieth century goes generally by the name of modernism, and later in the century, postmodernism. A common interpretation of the Modernist movement has it that writers of the early twentieth century were moved by the horrors of the First World War and influenced by thinkers like Sigmund Freud to question the idea that the mind was rational. Deciding against, they turned to a self-conscious rejection of all traditional forms in poetry and in prose. Among the early modernists, T. S. Eliot, claimed by the British as one of their best (though he was born in America and never formally rejected his Missouri roots), wrote the famous poem *The Waste Land* (1922), deemed a central work of early modernism, often interpreted by critics as representing the disillusionment of a generation in the shadow of the First World War.

The verdicts of history are more definitive in the case of the Second World War (when the war to end all wars ended instead with the one that featured the Holocaust and the dropping of atom bombs on an all-but-defeated Japan). After the war, modernism began morphing into postmodernism, whose banner went further than rejection of simple rationality to the impossibility of any variety of stable meanings.

T. S. Eliot was still at it, writing long and difficult poems (he was awarded the Nobel Prize in Literature in 1948, for what were regarded as his pioneering contributions to modernist literature). The very structural complexity of his poetry is one central reason why his contributions are defined as modernist (as complexity is also said to characterize such novelistic counterparts as James Joyce's *Ulysses*, a work that one newspaper headline called "modernism's most sociable masterpiece").[42]

Then poetry and politics collided. If T. S. Eliot was sometimes deemed to hold intolerant political views (including anti-Semitism), he never proclaimed these from a hilltop or in print or in radio interviews, and he was never jailed on account of them—unlike his friend Ezra Pound, another American expatriate poet and critic, to whom Eliot had dedicated *The Waste Land.* Pound was infamous for his anti-Semitic views and fascist sympathies before, during, and after the Second World War—a collaborator in Mussolini's fascist government and a vocal supporter of Hitler's Nazi Germany. History nevertheless hails Pound as a great artist in his own right, one also credited with discovering and encouraging other famous writers besides T. S. Eliot (Robert Frost, Ernest Hemingway, and James Joyce, among them).

But not everyone was an admirer, and when in 1948 Pound was awarded the Library of Congress Bollingen Prize, a small avalanche of bitterly opposed commentary ensued.[43] At the time, Pound was still incarcerated in a Washington, D.C. psychiatric hospital, having been arrested in 1945 by American forces in Italy and subsequently deemed unfit to stand trial on charges of treason. Among those unable to separate Pound's politics from his poetry, was Arthur Miller, who, denouncing the poet as "worse than Hitler," said this: "In his wildest moments of human vilification Hitler never approached our Ezra."[44] Robert Hillyer, a Pulitzer Prize winner and president of the Poetry Society of America at the time, attacked the committee that had chosen Pound for the award; he was quoted in *The Saturday Review of Literature*, telling journalists that he "never saw anything to admire in Pound, not one line."[45]

Of course, "modernism," I hasten to add, is not invariably a term of disapprobation, even if some critics treated it as such well into the 1980s. Most modernist writers were never accused of treason and never acted as founts of hateful speech. Most were well deserving of their fame (the category includes famous all-time greats in addition to the already mentioned Frost, Hemingway, and Joyce, and to name but a few more: Samuel Beckett, Bertolt Brecht, E. E. Cummings, William Faulkner, D. H. Lawrence, Federico García Lorca, Robert Musil, Eugene O'Neill, Dorothy Richardson, Wallace Stevens, Virginia Woolf, and W. B. Yeats).

It was only well after the Second World War that galloping technology moved Western societies beyond the breach, proffering hope in the form of communication machines that ever since have been transforming the nature and meaning of knowledge. And with the twenty-first century's ever more powerful computers and online possibilities came, perhaps not strangely, a resurgence of interest, though sporadic, in scholarship generally and in the commonplace book in particular.

When I first googled "commonplace books," in 2015, the references were fairly sparse, but since then, they have gone forth and multiplied. By late June of 2017, they were numerous beyond count, and they continue to proliferate. Of course, that is the nature of online information: with profits based on number of "hits," and no librarians authorized to sort and catalogue the information, all kinds of references, variations, and repetitions abound. Many online finds are electronic forms of work previously or concurrently published in hard copy. Much of what you can find online is excellent and invaluable. Much is meant only to sell you something, including pornography and hate literature. Much else ranges from the mistaken and the misleading to the outright inane, repeated and propagated about as religiously as any bromides of a previous age.

But you can also find online some of the latest intelligent commentary and innovative scholarly work on commonplace books and on the practice of commonplacing. Some of this work represents the attempts of academics and other writers to retrieve particular commonplaces from obscurity and to reinstate ordinary (undervalued and overlooked) people and groups to some sort of official acclaim or at least recognition.

One writer at the University of Alberta rescued a relative's nineteenth-century commonplace book. During an online search, I came across his academic paper: "Reading Fletcher's Commonplace Books: The Breadth of Cultural Influences in New Westminster, British Columbia, 1887-1897."

The writer had acquired two commonplace books written by Fletcher, and the paper's stated intent was to contribute to an understanding of the "social networks and cultural milieu of late nineteenth-century West Coast Canada." According to the paper, Edward Taylor Fletcher was born in Canterbury, England, in 1817, came to Canada at age 11, and then spent most of his life in Québec City, where he had worked as an architect, and in Toronto, where he was a long-acting president of the Toronto Literary Association, before retiring to the West Coast in 1887, where he died in 1897 at age 80. The paper's author, one James Gifford, also discovered in the course of his research that Fletcher had played the cello and was a published poet of some note, mentioned as the author of a book of poetry in the *Dictionary of Canadian Biography*.[46]

Scholars have generally undervalued the commonplace books of women (as they have generally ignored women's writing ever since Sappho left no doubt she had the nerve).[47] Quaker women kept commonplace books and saw the creation of knowledge as a community thing: they understood invention as a social process, a product of friendship and dialogue, not as history fuelled by individual great minds working in aerial isolation. And if history has rarely missed an opportunity to downplay the works of women, women have never stopped trying to redress the imbalance. To this day, women are routinely excluded from and under-represented in diverse fields in the arts as in the sciences.

Among attempts to rescue women from history's general disowning and, more specifically to restore their place in the commonplace books of the early modern period, is a 2016 doctoral dissertation entitled, "Romantic Women Writers and Their Commonplace Books," in which the author argues that women writers of the eighteenth and nineteenth centuries, aided by the march of print culture, "changed the genre of commonplace books."[48] They adapted the practice to suit their own needs and purposes, and in the process shifted the emphasis "away from classical texts and conduct literature toward colloquial, individualized compilations." The dissertation features case studies and suggests that these commonplacing women used the practice for private use and for communication within a social network. The writer comments finally that the need for such networks to store and share knowledge remains necessary, and finds their further evolution in online sites like Facebook and Pinterest. Lest I appear unduly naïve about the downsides of online communication in learning and community building, I quote:

> "We now know, beyond any doubt, that we are dumber when we are using smart phones and social media. We understand and retain less information, comprehend with less depth, and make decisions more impulsively than we do otherwise. This untethered mental state, in

> turn, makes us less capable of distinguishing the real from the fake, the compassionate from the cruel, and even the human from the non-human. [...] Engagement through digital media is just a new way of being alone. Except we're not really alone out there—the space is inhabited by the algorithms and bots that seek to draw us into purchases, entertainment, and behaviors that benefit the companies that have programmed them."[49]

By now, among the general public well into the third decade of a new millennium, the commonplace book is but a quaint relic: most contemporary mentions occur online rather than off and refer to electronic notebooks that obviate the need for paper-paper even when they suggest that reader response is advisable.

Thinking about the online environment of the digital age, my mind floods back to the later years of my teaching career, and to the day when a professor in the faculty of arts sent an email to the entire arts list, with a surprising if not shocking revelation. He'd just come from a class where he had returned marked-up student papers, on which he had noted in addition to a grade, comments on the students' work, made in longhand in the margins of the papers. When one student approached him with a question, the professor pointed to the passage he'd written on the student's paper, about to elaborate on the written response, assuming the student needed more information to get his meaning. But the professor didn't get far before the student casually allowed that, "Oh those, I can't read those, I can't read longhand writing."

The professor took an informal poll on the spot, and discovered, as his email reported, that none of his students, most in their late teens or early twenties, could read or write cursive. Even more startling, this was the first mention any of his students had made about the abundant squiggly marks on their papers, marks that in fact they could not decipher. Some among the arts faculty were duly alarmed, including me. Others defended this inability as a matter of no consequence and accused those of us who disagreed of being outdated and, heaven forbid, un-cool. There was one such belligerent who whipped back (I mean the thing arrived in my inbox roughly five seconds after the original email) with an angry and demeaning response: "If it's paper you're after," said the man, "there's plenty of that in the bathroom."

***

There are good personal reasons, assuming you like to read, to keep a commonplace book (or a series of them): in order to preserve your favourite passages and your responses to them (so that returning to them will be meaningful and productive, because as previously noted, just to copy the passage without your own annotations will have you scratching your head and wondering why ever you did). The work invites a pleasure of absorption and results in greater clarity of thought as it triggers reflection and lights a path to insight. You might even choose to share that work with a select readership (a group of close friends, maybe, or family members)—a testament to what you've learned about life and love and work and whatever else of your acquired wisdom seems to you worth preserving and passing on.

A commonplace book (even more than a diary) is useful if you're at a crossroads and considering a career change but aren't sure what you want to study or do (next) with your life; it can help you gain insight into your strongest interests and capacities. It can also help you know if your writing habit is meant for personal use or for publication, whether or not you want to publish what you write. The two are not necessarily opposed: even if you pursue writing as private pastime, you still might want to publish, especially given the ease of on-line publishing—from blogs to e-books.

Of course, it's well-known that any kind of personal writing at any stage of life can be therapeutic: a key to your deepest, most ingrained self and its aspirations, to what makes you as an individual tick. Better than a diary, which is almost by definition entirely self-centered, a commonplace book can help you to expand your everyday frames of reference. It can help make sense of a life. Commonplacing, especially done as I advise, in a process that ends with the keeper's own prose, provides a record of your evolution in thought and emotion, a storehouse of abiding themes in what I think of as the natural history of compassion.

You could keep a commonplace book for educational purposes (whether as someone enrolled formally in a course of study or as a self-directed learner). The efficacy of commonplacing for this purpose, for building, maintaining, and deepening knowledge and expertise, in virtually any discipline or field, is widely accepted, even if its use in education has waned over time. In the latest revival of the practice in recent decades, some teachers have acknowledged its efficacy and begun to use commonplacing to help their students gain fluency in specific subjects and in their powers of self-expression. Among adults long removed from formal education, especially those who've always wanted to write, commonplacing can be the spur that finally moves the avid reader to take a deep breath and pen in hand.

You could keep a commonplace book as a treasured hobby, just for the fun of it, and for the comfort that a life with books can provide beyond the escape from daily routines and demanding schedules. Or you could keep a commonplace book for what I think of as political reasons: to retain and assert your individuality in the face of tremendous pressures not to. It seems to me a clear obligation as well as the fulfilment of this obligation in a participatory democracy: this exercising of the ability to think for oneself. Steven Pinker wrote somewhere of the two main but contradictory psychological drives that move humans: on the one hand, to be part of the larger collective, part of something larger than a single self, and on the other, to stand apart from the crowd and distinguish oneself as an individual. I think the only way finally to reconcile this contradiction is love. (Maybe Buddhism with attitude makes a close second.)

For whatever reason you decide to take up the keeping of a commonplace book, I salute you, and wish you all the best in the endeavour. The practice will take you from reading to writing, and may lead to further forays in the art of writing and perhaps publishing, but even if it doesn't, the personal benefits as detailed are reason enough to proceed. If you're a professional or aspiring writer, the practice of commonplacing can spark your creative urges and enhance the quality and power of your prose. So, matters of money for the moment aside, what can a commonplace book do for the writer?

It can help you come up with writing topics/ideas. For many, the most pressing question is often what to write about—what the classical rhetoric of the ancient Greeks called *inventio* and what many contemporary teachers say is still the hardest thing for students to grasp. Even experienced writers may find themselves at a loss for something to write about, especially when they are between projects. Commonplacing can also help you establish what kind of thing you want to write (fiction or nonfiction, movie or television scripts; essays, technical manuals, scholarly books; hybrid and interactive forms, and genres yet to be invented).

The habit of commonplacing will reveal themes worthy of extended treatment, the ones that keep recurring in your notebooks. By showing how your ideas and feelings as reflected in your commonplace books change over time, the practice can expand your tolerance for new or opposing ideas, and with discipline, strengthen your critical faculties (so that you become better able to assess your own ideas and not waste time with unwarranted assumptions or blind prejudice as the basis for a writing project).

The commonplace method is excellent for bolstering and honing your existing writing technique, for deciding on the appropriate structure and point of view for a given work, and even for helping you to arrive at a work's basic themes, at what it is you're trying to say. (Any writer, genius or not, who claims never to have been at a particular loss in this respect is flat-out lying.)

Copying out passages that strike you as worth the effort and then following with your own responses can provide much explicit instruction and consequent learning about your own authorial strengths and weaknesses. As commonplacing strengthens your writing, it will also enhance your reading technique, since the two activities are enmeshed. Having adopted the practice, you will find that you begin to read with more focus, greater depth, and heightened powers of attention. When I speak of practice, I mean practice as activity, not as something necessary only for the less than perfect among us—since that would be all of us. I mean it not as a putdown but as an article of faith. The idea that "talent" should obviate an expenditure of effort, that a hard thing should always come "naturally"—read: easily—is so superficially and rigidly egotistical it's a wonder anyone still buys it, much less pretends to it.

Commonplacing unleashes your desire to write and feeds the flow of writing (I can testify to that), especially because it provides a kind of self-permission and even an excuse to write without a plan or a publisher. It hones technique almost by osmosis (you know the old saw: stealing from one writer is plagiarism, but stealing from them all is style). Thus the hope that talent or style will rub off on you is, at least in the case of the commonplace book, never nursed in vain.

And now, about the money thing: There's no law but the long-gone Samuel Johnson's that says you have to write for money. And Dr. Johnson's famous dictum, "No man but a blockhead ever wrote except for money" has been nicely corrected by one contemporary writer to read: "Of course a writer writes for money, but only a blockhead writes only for money."[50]

Still, you do have to do something for money; that, after all, is the modern taboo—not sex, but how you get money enough to feed and house yourself and yours, and if that's not an issue, then how you get money enough to compete in the dollar-status sweepstakes. It's a question one does not ask overtly in good company, this question of how one makes a living, but fortunately (or not), there's a polite rendition. One of my favourite sisters had an ace comeback for that polite standard question put by strangers to other strangers at social gatherings: Asked "And what do *you* do?" she would shoot back: "About what?" The point here is that keeping a commonplace book might even help you figure out, if you don't want to try to make a living from your writing, what you do plan to do for money. So, by "advance" your writing, I don't mean to try to show you how to make a ton more or even modestly more money at it. For starters, I wouldn't begin to know. I certainly can't tell you how to write a runaway best-seller, or advise you with authority on the business side and tax implications of professional writing. There are many good books that can so advise, and I have nothing against most of them.

Even if I were to try to advise you on advancing your writing career, my advice would amount to nothing new: learn a marketable skill and don't give up the day job until you see you can earn a living by your more-than-ever metaphorical pen; study the works of writers who write the kind of thing you would like to and study much else besides; have a heart for your eventual readers and master basic writing skills before you demand critical acclaim. Take advantage of the many good books on writing well.

Finally, and just saying: if money (independent means) were the deciding factor in who becomes a successful professional writer, then most writers would come from the ranks of the independently wealthy, which is decidedly not the case. I'm certainly not advising you to throw financial caution to the wind, to persuade you for instance to do what you love and the money will follow. I don't actually believe this or anything like it. In retrospect, from my now senior citizen perspective, it does indeed appear as though I did what I loved and the money (but never tons of it) did follow, but that's not because of the nature of money-making; it's because of the nature of retrospect. It would be more accurate to say that I persisted through good times and hard times in doing what I love (even when I didn't), that I followed my nose, that I kept putting one foot in front of the other—and that I got lucky.

It's destructive, I think, to advise the young (or the gullible hopeful of any age) to ignore pressing realities in favour of "believing" as a kind of propitiatory offering to the gods, the powers that be, of your sincerity or innate merit or deserving-ness. The fact is that publishing (like every other business or career pursuit) is a bit of a crap shoot. It makes sense to have a basic game plan and to exercise intelligent control over what you can, but it also makes sense (wisdom, even) to recognize and accept that much depends on matters outside your sphere of control, an insight common to those of my generation, now looking back.

So: may you write well, may you make many friends, may the fates look kindly on you, and as my grandfather used to say: If you get a choice in this life between brains and luck, pick luck.

Chapter 3

Language, Meaning, and the Trouble With Words

The subject of language fascinates many (as numerous tomes on the subject will attest), but once you begin to think about words and what they mean, you end up in a mess of trouble. Though we use words to express meaning, meaning remains elusive, for words and their meanings change over time and across cultures and contexts. Though they comprise the basic ingredients of language, words in themselves have no set or "objective" meanings. Words allow us to express all kinds of meaning, from simple reference to abstract reasoning. But these meanings are not absolute or static; they are relative and ever shifting, over time and even from one generation to the next.

The word "longhairs" referred in the 1960s to hippies or intellectuals or people banished from restaurants for going shoeless, but in an earlier era the word was used to refer to classical musicians and intellectuals in general. Adjectives like "psychedelic" and "groovy" were staples back then but are not used today, even by the now senior citizens who coined them. You can still find them in the dictionary, though: usually labeled slang, and effectively obsolete. Members of my daughter's generation (now in their forties and fifties) use the expression "on the spectrum" to describe mildly crazy but still likeable people; my generation (we of the once famed and now faded 1960s) might have described such people, more approvingly, as "far out."

Over longer periods of time and with more abstract terms, shifts in meaning across different languages become much harder to track. George Makari gave it a good try in his book *Soul Machine*, where he traced the trajectories of translated words over the centuries of early modernity, when "long histories attached to powerful words collapsed and became confused."[1] Makari was referring to abstract nouns, to words like these: mind, spirit, soul, and consciousness.

For example, back in the seventeenth and eighteenth centuries, the English word "mind" had no precise or synonymous term in French. John Locke used "mind" to refer to the so-called rational soul, meaning the capacity for reason. The closest noun in French was "*esprit*" (from the Greek word meaning "breath"), but that word had strong religious connotations. Even today the French word "*esprit*" is translated first as "spirit" or "ghost" and only fourth as "mind" or "intellect" or "intelligence." Those of Locke's French contemporaries who agreed with his emphasis on reason tended to translate "mind" with "*âme*," but this translation also proved less than precise, obscuring Locke's intended distinction "between a natural thinking entity and the spirit of God in man." The word "*âme*" is defined first as "soul" or "spirit," and second, as "mind" or "heart"—a distinction that holds in the contemporary idea of reason as different from and opposed to emotion. Major cross-cultural glitches over how to construe other basic terms referring to inner life persist, and in persisting, foment the kinds of miscommunication that translation may entail.

The meaning of the word "consciousness," for instance, is contested not only in philosophy but as well in the so-called hard sciences, especially modern neuroscience. The word itself entered the English lexicon only in the early seventeenth century. The French word for consciousness, *la conscience*, wasn't really synonymous; like the English "conscience," the French "*conscience*" implied ethical awareness. The alternative French word for "consciousness" is *connaissance*. But in French, the word *connaissance* is defined first as knowledge; second, as learning; third (in law) as competence; and only finally as "consciousness" or "awareness." Other words employed by Locke (such as "perception") also had no straightforward or adequately equivalent translations. For instance, the term "psychology" dates back to the sixteenth century, but back then it meant the study of the soul.

> "The central terms Locke proposed for consciousness and the mind, pivotal concepts he employed to naturalize aspects of the rational soul, would grow dark as they were given over to French words that also implied their antithesis. Consciousness might also be conscience, and mind was linguistically indistinguishable from soul and spirit."[2]

Like French, German:

> "… possessed clear words for soul (*Seele*) and spirit (*Geist*), but it possessed no derivative of the Latin *mentis*, no word for the mind. … As a new German discourse emerged on subjectivity and inner life, it would be plagued by this kind of semantic slippage."[3]

Thus we see that words are not precisely translatable between different languages, at least not word for word. Yet this "slippage" is often employed creatively, which indicates that despite the trouble with words, meanings can cross cultures and transcend them. In his commonplace book, *A Certain World*, W. H. Auden mentions a French author's dedication to her publisher: *Je mediterai, tu m'editeras*. Roughly translated, that means "I will think it over, you will edit me." But in the English translation, since there's no rhyming, the pun is lost. Taking liberties with words and the French language, the closest I can come to an English equivalent is this: "I will think, you will tinker."

The impossibility of direct or precise translation from one language to another underlines a more important insight: different languages make possible different thoughts, with subtly different meanings. Some expressions, for example, seem to me more meaningful in one language than in the other. Consider how much more poignant is the French "*Tu me manques*" (literally, "you are missing from me") than its comparatively flat English phrase "I miss you." The French "*je t'aime*" (with the final "e" voiced: tem-eu), also seems to carry greater resonance in French. When my granddaughter Clementine was first learning at age six to speak French as a second language, I asked her, "How do you say 'I love you' in French?" Translating literally, she answered: "*J'aime toi*"—a more literal but less idiomatic (and less moving) string of sound. Can't you hear the difference?

When I was young and reporting for the Canadian Press in the bilingual Montreal bureau, I used to go to lunch with a francophone colleague: she would help me with my French and I would do the same for her English. She used to say, when I complained about my lack of fluency, that the best way for me really to acquire the language, to learn to think in French as opposed to thinking in English and then translating into French, would be to take a French lover. She also said that I would know when I'd internalized my second language once I began to dream in French.

Years later, teaching journalism at a small-town university in British Columbia, the only French I could hear was that emanating from the French arm of the Modern Languages department—and that sounded more than ever like music to my ears. My closest friend at that university was Anne Claircy Gagnon, a francophone historian who grew up in a small town in the Peace River district of Alberta and who didn't speak English until she got to college. I'm not sure what our enduring friendship has to do with bilingualism, Canadian style, but I do know that we understand each other in either language, and that in terms of meaning and emotion, "translation" across the divide of one consciousness to another remains rarely necessary.

Meaning: Denotative and Connotative

Sticking strictly to denotative (dictionary) meanings, even in a single language, won't overcome the trouble with words, because words by themselves, out of context, don't have set meanings. The best that even the most hyper-authoritative dictionary can do is to offer various synonyms. In standard dictionaries (illustrated ones can "depict" only concrete nouns), the definition of words relies entirely on other words. Thus denotative meanings are rendered rather less than definitive. In fact, if you play the dictionary game along with me, you can see that definitions are ultimately, irrevocably circular. Take, for example, the word "matter." According to my *Concise Oxford Dictionary of Current English* (ninth edition, 1995), matter is "a physical substance in general, as distinct from mind and spirit; that which has mass and occupies space." A "substance" is a "particular kind of material having uniform properties," and "mass" is "a coherent body of matter of indefinite shape."

What about the word "element"? Though invisible to the naked eye, an element is presumed to occupy space. In chemistry and physics, an element is defined as "any of the hundred or so substances that cannot be resolved by chemical means into simpler substances, each consisting of atoms with the same atomic number." A chemical is "a substance obtained or used in chemistry." And chemistry? Well, coming full circle, chemistry is "the study of the elements and the compounds they form and the reactions they undergo; the chemical composition and properties of a substance."

If we were to arrange these terms in descending order, "matter" would be the largest category (all the other terms being some kind of "stuff" that could be subsumed under the category "matter"). Much defining depends on saying what something is *not*. Recall that "physical substance" is defined as distinct from mind and spirit, and in more contemporary parlance, from energy. Matter, in other words, is precisely not energy, except perhaps as immortalized by Albert Einstein's famous formula: $E=MC^2$ (where energy equals mass times the speed of light squared).

And so we arrive back where we began: words remain slippery.

Dictionaries do the best they can with the only means at their disposal: other words. And that's just denotative meaning. Connotative meanings complicate exponentially; they are and must be as various as individuals, within and among whom meaning is ultimately negotiated. "The relationship between words and things, i.e., meaning, is indirect, mediated by concepts in the heads of language users."[4] Any yet, words must carry some basic meanings in common; otherwise, communication with words would be impossible, as if words were written in a non-human language, one "foreign" to all (and not just, as in higher mathematics, foreign to most).

It's the same with concepts, with for example the concept of time, perhaps the most pressing illusion of all. The idea of time is quite beyond defining, and yet, as William James wrote: "The time quality of experience is its most significant trait." Words (spoken or written) unfold sequentially in time. We think of time as something that progresses, but time is not some "thing" that can be isolated for testing in a laboratory. When she was five years old, granddaughter Clementine put to me her nascent theory on the subject. From the mouth of the babe, this: "It's funny. Yesterday was today, and tomorrow will be today, but really, it's always now." How is it possible for time to be an eternal present (an always-now)? Then again, how could time be otherwise?

Despite the availability in English of past, present, and future tenses, words cannot record reality "in real time"—not even when a writing project aims to do just that, to capture time and pin it down, as Marcel Proust is said to have attempted with his monumental novel *À la recherche du temps perdu*, or as Michel de Montaigne, who tried in his famous essays to lasso consciousness and in the process pioneered the essay form.

The compulsion to write things down, to capture reality on a page, to "record" reality in order to understand it, may well lead to insight, but the goal in real time is not capable of fulfillment: at some point you would have to lay down your pen (however metaphorical), and so you could never have a completely true or accurate record of time, in time: you would always be backtracking. The attempt would be endlessly recursive, rather like the attempt to define or locate consciousness—no matter how closely you stuck to just the facts (never mind, for the moment, *which* facts). Or, as Tracy Kidder put it in *Good Prose*: "What you write about can never be co-extensive with what you are writing about."[5]

Although simple words that denote physical objects (concrete nouns such as "tables" and "chairs") are widely held in common among people who speak a common tongue, meaning remains ultimately subjective.

> "The mystery of intimate utterance remains. The communication of intimacy passes through the words and enlivens its sound, but it cannot be held by the word. … It depends not on words but on persons."[6]

Annie Dillard saw emotions, not words, as the source of meaning when she described the experience of watching, along with other spectators, an eclipse of the sun: "The heart screeched," she wrote. "The meaning of the sight overwhelmed its fascination. It obliterated meaning itself." For Dillard too, significance is a matter personal and inter-personal:

> "If you were to glance out one day and see a row of mushroom clouds rising on the horizon, you would know at once that what you were seeing, remarkable as it was, was intrinsically not worth remarking. No use running to tell anyone. Significant as it was, it did not matter a whit. For what is significance? It is significance for people. No people, no significance. This is all I have to tell you."[7]

Meaning is not in words or even images per se, but in the context of their use, and in the chain reactions that words may evoke. Thus dependent on context, meaning is multidimensional. As William James noted more than a century ago:

> "Every definite image in the mind is steeped and dyed in the free water that flows round it. With it goes the sense of its relations, near and remote, the dying echo of whence it came to us, the dawning sense of whither it is to lead. The significance, the value, of the image is all in this halo or penumbra that surrounds and escorts it."[8]

And yet meaning is not necessarily evident or obvious from its context.

> "Like Rorschach blots, words need to be constantly interpreted, and always require us to do some filling in. In any given situation, the meaning of a word, a phrase, unfolds dynamically. It cannot be second-guessed."[9]

Still, we second-guess routinely, as when, for instance, we try to figure out what someone else is meaning by the words that someone else is speaking or writing, and we even second-guess ourselves (she wrote), especially when we're writing. This business of second-guessing is how we try to arrive at meaning, and our conclusions may be mistaken as easily as they may be well-founded. It's like the old joke I once heard about two psychoanalysts in conversation. The first analyst asks after the health of the mother of the second analyst, who says: "You know, something really strange happened the other evening. I was having dinner with my mother, and I meant to say, 'Please pass the salt,' but it came out 'You f-ing bitch, you ruined my whole life.'"

Some, like Rachel Carson, find soothing significance in nature:

> "There is a common thread that links these scenes and memories—the spectacle of life in all its varied manifestations as it has appeared, evolved, and sometimes died out. Underlying the beauty of the spectacle there is meaning and significance. It is the elusiveness of that meaning that haunts us, that sends us again and again into the natural world where the key to the riddle is hidden."[10]

The trouble with words is essentially this: while we rely on the words of a language to communicate, the possibilities of contradiction and ambiguity are ever-present. And as we have seen, in terms of overcoming the trouble, synonyms won't do the job, for words have no exact synonyms. In fact, the more synonyms that a dictionary lists for a given word, the more troublesome definition becomes. Most dictionaries provide at least several synonyms, and often more than several, complicating the issue by simple addition, especially for abstract nouns like "meaning" itself. Usually listed first are such as these: "what is meant by; significance; indication; reference; intent."

Isn't it interesting that in definitions of the word "meaning," the word "intent" is usually listed last, if at all? As far back as my 1933 two-volume *Shorter Oxford English Dictionary*, "intent" is listed last, and almost as an afterthought, labelled "archaic." Consider that words may signify, indicate, or refer to, but only living beings possess the power of intent. If you look up and compare the verb forms of these synonyms ("to mean" and "to intend"), the fog begins to clear. You find that of the various synonyms, only this one set approaches equivalence. "To intend" and "to mean" are both defined as transitive verbs, to intend as "to mean or have as one's purpose"; and to mean as "to have as one's purpose or intention."

We could venture ever further into the meanings of meaning, but we won't. (I've been down that rabbit hole many times: it's a rabbit hole.) Suffice for the moment to say that meaning is not encompassed by words in themselves or by their synonyms or even by their (changing) contexts. And while the trouble with words may begin with dictionary definitions and bodily perspectives, it doesn't end there. When I use the word "meaning" in this text, I will be referring mostly to intents and purposes. But before I can continue with an analysis of the trouble with words, of how words may interfere with or pervert or negate meaning, I must define as best I can, what I will mean by three foundational words used repeatedly in this book: fact, reality, and truth.

***

According to the *Concise Oxford Dictionary*, a fact is defined, with characteristic circularity, as "a thing that is known to have occurred, to exist, or to be true; truth, reality." Reality is "what is real or existent or underlies appearances." And truth is "the quality or state of being true or truthful; what is accepted as true." Thus both facts and realities are widely accepted at face value, while truth is a matter ("a state of being") widely considered searchable and debatable. We seek truth in all disciplines and often argue over the truth of a matter, including matters of historical fact.

Truth, then, is a relation (a correspondence) between something claimed and the underlying or relevant facts and realities; falsity is also a relation, but one of contradiction. I reject categorically the idea that truth (unlike opinions and interpretations) is relative. Instead, both true statements and false statements are relative only to the facts that obtain; that is, to those facts that stand to reveal whether a statement is true or false (whether the relation is one of correspondence or of contradiction). The introduction into the political lexicon of the phrase "alternative facts" is the product of an addled mind (she knows who she is); it works to undermine the very concept of truth, to surreptitiously peddle the notion that matters of fact and matters of interpretation or opinion are equivalent and interchangeable. Instead, facts are what underlie and form the foundations of truth; they are the tools we use to try to establish what is true. Even though facts in themselves don't "add up" to truth, there is no fact in which truth is not implicated and no truth without reference to some sort of facts.

Years ago, thinking about how to teach my journalism students the way to write a "lede" (the opening lines of a news story), I discussed the issue with an old newspaper friend, and he told me a story that nicely illustrates. The novice reporter, so the story goes, comes back from his very first assignment—a news conference at City Hall about the vote on an important local resolution. Back in the newsroom, the cub reporter struggles to write the piece, his very first, by deadline (maybe, if he is very lucky, three hours hence). The crusty city editor is growing impatient as the hours pass and the cub reporter has yet to turn in his copy. Finally the editor calls over to the reporter, stationed several desks away. He has already asked for the story two or three times, but the reporter pleads for yet more time. As the deadline hour draws near, the editor raises his voice to be heard amid the typical noise of the old-style newsroom.

"What's the lede?" Crusty demands.

"I thought I'd begin with a comparison between ..." Cub begins to reply.

Crusty: "No, no. The lede, what's the lede?"

Cub: "Well, I'm going to start with ...

Crusty: "Geez, what is the lede?"

Cub: "Some people say ...

Finally, at wit's end, the editor translates: "Okay, okay," he says. "But what happened?"

"Oh," says the cub reporter as the light goes on upstairs, "they voted in favour."

In news writing, the body of a story is supposed to present "just the facts," and the lede (often limited to a single sentence) is expected to present the most important fact, and then subsequent facts and related opinions (in the form of quoted sources) in descending order of importance. News editors cut stories to length by cutting from the bottom of the story, which is one reason why the lede is crucial and why the art of lede writing depends on the reporter's grasp of the significant facts. Despite the truncated length and limited parameters of most news writing, the selection of significant fact is not always straightforward or obvious (especially to the cub reporter).

How we go about ascertaining the significant or applicable facts depends on the discipline in which we are engaged. For example, to establish the truth of past events, of history, we examine available sources, and we compare sources to see where they agree and where they diverge. To arrive at the facts in science, we form hypotheses and conduct experiments to prove or disprove these hypotheses. In both cases, we seek to know, on the basis of confirmed facts, the truth.

Knowledge in any field progresses not only by the accumulation of significant facts, but also by questioning the meaning of those facts. To question the accepted knowledge of earlier thinkers does not negate the search for truth; it enhances this search, for knowledge and its progress depend not only on embracing the meanings of earlier thinkers but also on questioning them, a process through which new facts may come to light. For instance, the way to unravel the skein of history is not simply to abide by long-held views, but to follow the thread of conflicting narratives; and the way science advances is not just to stand on the shoulders of giants so to see farther, but also to question previously accepted facts and so to arrive at compilations of new facts that may amount to groundbreaking theories.

In other words, the progress and prospect of knowledge depend not only on the assimilation of previously established facts, but also on the scrutiny of these facts and of the accepted knowledge they are based on. For instance, Einstein had to fully understand the meaning of Isaac Newton's theory of gravity, and he had also to question it at length before he could arrive at the theory of relativity that all but replaced it. This basic principle applies to all honest inquiry across disciplines. Humanist thinkers of the Enlightenment had to question the idea of social class or "station" as divinely ordained before they could recognize the repressive and superstitious aspects of church and state that they opposed, before they could begin to expound the virtues of reason and thought in an imagined world ruled not by religious or state authority but by common human values. Many ideas once thought the result of divine or natural law, ineffable and unchangeable, have turned out to be man-made distinctions quite amenable to questioning.

While facts and realities may change with temporal and environmental developments, the truth is always a relation. When I speak of truth in this text, I will mean the truth about something (as opposed to a philosophical consideration of the term). In both the humanities and the sciences, methods for ascertaining the truth of a matter may vary somewhat—but all methods rely on facts.

In philosophical thinking, however, the concept of Truth is abstracted and does not depend on facts. The only formal method for establishing truth is the syllogism. Consider that a syllogism is a three-part operation that begins with a major premise and a minor premise, both of which are statements assumed to be true. The syllogism's third element, its conclusion, is considered to be correct based on the assumed truth of its major and minor premises. For example, indeed the classic example: 1. All men are mortal; 2. Socrates is a man. 3. Therefore Socrates is mortal.

Syllogistic thinking is deductive (it proceeds from a general statement to arrive at a particular conclusion), but the worth or truth of a syllogism's conclusion depends finally on the truth of its premises (which, recall, are only assumed to be true, for the sake of the syllogism). Syllogisms may thus easily arrive at false connections and conclusions. For an example (of my invention) in which the major premise is false: 1. All men are intelligent; 2. Donald Trump is a man; 3. Therefore Donald Trump is intelligent.

Some premises may seem unobjectionable at the time of first figuring but become debatable as new claims to knowledge arise. In his book *The Master and His Emissary*, Iain McGilchrist gave the following example of a syllogism with a false minor premise: 1. Major premise: All monkeys climb trees; 2. Minor premise: The porcupine is a monkey; 3. Implied conclusion: The porcupine climbs trees.[11]

Checking this out online, I read that while porcupines are good swimmers and also good climbers, they spend most of their time on the ground. Then again, I also read online a 2013 article that said biologists from the Federal University of Paraíba in Brazil had discovered a tree-hugging hybrid species (a monkey-like porcupine) and named it the "monkey-pine."[12] I found as well an article dated several years later (July 2016), by one Richard Irwin: "Dr. Iain McGilchrist: The Porcupine Is a Monkey, or, Things Are Not What They Seem." It began like this:

> "Iain McGilchrist will contend that the world in which we live in the West is shaped by a set of beliefs about reality which we know from experience, and feel intuitively, to be almost certainly false. Though the consequences of this are widely deplored, we seem strangely powerless to resist it. We are as if in a trance, whistling a happy tune as we sleep-walk towards the abyss."[13]

The kind of thinking we call "inductive" (as opposed to the "deductive" reasoning of the syllogism) provides major advantages in both philosophical and scientific approaches to truth seeking. Though the two approaches are often considered opposed, and though deduction, especially in science, is considered more reliable, they share long common roots. The earliest term for what we now call "science" was "natural philosophy," which began with inductive thinking. As William James long ago noted:

> "One of the most successfully cultivated branches of philosophy in our time is what is called inductive logic, the study of the conditions under which our sciences have evolved. When the first mathematical, logical, and natural uniformities, the first laws, were discovered, men … believed themselves to have deciphered authentically the eternal thoughts of the Almighty. His mind also thundered and reverberated in syllogisms. … But as the sciences have developed farther … investigators have become accustomed to the notion that no theory is absolutely a transcript of reality, but that any one of them may from some point of view be useful.

> Their great use is to summarize old facts and to lead to new ones. They are only a man-made language, conceptual shorthand … in which we write our reports of nature; and languages, as is well known, tolerate much choice of expression and many dialects."[14]

In everyday discourse, such as journalism and other nonfiction genres, a truth claim can be proven or disproven by reference to external facts. When the claim coincides with the relevant facts, we deem it true; when it doesn't, we reject it (or ought to reject it) as false. Because facts form the basis of any attempt to arrive at truth, the term "alternative facts" and other such dissembling phrases represent self-contained lies; they negate the very possibility of discovering the truth about anything at all. One is of course entitled to one's opinion, but there is a necessary divide between matters of fact and those of interpretation. Moreover, the relative value of a given opinion still rests on its basis in fact (or its lack of such basis). In other words, while everyone is entitled to an opinion, not all opinions are equally valid (not all opinions are based on facts).

To recap: when I speak of truth in the pages that follow, I will refer to truth relative to a given question about reality (that is, the truth *about* something), and not to a philosophical notion of absolute Truth. And to reiterate: I expressly do not mean to say here that truth is relative (which would negate the meaning and possibility of truth); I mean that the truth is a relation: that the truth about something is relative only to the facts of the matter under consideration, and that the truth can be (and should be) ascertained by reference to these verifiable facts. A lie about something may also be revealed by examining the "facts" on which the lie claims to be based.

> "It has lately been fashionable to say, quoting Nietzsche, that there is no fact, only interpretation. This itself is an interpretation of the fact that in our efforts to understand the world, we ordinarily get things a little wrong—sometimes very wrong. … this bias away from truth is reinforced by the character of language itself. Language makes sense without reference to the truth, or with an oblique or even an inverted reference to it."[15]

***

Language is a tool of communication, and can, like any tool, be used to advantage or misused for ill effect. Like a double-edged sword, language can cut both ways. Words can be heuristic, used to explain and enlighten, or they can limit discovery, fixing ideas like blinders. You can use words to speak truth to power or lie shamelessly to gain advantage; to comfort a friend or incite an enemy; to aid or obstruct. Words can help and they can hurt.

Language can be used to encapsulate lies and engender passivity, for example, to get people to believe that the truth is, Alice-in-Wonderland style, whatever you would like it to be, or that facts may be opposed by "alternative facts"—both of which viewpoints suggest that thought about or resistance to tyranny is not only pointless but moreover unthinkable, and thus impossible.

But language can also be used to encourage and inspire. Even in the inner thought of a single individual, words, for good or ill, manipulate. For instance, if I manipulate myself to get things done or see them through, I call it self-discipline, or purpose, or other high-level ideals. If I manipulate myself to fail, I call that neurotic. If I manipulate the facts I am in possession of to gain an advantage or licence of some sort over another or others, I call that deceitful. I do not believe, however, as some do, that the central or inevitable purpose of language is deceit.

"Language was given to men so that they could conceal their thoughts," said Charles-Maurice de Talleyrand. I disagree: that words may be used to conceal thought does not negate that they may also be used to reveal it. I don't even believe that language was somehow "given" to men. (I briefly note here, as I will have occasion to note at greater length later and with reference to other quotable authors, the absence in Talleyrand's universe of speaking women.)

Of course, there are many ways to lie with words. The term "genocide" was coined in 1944, by Raphael Lemkin, to refer to the murder of European Jewry during the Second World War, and genocide is now a crime under international law. Instances of targeted killing of ethnic, racial, religious or national groups of people have occurred throughout human history, and occur still. Today, however, we have a newer word for such targeted killing, routinely employed by presumably objective news reports: "ethnic cleansing." Earlier euphemisms were even more darkly suggestive. During the Holocaust the term for mass murder was "extermination" (to suggest that those to be killed were more like bugs than human beings). There are writers who still refer to the butchery as "extermination." Then and now, propaganda involves the wholesale reversal and perversion of meanings. Euphemisms are invented precisely as a kind of shorthand to prevaricate about things that people find odious or disturbing to contemplate.

Euphemisms seek to avoid, but lies per se occupy a different and darker territory. Within the play of language, the essence of the lie remains the intent to deceive. For example, the debate about whether journalists should lie to or mislead the subjects they would write about is often construed as an ethical issue somehow muddy or complex. I find this curious; it's not muddy at all: to lie is to lie and to mislead is to lie, and unless a lie is in the service of life (No, Mr. Gestapo Man, no Jews here; no, Mr. Leader of the Free World, no Muslims here; no, Mr. Holier Than Thou, no Catholics, no Hindus, no Quakers, no Buddhists—pick any object of organized hatred throughout human history), a lie is pernicious. In fact, in personal relationships and interactions, the lie is the most manipulative thing you can do with words.

To lie is to mislead and deceive with intent. Thus a lie is different from an error (from being mistaken about or ignorant of the facts). If I say that $10 plus $14 equals $35, I am in error, ignorant of the mathematical facts. If I know the correct total but overestimate it intentionally, then I am lying (perhaps intending to cheat you out of one dollar). A lie meant to deceive others is also different from a lie in the service of self-deception. If I tell myself I can afford to charge to my credit card $35 when I have no dollars to my name, I am lying to myself in order to deny a truth I'd rather not acknowledge (and incidentally keeping the credit card companies in business). The point is that in all these cases, the conclusion that 10 plus 14 equals 35 remains untrue.

Inconsistencies of numbers, however, are much easier to navigate than those of words. Consider for instance that numbers, unlike words, have no synonyms. The major promise or potential of words is their heuristic value, one perhaps under-estimated in the digital age; their major pitfall is the tendency of words to colonize minds when words are used by rote, with little meaning or precision. When words are used with a kind of automaticity, without considering their meanings, they render individuals more vulnerable to confusion and thus more likely to be misled by others, by means of words. The ill effects of rote usage can extend to words meant, as in news coverage, to convey facts (as opposed to interpretation or commentary). For example, during the Vietnam War, journalists had trouble describing in words what they saw, not necessarily because:

> "… it was so uniquely horrible; it was that the brutality and confusion one experienced seemed to lose something when rendered into language. Somehow, describing the situation so that it could be set in columns of type always seemed to be cleaning it up."[16]

What happens if language as it is now employed—when "information" is so readily available and so easily manipulated—in just such routine fashion?

What happens if language itself becomes a kind of rote, a kind of social displacement activity, with people speaking (and sometimes writing) without much meaning of any sort, as a kind of social nicety, saying what they feel they are expected to say at designated "appropriate" times and in common circumstances? When acquaintances meet on the street, for example, they routinely exchange such niceties. One says "Hi, how are you?" and the other answers "Fine, how are you?" though they may be genuinely uninterested in the first instance and lying to "save face" in the second. Because words can be misused on purpose, to lie or misrepresent or deceive, many people use the word "semantics" in a derogatory sense, as in "that's only semantics"—words devoid of meaning.

And this, in a nutshell, is the trouble with words: they are by nature relentlessly dual, capable of meaning one thing or another quite different thing depending on the context and the intent of the speaker or writer, the listener or reader. In fact, as noted, it is a persistent quality of words that they may often be defined most clearly in opposition. What is the difference, for example, between a need and an addiction?

I distinguish the two this way: a need can be satisfied; an addiction can only be maintained. You could argue that eating is an addiction too, because you need to keep eating to live; but an addiction to food (as opposed to a need for food) is a vain attempt to fill an internal emptiness and over-eating is the proximate result. As the saying goes: "Some people eat to live, and others live to eat." If you eat to live, you are not addicted, only hungry and doing the necessary decreed by bodily appetite. If you can't stop eating even when you aren't hungry, you are addicted to food.

The opposite eating disorder, anorexia, may also be defined in opposition. An addiction to avoiding food is not motivated (as over-eating is) by a need to fill the void and feel oneself a part of something larger, but by its virtual opposite: the need to exert some kind of control by establishing a boundary of the self, to feel apart from something larger. Fast metabolisms may account for people who are naturally thin, who have trouble gaining weight instead of the more usual goal of losing it. If you can't eat any more because you feel full, you are inclined to thinness; if you won't eat in a bid for at least one circumscribed area of life that you can conceivably control, you are inclined toward anorexia.

Both eating disorders (stuffing and starving) signify a kind of trouble with boundaries, and neither one achieves its purpose; like all neuroses, these are inappropriate responses to emotional pain. They don't work, except to bind the pain (keep it "under control"); they don't alleviate the pain or allow it to dissipate.

When she was almost five years old, granddaughter Clementine threw a tantrum one evening while her parents (my daughter Lienne and son-in-law Daniel) were out of town and I was in town to look after her. I was amazed by the explosive nature of Clem's temper (I had by this time forgotten my own, softened, I believe, by the passage of time, and by my love for and learned reliance on words), as well as by the sheer physical strength of one so small. Once Clem had stopped throwing things, I began picking them up, which sent her into a second frenzy of throwing things. I gave up on restoring order and said: "You know, Clem, everyone has to cope with bad feelings, and flying into a rage and throwing things around doesn't actually help. Would you like to talk about this feeling?"

"No, I want you to get away from me!" she yelled. Then broiling silence.

"Well then, I'm going into the guest bedroom to read, and that's where I'll be if you change your mind."

Stubborn could be Clem's middle name (she comes by it honestly: "stubborn" could be my middle name, too). She held out for a good ten minutes before appearing at my door, tears streaming down her beautiful face.

"Bubby," she began, "the bad feeling keeps coming back."

"That's okay, my darling," I consoled. "That's how it is with feelings sometimes. Just feel the feeling and let it pass."

The heuristic potential of words is immense, even unarguable, but it is nothing like absolute. On the one hand, words allow us to analyze and to imagine what does not (or does not yet) exist. On the other hand, words also allow us, and maybe even encourage us, to confuse the map with the territory. The territory, the land area described by a map, can't be erroneous in the way a map can be, but the territory does not speak and is not say-able. We have maps in order to re-present to the mind a land mass that exists in reality. Similarly, we have words to describe and communicate feelings and thoughts that logically must precede their expression in words. It is the nature of language, however, that as soon as you use words, you open a path to other, potentially contrary, denotative and connotative meanings. And so again, we come full circle: once we use words to describe or delineate feelings or ideas, the words become some sort of map. This dual nature of language allows for binary distinctions that don't exist in reality, even though most people, for example, "understand, intuitively, that the distinction between structure and agency is—like the distinction between 'nature' and 'nurture'—an artifact of explanation, not a part of reality."[17]

To complicate matters, what's wrong with words is the very "same thing that [is] right with them, presumably." To take a position on any matter of debate is to enter the minefield, for regardless of your argument, the "fact is, as soon as you start with words, you're locked into a debate, forced to take a position with respect to others, confirming or rebutting what has been said before."[18]

Thus the trouble with words is at least twofold: on the one hand, the difficulty of expressing meaning, because what you mean by the words you use and what others understand by them depends largely on a corresponding or shared understanding of the meanings of those words. On the other hand of trouble is the rote use of words: words spoken or written without much intention to convey meaning, usage that undercuts the import of meaning or even the possibility of its expression. Though words are an essential element of communication, language may foster an "illusion of knowledge":

> "When we all use the same words, we can easily get lulled into thinking we are having the same experience, when in fact our experiences may be very different. ... Our experience is in motion, but our language holds that experience still. ... Language ... often binds us to a single perspective."[19]

Paradox, Metaphor, and a Final Philosophical Detour

Word sense relies, as noted, on divisions that don't exist in reality. It's not just that language is not synonymous with all of reality, and not able even to "mirror" tiny parts of it. It's that language and reality are at standing philosophical odds. A mirror, however faithful its image, is still a mirror, not a lens. For example, when I regard myself in a mirror, my right and my left are the same as they are from my own perspective; when I regard another person, the directions are reversed: facing you, my right side is opposite your left side, and vice-versa.

Words treat reality as if it were dissect-able, but the real world is indivisible. Language separates, but reality is whole. Language is digital and linear, but the real world is analog and multifaceted. Ray Jackendoff put it pithily in his book *A User's Guide to Thought and Meaning*: "Words have a tendency to sharpen boundaries—the 'handle' is more discrete than the concept it's a handle for."[20]

Words split linguistic hairs; they divide, and by dividing, they may reinforce illusions of binarity, the idea that everything has two sides (and only two sides), and thus they may encourage either-or thinking. In other words:

> "Language itself may be misleading us. Appalled by inequality our minds turn immediately to its opposite. Sidestepping that impulse … requires giving up a satisfying rhetorical clarity, but it may bring us closer to our moral common sense."[21]

The postmodernist trend in literary studies goes further than conflating words with reality; it sees discourse as the ultimate reality, as if reality itself were a product of words. Robert Darnton commented on this tendency to confuse reality with statements about reality. In a review of Roger Chartier's book *Forms and Meanings: Texts, Performances, and Audiences from Codex to Computer*), Darnton wrote this:

> "… like some opponents of post-modernism, he [Chartier] takes a strong stand against the so-called 'linguistic turn,' or the tendency to interpret meaning, behavior, and reality itself as the product of discourse. The current fashion of discourse analysis, as he sees it, is fundamentally misguided, because it treats non-discursive practices, such as everyday behavior, in the same way as messages printed in books. It confuses experience with texts and threatens to replace social history with literary criticism."[22]

Language is a paradoxical, second-order reality system, distinct from reality but easily confused with it. Words are the units of this system, but as we have seen, the more you try to define a word, the more nebulous its meaning becomes, the emptier of meaning the word is seen to be. It is not texts as such but word-wielding humans in context that bear the essence of meaning.

The word "paradox" comes from two Greek words: the prefix para, meaning "beyond or distinct from but analogous to" (think "paranormal" or "paramilitary" or even "paragraph") and doxa (opinion). Oxford defines "paradox" as a seemingly contradictory statement that turns out to be true, to be not self-contradictory; but also as a phenomenon that seems unreasonable or impossible, that flies in the face of existing (pre-conceived) ideas. Notice how much more clearly the word "paradox" applies to statements than to phenomena. If phenomena exist in reality, they have being other than words, being that words can refer to. Literacy is a paradoxical system, but in analog reality, there is no paradox. For paradox, you need words.

As the famous liar's paradox has it: "This sentence is a lie." The sentence is self-contradictory. If the sentence is true, then it asserts a falsehood about itself and cannot be believed or taken at face value; and if the sentence is false, it suggests, in perfectly circular fashion, that it's true (that it's false). But such self-contradiction is possible only in language. The sentence works as paradox because it refers only to itself. In this sense, all sentences are lies—but in this sense only. Because language re-presents in words "things" in reality, it introduces the possibilities inherent in representation: both truth and lies, language revelatory and language inept.

If words are ambiguous and meanings elusive; if viewpoints or perspectives are "merely" subjective; and if facts are contestable and don't "speak for themselves": then what of meaning and whither truth? In terms of the truth about something, William James's pragmatism has yet to be outdone as "a method of settling metaphysical disputes that otherwise might be interminable":

> "Is the world one or many?—fated or free?—material or spiritual?—here are notions either of which may or may not hold good of the world; and disputes over such notions are unending. The pragmatic method in such cases is to try to interpret each notion by tracing its respective practical consequences. What difference would it practically make to any one if this notion rather than that notion were true? If no practical difference whatever can be traced, then the alternatives mean practically the same thing, and all dispute is idle."[23]

In fact, according to James's pragmatism, any statement without practical implications is relatively meaningless, and debates about such statements amount to "vain wrangling":

> "The serious meaning of a concept ... lies in the concrete difference to someone which its being true will make. ... if it can make no practical difference which of two statements be true, then they are really one statement in two verbal forms; if it can make no practical difference whether a given statement be true or false, then the statement has no real meaning."[24]

On the other hand, as amply demonstrated by major accomplishments in both the arts and the sciences, our meaningful narratives (our language, our thought) have indeed opened once-locked doors into reality. Slippery as it gets, language exerts remarkable agency. Though words can never constitute or even represent the whole of reality, it is words (and the increasingly sophisticated technologies based on them) that allow us to apprehend reality by naming it, and to circumscribe inquiry in order to discover some of reality's secrets, despite that those discoveries are limited by our own capacities (as also by their technological extensions).

Through the power of language, we gain a modicum of understanding and control. Reality, like territory, does not speak, yet maps remain eminently useful. Words are like that: not substitutes for, but guide maps to, reality. Yet the tendency to confuse or conflate language with reality (the map with the territory) appears practically hard-wired. Language originates in the unconscious, but as long as this fact is not rendered invisible, language still stands to raise consciousness. When, however, the tendency to confuse the two operates without awareness (when we don't notice the contradictions), we get into flattened out, either-or thinking and binary oppositions.

The dualism built into the structures of language is what enables paradox. Yet it is not paradox but metaphor that makes the heart of language. For if paradox were the essence of language, then language would be only a maze of tormented misconception and there would be no sense in speaking or writing, no sense in seeking truth or meaning, and no redeeming qualities in the love and potential of language.

Instead, since language affords and can hone the capacity for comprehension, there is every possible reason to learn to speak and write truly, to learn to listen and hear, not just take turns talking, and to eschew as much falseness as you are able to face (to recognize and resist). Without the ability to capture in thought what reality is like, without metaphor, the true and the false appear equally real—that is, equally relevant or irrelevant, and so, equally unhelpful.

More than mere literary trope, metaphor is the beating heart of language. Paradox can deal only in self-negating dualities like doors that open in or out; metaphor, on the other hand, can suggest, and its horizons are not like the single horizon that separates the heavens from the earth, but more like the imagined horizons of many-sided perspectives, more like the prisms of a diamond. Perhaps, as Annie Dillard suggested, the truth (as relation) outlives paradox (as structure). In her book *For the Time Being*, Dillard wrote that many "spiritual thinkers" possessed "a sort of anaerobic capacity to batten and thrive on paradox."

All those old saws about truth are true; the search is worth the candle. We can know the truth, and the truth shall make us free. Or, as per one of those philosophizing posters of the 1960s (accompanied by a photo of a frog clinging tenuously to a thin branch): "The truth shall set us free, but first it will make us miserable." The difference between paradox and metaphor is what Wallace Stegner got at when he wrote that:

> "... a good writer isn't really a mirror. He's a lens. One mirror is like another mirror—a mechanical reflector. But a lens may be anything from what you have in your Instamatic to what makes you handle your Hasselblad with reverence."[25]

Despite the limitations of words, literacy has proven a consequential work-around in human evolution. And if words are only secondary phenomena attached to something called "reality," they are yet clearly powerful within history as within individual lives. Language allows for abstract thought, including the kind we call imagination.

> "In terms of the brain, we know that concepts are somehow stored there, but we have little idea of exactly how. ... If you are uneasy about this, think of the nineteenth-century search for the source of the Nile. People knew the Nile must have a source, as all rivers do, and they knew it was somewhere in the middle of Africa. Eventually it was located. The phrase the source of the Nile was not a meaningless phrase just because no one had yet pinpointed its referent."[26]

Language does not work as a substitute for reality, and if language is unable even to describe objective reality objectively, that's only because there's no such thing as objective reality. Our thought and our language don't mirror or represent the whole of reality because they can't. Yet just because there's no such thing as objective reality, doesn't mean there's no reality. Just because our human perspective is limited by subjectivity doesn't mean that a given perspective isn't real or doesn't matter. It just means that if there *were* an objective reality, we, the human species and/or individual humans, wouldn't be in charge of it. And yet language gives and feeds the illusion that there is and we are.

While there is no such thing as objective reality, there is a difference between truth and lies.

Philosophical attempts through the centuries to find and define or name the Absolute Truth have predictably proven unsuccessful (though they nevertheless persist). Everyday truth, on the other hand—the truth *about* something—can still yield, and the search is still worth the effort. That we can possess only relative truth, is no reason to give up on the truth about something. The idea of Absolute Truth amounts to a kind of wishful thinking. But that doesn't mean that our pining after absolutes (what George Steiner called "nostalgia for the absolute") doesn't affect our behaviour or that it bears no relationship to reality or to real-world consequences. For a clean cut through the jargon, ask a great journalist:

> "... while I am aware that there is no Truth, no objective truth, no single truth, no truth simple or unsimple, either; no verity, eternal or otherwise; no Truth about anything, there are Facts, objective facts, discernible and verifiable. And the more facts you accumulate, the closer you come to whatever truth there is."[27]

If truth is a relation between language and reality, the truth about something is theoretically at least both ascertainable and verifiable. If language can express a more or less true relation (to reality), then the truth is discoverable, though the process may not be easy, nor the findings to our liking.

We can come to know the truth about something, as long as by "truth" we mean the facts of a given matter, and as long as the matter is one of fact and not one of opinion. Opinions may be well- or ill-founded but they can't be true as such. The only case in which an opinion can be considered true or false is that in which one voices an opinion contrary to the opinion one actually holds, or when the opinion one professes contradicts one's behaviour, and in these cases, we would call the opinion and/or the behaviour, hypocritical rather than untrue.

Truth in Everyday Journalism and Politics

Recent years have seen books proliferate to argue that words and truth do matter—because their writers are protesting that they don't seem to matter at all, especially in political speech. Do they protest too much? I think not.

Of course, there's nothing new in political double-talk and the well-rehearsed non-answer. By such means, many politicians get away clean not just by refusing to respond to questions posed but also by promulgating bald-faced lies (known in the business of Public Relations, which reporters used to call "the dark side," as the more congenial "staying on message").

I began thinking about these changes decades ago, while working for the national wire service Canadian Press in the Montreal bureau, when CP was still a not-for-profit cooperative, before it announced plans to privatize in 2010. Before then, CP was owned and operated by its member newspapers, whose clout within the co-operative was based on the member newspaper's circulation size (and thus its fees due to the co-operative). The move to privatize came to fruition in 2010, but the trend was evident years before. In the newspaper business, journalistic ethics 101 says: keep your opinions out of it; tell the story down the middle, without taking sides. In practice, that often amounts to figuring out and then telling the truth about who is lying to whom and why.

Broadcast and print media began at some point—I noticed it in the late 1980s or early 1990s—to use the term "narrative" to explain various views and accounts of real-world events. That seemed to me then a kind of professional cop-out: a sanitized version of Cover Your Behind, as if even reporters and their editors had given up on the truth, implying one story is as good or bad as the next, that the truth is not attainable to be told. Today, the same word "narrative" sparks different feelings: when video-recorded incidents of police brutality and other evils go viral, sparking mass protests around the world, and when critics and the protesting public in general use the word "narrative" to indicate their awareness that a standing narrative may belie the truth, and when they unite to make common cause, I feel proud instead of ashamed to be human, and my faith in humanity is restored, if only for the moment.

In the early 1990s, I interviewed a government official about the Canadian tainted blood scandal, in which thousands of Canadians undergoing medical transfusions had been infected with bad blood from officially (and presumably safe) sources. The report argued that the public health disaster was preventable, theoretically at least: had anyone been prepared early on to take responsibility and blow the whistle. In response to my questions, the official kept repeating that while she "wasn't there then," she could assure me that no one got tainted blood from the federal blood system. How could she possibly assure me of that when the bad blood had infected so many with the AIDS virus, and when the scandal was widely reported?

I persisted. If nothing untoward occurred, if no mistakes were made, how did the blood make so many Canadians sick? But the official just kept repeating official policy, chapter and verse—as if the words themselves were unrelated to truth, as if the words she spoke were an expression only of her official position in the power grid, bearing no relation to reality: words as a *substitute* for truth. Her job was to speak certain words, not to understand or remedy anything, certainly not to take any kind of responsibility. How could she? She "wasn't there then."

It seemed clear to me at the time that the official wasn't there now either. Was it a presumed part of my job as a reporter to quote authorities and politely fail to notice when they lied outright or made no sense whatever? How could I complete my assignment without quoting the source I'd been sent to interview?

All I could do, in the truncated language of newspapers and wire services, was to quote other sources rebutting the official—of course a better option than not quoting rebuttals, but hardly ideal.

In terms of truth-telling, perhaps no publishing outlet provides an ideal venue: everything depends on the devil in the details, and all venues provide options and all have limits. Years after reporting on the tainted blood scandal, years after I had left the business of daily reporting, I had a chance to comment more freely (than possible in newspaper accounts) on Canada's access-to-information laws and the public's right to know, when a report ("Fallen Behind: Canada's Access to Information Act in the World Context") quoted from my 2008 book *Investigative Reporting in Canada* on the matter of Freedom of Information requests filed by reporters:

> "If the reporter can be dissuaded by this initial [access request] refusal, and many can be, the government learns how well the strategy works and the information remains locked away. Thus the battle to pry loose government data that ought to be public is a battle for more than information—it represents the larger struggle for freedom of expression and the public's right to know. [...] It's a commonplace among reporters of investigative stripe: the various freedom-of-information acts have actually made it more difficult, not less, to pry loose information from government holdings."[28]

The report showed how good intentions can go astray and underlined how legal measures meant as remedies can become policy measures that counteract them. Before the institution of access-to-information acts, information was actually easier to get from places like police stations and government departments. The law ostensibly meant to provide greater public access to the facts actually made it easier for those in positions of power to hide information that should be in the public domain, to hide documented facts that had been accessible before the coming of the laws (perhaps by tipping off sources that enquiries were being made, that an enterprising reporter was sniffing around). One way to oppose this trend would be for more journalists to file more access requests. Of course, the double bind here is that the time spent on formal requests could well prove wasted (with "sensitive" information blacked out when a written response is finally obtained). Nevertheless, the tendency of official sources to find ways to pervert the stated intentions of the law and to hide information rather than reveal it still underlines the importance of documentation in establishing the truth of a matter.

Why else would official sources work so hard to keep such documentation secret? Clearly, words can be used to pervert stated intentions, flouting or frustrating those intentions rather than fulfilling them. You could say that officials are after all only people with jobs, going along to get along, following orders to keep their jobs, but then you would also have to admit that there remain people of conscience who refuse to "go along" and who risk jobs and more to resist.

In a story about alternative treatments for cancer that I wrote while working for the Canadian Press in the Montreal bureau, I interviewed a spokesperson for media relations at Health Canada about why the department refused to test Gaston Naessens's 714X, an immune based alternative treatment for cancer. No matter how hard I tried to get a straight answer, the spokesperson just kept sending me general documentation saying how the process of medical trials is supposed to work. My protestation (that the reality was inconsistent with the documentation, that how it's supposed to work wasn't how it was working), no matter how often or firmly reiterated, met with a curiously passive resistance, an imperturbable wall of non-response. I couldn't get a straight answer to any of my questions, but the supposedly relevant policy documentation just kept coming. In fact, I felt as if I were being beaten about the head with it.

In the matter of alternative treatments, one Montreal woman who fought for her cancer-stricken daughter and got the attending doctors to use 714X in conjunction with chemotherapy, got it exactly right. She said the doctors practising traditional medicine and those advocating for alternatives could work together: the problem is they don't.

The same basic ploys are used by officials in all reporting on medical "alternatives" (or, for that matter, on all kinds of alternative and oppositional views and paradigms). Mostly, such alternatives are dismissed with the preferred explanation for this dismissal: that any evidence that does exist is merely anecdotal. Consider that the dismissal of anecdote in medicine, as in other fields, amounts to the dismissal of individuals, of subjectivity.

The kind of circular "reasoning" that characterizes rejection of the unorthodox effectively closes the gate on debate. As Candace Pert describes the situation in a book that deals with her 1986 discovery of opiate receptors in the brain (and how it took decades for these findings and their implications to be accepted), the scientific and medical establishments did what they usually do when they come across informational claims or data that don't fit the reigning paradigm: they ignore it. If upstarts persist in speaking up, stronger measures are taken to discredit the speakers, usually with little data but lots of ad hominem attacks.

The patterns faithfully repeated themselves when I chased another alternative health story in the early 1990s about a then new diagnostic procedure for finding tumours in the breast. Called Lintroscan, this new technology had been developed by researchers at the University of Miami and was making its way through proper channels, soon to be adopted in Canada, according to officials I interviewed at Health Canada. The Montreal bureau of the Canadian Press published my first article on the subject in 1992.[29] When I left the national wire service in 1995, determined to duke it out as a freelancer, I wrote a follow-up story on Lintroscan, which was published in a tiny Montreal weekly called The Hour.[30]

When I re-interviewed the American doctor I had consulted for the first Canadian Press story on Lintroscan, the doctor told me he had used the device successfully for a few years (he even did a scan for a woman who travelled from Quebec to Ohio for the purpose, and he did it for free because neither the woman's health insurance nor the Quebec government would pay for it). He said he had been forced to stop using Lintroscan in 1992, shortly after my original CP story ran, when field officers arrived unannounced at his office and carted away his Lintroscan machine, claiming that the U.S. Food and Drug Administration had ruled it illegal.

"The FDA can do that?" I asked him.

"The FDA is omnipotent," he said. "It's about $110,000 a [mammography] unit—that's a lot of money to throw away. I really think a lot of it had to do with the fact that Lintroscan would have put mammography out of business for the most part."

Shouldn't it?

I called the FDA to ask about this ruling, and officials there verified: Lintroscan had been ruled illegal. I had unwittingly fed the good doctor to the FDA police, yet the doctor was so kind in that follow-up interview. "Don't blame yourself, Maxine," he said. "You tried to do a good thing." Clearly, all manner of good intentions may go astray as they navigate the shoals of publication.

Of course, instruments of disinformation have always existed and been employed by governments and large corporations and others who can afford them as measures of social control (read: to maintain power and profits). But these days, the phenomenon is normalized: it appears to be widespread not just among politicians but among many more minor officials charged with some kind of public responsibility and presumable accountability (not to say "trust")—as if everyone has read from the very same political playbook.

> "There is a small industry out there called media training. It offers instruction on how to 'control a narrative,' to use that awful term. Most politicians are clients. The prime directive of media training is that the question never matters. That an honest response is for amateurs. Media trainers advise memorizing a set of non-responses and repeating them no matter what question is asked."[31]

When officials speak now, many are not defending the content of their speech but only their "right" to speak an official line. Worse, the evasion of answers and the propagation of lies, both so central to the playbook, sometimes appear impervious to exposure by journalists and others. The unofficial playbook knows no national boundaries: Canadian government officials and other power holders are at least as well practiced in its techniques as those of any other nominally democratic nation.

Elements of the playbook were in full play, for instance, in February 2020, when Canadian news media reported on native protests against a proposed gas pipeline. The Wet'sewet'en (pronounced: Wet-Sue-Wet-In) people of British Columbia had set up railway blockades to oppose the building of a pipeline on their territory. Other native groups across the country, including the Mohawk in eastern Canada, had joined in support. The blockades were more than inconvenient for cross-country travellers; they blocked shipments of propane and other materials essential to the livelihood of farmers and other groups across the nation. It took sustained native protest to finally get the federal government to engage in the talks that government had promised in its election campaign of 2015.

Yet the idea that public protest and public discussion don't change anything is badly mistaken. Thirty years earlier, as a reporter for CP, I had covered the 1990 Oka crisis. That protest was over the plan by some entrepreneurs in the town of Oka, led by the mayor of the town, who wanted to build a golf course on Mohawk burial grounds. After a police officer was killed in a standoff with natives, the Quebec government called in the federal army and people could watch from the comforts of home the televised government-approved violence that followed.

Anyone who thinks that nothing has changed must, like the Canadian official spokesperson on the tainted blood scandal, not have been there then. Anyone who thinks that the native protests then were without foundation (they were and still are about land disputes that go back to the days of the nation's founding) or that the federal government's brutal suppression of the protest was less than brutal, must not have seen soldiers beating women and children as they fled, on order, from their own homes. Thirty years later, popular understanding of and support for native land rights is much higher than it was during the Oka crisis. Said one woman interviewed on a television newscast from Toronto's Union Station about the 2020 rail blockade: "Of course the train cancellations are inconvenient. But there's a big difference between inconvenience and injustice." (Bless her justice-loving heart.)

What hasn't changed as much are the mechanisms, the algorithms, of official power, its made-to-order policies, and if need be, made-to-order laws backed by the ultimate insurance of armed force. For example, in politics, in order to justify the use of armed force, official spokespeople may imply that there is no alternative by saying that peaceful negotiations have to date proven unproductive, when the truth is that no negotiations have taken place. This sort of tactic is used routinely, straight out of the how-to-tell-whoppers-and-get-away-with-it political playbook.

But while government authorities may ply the same old, same old lines, at least some portions of the people have grown more aware of the nature of political lies as such. In an interview with Canadian journalist Eleanor Wachtel, famed linguist Noam Chomsky commented on the difference between official discourses and a kind of public (human) wisdom:

> "Intellectual discourse has followed a rather normal path in times of crisis, shifting towards greater subordination to power, sometimes with a kind of fanaticism. The general public, in contrast, has become more open-minded, concerned, engaged, in ways that cannot be characterized in simple terms."[32]

Though the native protests of 2020 were eerily reminiscent of Oka thirty years earlier, it was clear that something had changed in the interim, at least in the attitudes of those not seeking political office or the dollars of campaign donors (without which their hopes of ballot-box victory are effectively nil). It's the same with alternative health news and views: Lintroscan may be suppressed, but women are hardly beating down the doors for mammograms, which have been shown to cause more breast cancer than they detect. Mammograms are now advertised quasi-privately, with letters to target audiences (aging women), and widely offered free of charge.

What applies to public crises generally applied with ferocity to the worldwide crisis with the advent in early 2020 of a deadly corona virus. Varieties of political manoeuvring may change only slowly, over decades; not so viruses. The U.S. administration of Donald Trump didn't just engage in the lying that Trump was infamous for, but so badly bungled the initial response to the pandemic that the U.S. in early 2020 had by far the largest number of cases of covid-19 and the largest number of deaths from the disease worldwide. Such an outcome can hardly reflect the "consent" of the governed, regardless of the machinations that govern the election process.

While many politicians proceeded with politicking as usual, so-called "ordinary people"—especially those on the front lines of the battle—showed remarkable courage and compassion. In the great city of New York, which had been badly hit by the virus, people in Manhattan opened their windows and came out on their balconies at pre-arranged times to cheer on hospital workers in a show of appreciation and solidarity, an action undertaken with gusto around the world. People in Italy, with one of the highest death tolls in the early days of the pandemic, had done the same. In fact, people all over the world found ways to stay in touch without physical closeness. It was a time to be thankful for the Internet and for the other means of virtual communication that we take so much for granted. Even more than that, love in the time of covid-19 was a time to be grateful for the so very many who did—and continue to do—what they could and can to help and care for others. This too is human.

The Personal, the Political, and the Playbook

The feminist insight that the personal is the political retains its import in terms of the prospects for truth telling amid the widespread tactics of the political playbook: the personal really is the political in numerous ways. Lying, equivocating, misleading, suppressing information—all of this is quite ordinary stuff in the political playbook. Also common is this: don't just accuse your adversaries of this or that; accuse them of the very wrongdoing and lies that you yourself are trying to commit and perpetrate.

When I was teaching journalism, and especially in the years that I was chairing the department, one of the department's teachers was a man who repeatedly challenged my authority, but not in an effort to call to account or modify my behaviour (he never offered alternative measures for change). Rather, the man dogged my every step only to contest what he clearly saw as the illegitimacy of any kind of authority I might have the chutzpah to claim. It's well recognized among academics that chairing a department, especially one as raucous as a journalism department, is a position nearly thankless. In the event, though, I discovered two important things, one about power and one about myself.

About power, I learned that with a little power one really can make positive change. About myself, I discovered that I *like* being the boss. This journalism instructor who opposed my every move in the department was apparently well acquainted with the modern playbook—but he was only slightly aware of his own motives. That's why, I think, he would invariably end up losing his staged battles and causing more damage to himself than to me, wasting only my time while simultaneously exposing his own corrupt motives and behaviour, like the naked emperor clothed in imaginary finery. In one of these enactments, the man complained directly to the university's Human Resources director. He demanded a meeting, claiming that I had discriminated against him by scheduling him for a next-semester class at 4:00 p.m., when he had to pick up his son from school because his wife couldn't. Thing is, the man had never mentioned to me that my schedule created a personal problem for him (instead assuming and implying nefarious motives).

Here's how a lack of self-awareness can hamstring anyone intent on mimicking the ploys of the political playbook: During the meeting, the man began by saying to me: "I'd like to help you, Maxine, but ...". Lippy as ever, I interrupted him and shot back: "I'm working on my third book for Oxford University Press, and I don't need your help." The man turned beet red, tossed off a remark about how he didn't have to put up with this, uh, stuff, and then he stood, making as if to leave. Before he reached the door, however, his cursory understanding of playbook strategy kicked in: the revelation showed first on his face and then in his post-immediate reaction. He realized how bad it would look were he to angrily depart a meeting he himself had requested, indeed, insisted upon.

Failure to grasp the manoeuvres of the playbook, otherwise known as naiveté, also has consequences (not invariably negative). As a young woman, I got my newspaper internship at the *Edmonton Journal*. In my application for the internship, I had listed on my résumé, along with my qualifications, the fact that I'd led the drive to start a union at the first paper I worked for (a sleazy supermarket tabloid once known as Midnight, with hysterically funny headlines, and an enviably large circulation). Just before the scheduled week of the membership drive, a voice on my home phone messaging system threatened to break both my legs if I didn't desist. It doesn't just happen in the movies, though if I remember correctly, for some obscure reason, I was unafraid (I giggled). Today, chastened by age and experience and the sad fate of dailies, I think I might well be afraid. Worse, I would certainly be less optimistic about the prospects of unionizing or about the light unto the public that is supposed to be the press.

Cases in point are the so-called "catch and kill" strategies used by some major media, strategies that work less auspiciously, more smoothly, than direct confrontation in the interests of media manipulation, at least for media organizations who can afford the hefty price tag. What happens to a reporter trying to tell a true story these days is a lot more harrowing than anything I experienced back in the day. And yet with perseverance and a little help from freedom-loving friends and publishers, true stories still manage to get told. Just ask the two female reporters who broke the story of sexual predator Harvey Weinstein in the *New York Times*. Ask Ronan Farrow, who wrote the full story, first in the fine *New Yorker* magazine and subsequently in book form, of a famous movie mogul and his serial-rapist ways (*before* Weinstein's trial and conviction).

The truth about something can still be discovered. Just ask Robert Caro, who spent years of his life to tell the truth, in his book *Working: Researching, Interviewing, Writing*, about what everyone believed could never be known: whether Lyndon Baines Johnson had stolen his 1948 election as a United States senator from Texas. Caro did finally ascertain the truth (yes, LBJ stole it). To do so, Caro went far beyond textual sources, moving to the "hill country" where LBJ grew up, getting familiar with the locals, and getting them to open up and tell him their own stories about LBJ. In March of 1986, he interviewed Luis Salas, who it turned out had "fixed" the vote tally in his district to Johnson's advantage. It was in this interview with Salas (forty years after the fact), that Salas not only admitted he'd lied in court all those decades earlier, but also revealed he'd written a 94-page-long manuscript about the whole affair.[33]

Caro copied the manuscript, with the author's pleased permission (Salas said he wanted the truth to be told before he died). Thus Caro managed to publish in book form the truth about a long-ago election controversy, to answer the question that "everyone" thought could never be answered. That the event was decades old disqualified the facts as "daily news," but not (and never) as truth. This may explain why in recent years some previously unearthed truth is emerging in the narrative long-form journalism of books (and sometimes magazine articles) more than in the daily news (which reports "just the facts, ma'am," especially those facts less than 24 hours old). I do not mean here to disparage the work of daily news reporters; on the contrary, that work is often brilliant and remains, as "the first draft of history," indispensable to longer-form accounts (not to mention that many daily news reporters realize the limits of the newspaper platform and have responded by writing books of their own). Of course, no conspiracy is required to conduct the business of daily reportage as usual—especially when no conspiracy is reported. So hats off to all intrepid reporters, to all those journalists who seek the truth, without, as it is written, fear or favour, and who against all the odds find the means to publish it. The poet W. H. Auden paid tribute:

> "With all that can be said, justly, against journalists, there is one kind of journalist to whom civilization owes a very great debt, namely, the brave and honest reporter who unearths and makes public unpleasant facts, cases of injustice, cruelty, corruption, which the authorities would like to keep hidden, and which even the average reader would prefer not to be compelled to think about."[34]

Auden himself maintained his authorial integrity by refusing to edit out critical commentary in a piece he wrote for *Life* magazine, about the fall of ancient Rome. At the end of the article, Auden wrote this:

> "I think a great many of us are haunted by the feeling that our society, and by ours I don't just mean the United States or Europe, but our whole worldwide technological civilisation, whether officially labelled capitalist, socialist, or communist, is going to go smash and probably deserves to."[35]

Asked to delete the passage, Auden refused, and Life declined to publish the piece.

People everywhere recognize the purpose of the lie. Liars in positions of power get this, and that's *why* they lie. Noam Chomsky put it plainly when he commented on the capacity of people to resist lies. He expressed a kind of "optimism about people's capacity to act in decent, humane ways when they understand the realities," and he noted that awareness of the nature and power of the lie is "shared by people in power almost universally":

> "If you look through history, or even today, you'll very rarely, if ever, see a statesman or a leader turn to the public and say, 'Look, it would

be in our interest to go slaughter those guys over there or to rob them or torture them or terrorize them, so let's do it.' … What you do find is an elaborate set of rationalizations and excuses and quite elaborate constructions developed by intellectuals, which make it appear as if robbing them and torturing them and killing them is right and just. Well, why bother with that unless you're afraid, at some level of your consciousness, that if people know the truth they're not going to let you get away with it."[36]

Chapter 4

Grammar: Sense and Nonsense

You might think people would appreciate grammar for its offer of order, an aid to written expression. Yet many discount the rules of grammar as oppressive; some seem to hate the very subject with a passion that merits the verb.

The grammatical structures that underly meaning are tools for making sense on a page or on a screen. But the names of these structures remain unfamiliar to many, and so the subject of grammar mystifies when it might enlighten. What resists remedy is an ingrained contempt for the very idea of "rules," as if the conventions of literacy exist mostly to muzzle free expression. More commonly, grammar is not opposed but merely dismissed as of minor if any importance. But to say grammar doesn't matter is to say that words don't matter. It's a short step from there to "truth is relative." But to say that truth is relative is to gut the concept of truth—as that of falsity. In dismissing grammatical understanding, one forfeits its spyglass.

Ignorance of grammar appears blameless; the subject is dismissed with clear conscience by many, as if it's to be taken for granted that anyone who objects on the basis of correctness is just too out of it to count. Some disdain grammatical understanding because they believe it matters little in the practice of writing; they remind me of those who learned to hate math in school and never recovered and who in adult life tend to dismiss mathematicians sight unseen, as if these latter were speaking in a code of no consequence.

Some argue that grammar is just a matter of convention—and *of course* it is: that's *how* it aids communication. Others conclude that grammar matters only because you have to be more "formal" in writing—that writing and speaking have different standards (also true); that correct grammar is "nothing but" a matter of colloquial expression clashing with "standards." Such views fail to grasp the difference between the back-and-forth of spoken words and the inertness of written ones. In literacy, the marks on a page or screen are all the recourse a writer or a reader has to go by. That's all the more reason to embrace grammatical understanding, not for the sake of idle formality, but for that of meaning conveyed.

The point of grammar is precision. Writing requires more precision than spoken language because in speaking, you know when your meaning isn't getting across, and you can reiterate or expand as needed. In writing, there's no hearer available to clarify, to interject a "Say what?" or "Whaddaya mean by that?" In writing, you have no chance to notice that the unknown reader isn't getting it, and no second chance to explain what you mean. There is no tone of voice to be heard and no furrowed brow to indicate incomprehension, no bodily expression by which to assess attitude or intention. The failure to recognize this difference between the spoken and written word is at the root of much bad prose. When I was teaching journalism, I knew a professor who told his students he didn't need to bother with grammar because he was a "natural writer." That's laughable: I picture a newborn, brandishing a crayon.

On the other hand, grammatical error can be overrated as a source of bad writing, for such error is not the central factor in writing: it's meaning that's primary. I agree that a pedantic concern with correctness is a blinder that accounts for much stilted writing and accounts even more for deaf-ear editing. To stand up to bad editing and editors is after all a mark of honour among conscientious writers. ("When I split an infinitive," said Raymond Chandler, "I mean it to stay split." Hurray!)

Grammar stands to aid clarity, but some anti-grammar commentary equates clarity with the denuding of style, synonymous with simple, short, shallow. I regard clarity as among the highest virtues in writing (second only to truth). I see style as the fruition of voice, and clarity as the mark, the telltale sign, of this fruition. I mean that style is what a writer achieves when she has learned to rely on her own voice (the way, as a toddler, she first learned, and not without effort, to stand on her own feet). A writer speaks in her own voice once she has acquired the skill and marshaled the courage to deploy that voice. Voice is powerful. (It's said of Churchill that during the Second World War he mobilized the English language and sent it into battle).

Voice is the essence of style, what makes one writer's style different from another's, and when combined with skill, what makes a given style recognizable. When voice comes to fruition, clarity is crystal: there's no need to pander to critics, internal or external, once you know what it is you want to say and have found the courage to say it. While some would-be critics treat grammar as the enemy of artistry, I see it as a foundation of style, regardless of how well or not the writer can spout grammatical terms. That is, I distinguish between the operational understanding of an educated ear and the parading expertise of the pedant. Many good writers possess the former quite without (and quite without the need for) the latter; they possess an operational understanding, usually gained from wide reading.

Bad teaching and bad grammar books explain some of the resistance to grammatical precision. The advent of so-called "whole language" theory didn't help; the theory stands in strict opposition to phonics, the traditional method of reading instruction. Although the whole-language movement gathered renewed steam in the 1980s, the argument about how best to teach reading goes back even farther.

> "Noah Webster believed in phonics, Horace Mann in the word method. In the late 1920s, as progressive education became an influential movement, schools began to switch from phonics to whole-word reading instruction. The much-lampooned mid-twentieth-century Dick and Jane readers, and also Dr. Seuss's The Cat in the Hat, are based on whole-word theory: they try to get children to familiarize themselves with a limited set of simple words (to memorize them, phonics people would say, like trick ponies), not to use their knowledge of letters and sounds to decode words they haven't seen before. Rudolf Flesch's scorching 1955 best seller Why Johnny Can't Read turned the pendulum back toward phonics in the 1960s. By the 1980s, the glory decade for whole-language, the pendulum had swung again."[1]

Grammar phobia is still widespread, and not only among English students. The whole-language approach appears to have spread, to have infected other teaching subjects with the desire to jettison rules of any sort. For instance, the decade of the 1970s saw a rise in similar methods for teaching math, methods that also eschewed basics, doing away with such as instruction in long division and the memorization of times tables.

Since the traditional way of teaching children to read is phonics (sounding out words, letter by letter) and since whole-language theory proposes instead to teach the skill by getting kids to recognize whole words, one at a time, word by word, it would seem obvious that the latter method leaves kids up the creek when they encounter new words—but apparently it's not that obvious.

A 2019 article by linguistics professor John McWhorter stood firmly on the side of phonics and praised a book called *Teach Your Child to Read in 100 Easy Lessons*, which explained to parents how to use the phonics method to do just that.[2] Though this book had been published in the early 1980s, when whole-language theory and practice were gaining wide popularity, it was based on research from the late 1960s. McWhorter wrote that he and his wife, also a professor, had been able to use the book to teach their four-year-old to read in a matter of months. He noted that Siegfried Engelmann, one of the book's authors:

> "… was involved in the [U.S.] government-sponsored Project Follow Through, whose summary report compared nine methods for how to teach reading and tracked results on 75,000 children from kindergarten through third grade. The results, though some critics over the years have rejected them on methodological grounds, were clear: The approach that proved most effective was based on phonics—teaching children how to sound words out, letter by letter, rather than encouraging students to recognize words as single chunks, also called the whole-word system."[3]

The article concluded that while controversy over whole-language theory and practice may yet persist, the verdict is in: trying to teach reading as "a kind of elegant guesswork" instead of by sounding out letters is a recipe for illiteracy.[4] More disturbing still is the often blithe dismissal of the problem. When in doubt about the meaning of a word, most teachers would advise you to look it up in the dictionary. But in fact this is something I've wondered about before. Do young people who've been taught the whole-language way know how to look things up in the dictionary? Do students get alphabetical order if they were taught via whole language theory? How could they, if whole language theory expects the student to somehow imbibe the meaning of words without being able to sound out new ones, that is without understanding that letters mean sounds, and only secondarily add up to words and sentences—without, that is, the primary revelation of written language (that letters represent speech sounds)? From a more personal perspective, Anna Quindlen cited children's author Lois Lowry:

> "I remember the feeling of excitement that I had, the first time that I realized each letter had a sound, and the sounds went together to make words, and the words became sentences, and the sentences became stories."[5]

Quindlen noted:

> "The very beginning of a child's reading is even more primal than that, for it is not so much reading but writing, learning to form the letters

> that make her own name. Naming the world: it is what we do with words from that moment on. All of reading is really only finding ways to name ourselves, and, perhaps, to name the others around us so that they will no longer seem like strangers. … I am not alone. I am surrounded by words that tell me who I am, why I feel what I feel."[6]

Most unfortunately, whole language theory is alive in some circles, and still a matter of debate—something I was amazed to discover (not in a good way) by looking the term up online. I had assumed such nonsense would have bitten the dust by now. "No lie can live forever," said Martin Luther King, but it would seem that some missteps, though they may not live forever, at least enjoy much longer shelf lives (much longer than it takes for the truth to get its pants on and sally forth).

It appears that about the same time educational experts were ditching phonics, they were also set to forgo any instruction in grammar. The ill effects of such dispensing became apparent to me when I was teaching journalism: at least one entire generation with no idea about English grammar, without knowledge of the meaning of the phrase "parts of speech." In fact, I ended up writing my own grammar book because one day at the white board, after barreling on about the functional differences between the parts of speech, I turned to the students to see a virtual sea of incomprehension. When I asked the students to tell me by a show of hands whether they'd ever before heard the term "parts of speech," only one student in a class of about 30 raised his hand. He was 60 years old and taking the class for pleasure.

The same kind of deficit in the teaching of mathematics became apparent to me during the years I taught, specifically, on the occasion of an upcoming exam in the Research Methods course. I was in the habit of giving my students, in advance of an exam, a guide to precisely the kinds of questions I would be asking, and the kinds of responses I would expect (short answer, true or false, extended reasoning in essay form, and the like). I thought that if the students felt the exam was more predictable, they would be more encouraged to study for it. One young man (not unintelligent and not untalented but definitely unmoneyed: he lived in his van with his dog in the parking lot of a big-box store until he was there-from "evicted") raised his hand: Would they be allowed to use their calculators? he asked.

Well, you may if you like, I said, but the math questions I'm asking are simple things, such as figuring a percentage or percentage change with rounded figures. But I would need my calculator for that, he insisted. If I asked you what percentage is 50 of 100, I countered, wouldn't you be able to answer that without a calculator or even a piece of scrap paper? No, he said, he would use his calculator to be sure. He may have been, to press a point, exaggerating—but not by much. Another student complained about having to deal with numbers at all. "I'm not a mathematician, Maxine," she remonstrated. It's not a matter of higher mathematics, I advised, but one of being able to check, as a reporter, whether someone talking to you about increases or decreases or percentages is making any sense, a matter of not setting yourself up to be either cowed or snowed by "information."

Grammar Dread

> "To many people the very word [grammar] conjures up memories of choking on chalk dust and cowering in fear of a thwack on the knuckles from a spinster schoolteacher. … It should be thought of instead as one of the extraordinary adaptations in the living world: our species' solution to the problem of getting complicated thoughts from one head into another. Thinking of grammar as the original sharing app makes it much more interesting and much more useful. By understanding how the various features of grammar are designed to make sharing possible, we can put them to use in writing more clearly, correctly, and gracefully."[7]

In his book *The Sense of Style*, Steven Pinker lambastes pedantry that would suggest the rules of usage can and should be dictated by elite tradition with no regard to how people actually speak and to how language itself evolves. And on this count, for wonderful flights of rhetorical resistance, Pinker would be hard to out-do. He writes about how "people use their mother tongue, including words and constructions frowned upon by the purists," otherwise described with some choice epithets and phrases of severe disapproval like these: "pointless purist dudgeon," or "schoolmarm rule" —and many more. He marshals scathing attacks on pedants, denounced collectively as members of the "Gotcha Gang." But Pinker also states just as clearly his position against willful, self-satisfied ignorance, especially of the pedantic kind:

> "Language pedants hew to an oral tradition of shibboleths that have no basis in logic or style, that have been defied by great writers for centuries, and that have been disavowed by every thoughtful usage manual.

> Nevertheless, they refuse to go away, perpetuated by the Gotcha! Gang and meekly obeyed by insecure writers."[8]

Pinker himself is anything but insecure, and his book on style is peppered throughout with displays of disdain for language pedants with phrases like "purists, who are often ignoramuses," "more-grammatical-than-thou" readers," and with rhetorical questions like "Ready for another example of pointless purist dudgeon?"[9]

When Pinker really gets going on pedants, he often personifies his objections in the figure of the emblematic "Miss Thistlebottom"—a moniker actually coined years earlier by Theodore Bernstein, the American author of several manuals of style. (Aside: Note how Mr. Thistlebottom doesn't quite compute.) Miss Thistlebottom is usually a "spinster," and invariably the old fashioned, rule-based kind of grammarian found in classrooms and good textbooks. I must have been lucky in my experience with the Thistlebottoms of my grammar school days, for I remember them not as nitpicking obstructionists but as reliable models and even founts of wisdom in matters of sentence construction—of course, that was back in the day, before the advent of whole-language theory and the abandoning of expert instruction in basic grammar. Pinker must not have been as lucky in primary school; when he argues against a hidebound rule of grammar, poor Miss Thistlebottom appears stage centre to bear the brunt of the blame.

But Professor Pinker is no kind of anti-feminist or anti-intellectual—and, more to the point, no kind of anti-grammarian. In the opening pages of *The Sense of Style*, he notes:

> "... the book you are holding is avowedly prescriptivist: it consists of several hundred pages in which I am bossing you around. While I am fascinated by the linguistic exuberance of the vox populi, I'd be the first to argue that having prescriptive rules is desirable, indeed indispensable, in many arenas of writing. They can lubricate comprehension, reduce misunderstanding, provide a stable platform for the development of style and grace, and signal that a writer has exercised care in crafting a passage."[10]

I heard him speak at a B.C. university when I was teaching journalism there, about his book *The Better Angels of Our Nature*, and I liked him more than ever for the way he stood up to the Gotcha Gang—in this instance, not language pendants criticizing his grammar (I doubt they'd dare), but a collection of male full professors objecting to his research, calling the data "cherry picked." Since this particular gang had a special knack, largely unfailing, for getting female professors to do the bulk of the work for no credit, I had to wonder whether the gang understood the difference between picking cherries and marshalling evidence; they didn't, after all, offer contrary data.

Pedants Versus Sticklers

To reflexively rule out Miss Thistlebottom or to castigate her stickler ways may be to miss her pristine logic into the bargain. Visceral opposition to pedantry is, well, visceral. I get it, and I appreciate the erudition and the honorable motives that inspire this resistance. But I object when such resistance drives critics to grant no quarter to Miss Thistlebottom, even when she makes perfect sense. I have no argument with—in fact, I share—a passionate distaste for language pedants, for those who cite the sort of nonsensical grammatical dictates best consigned to the dustbins, especially those who do so as an expression of their status, their presumed authority to spout the rules. But there's a difference, after all, between the pedant and the stickler.[11]

Pedant: n. 1. A person excessively concerned with trifling details or who insists on strict adherence to formal rules or literal meaning at the expense of a wider view. 2. A person who parades or reveres academic learning or technical knowledge above everything.

Stickler: n. 1. A person who insists on something (a stickler for detail). 2. A difficult problem or puzzle.

In other words, although pedants are sticklers of a particularly unlovable sort, not all sticklers are by nature pedants. And sticklers don't deserve the opprobrium they often get, even from linguists, who rely on the so-called Cambridge grammar, which aims at scientific analysis (rather than writing technique), on providing a useful scaffolding for linguists (rather than teaching the basics of traditional "school" grammar). For the latter purpose, the Cambridge grammar would over-complicate reasonably simple matters.

The linguist's "generative" grammar does not distinguish between clauses and phrases in terms of function (it speaks instead of tree structure, for instance regarding a clause as a type of phrase, and speaking of coordinators as opposed to conjunctions). This difference in terminology from traditional grammar is one that pretty much guts the Cambridge system as a means of mastering English grammar: no one will learn from it the much-dismissed "schoolmarm" basics. (Aside: Note how school-man does not compute in the same way that Mr. Thistlebottom doesn't.) In this way, grammar for linguists and grammar for writers are at distinct cross purposes, which explains why relative ignorance of grammatical terminology doesn't necessarily translate into bad writing (since once again, good writing depends on operational skill rather than on expertise in the matter of grammatical terms).

The reasoning of the Cambridge grammar is aimed at insight into the underlying codes of language by quantitative and other analytical measures; the traditional grammar taught in elementary schools is meant to acquaint you with the basic structures and syntax of language—with some of the ways beyond count that words may be combined to make meaning and personal style.

Clearly, many linguists do not share an implicitly elitist condescension toward "traditional grammar," such as that expressed in *The Cambridge Encyclopedia of Language*, which defines six types of grammar (descriptive, pedagogical, prescriptive, reference, theoretical, and traditional). Of the lowly traditional grammar, the encyclopedia allows:

> "A term often used to summarize the range of attitudes and methods found in the period of grammatical study before the advent of linguistic science. … It is difficult to generalize about such a wide variety of approaches, but linguists generally use the term pejoratively, identifying an unscientific approach to grammatical study, in which languages were analysed in terms of Latin, with scant regard for empirical facts."[12]

This characterization ends on a respectful note: "However … there is now fresh interest in the study of traditional grammar, as part of the history of linguistic ideas."

What genuine language lovers tend to target are not all sticklers but those authorities (aka pedants) who think that grammatical rules should be observed slavishly, because a self-proclaimed cadre of experts says so (often experts who write little and/or not well). I think many among the anti-grammar contingent are aiming at magnanimity, putting down those grammarians whose motives are repressive; they mean to free people from fear of grammar. That's a motive I heartily endorse. But when they imply that the rules in general lack grammatical logic, I must respectfully disagree. As long as you are familiar with the rules, you are in a good position to abide by or defy them in accordance with your writerly intentions. But important grammatical rules are more than empty convention; the failure to observe them can muddy a writer's intended meaning.

In matters grammatical, some advise going with what "feels" or "sounds" right—and that makes a pretty good start. But such off-the-cuff procedure doesn't negate (in fact it underlines) the reliability of grammatical understanding. Sticking only to what sounds right can keep students (and even some professional writers) in the perpetual dark, thinking there must be something not only constraining but also ultra-mysterious and probably evil about "the rules."

The polar opposite is what I tried to show students: the rules of grammar and punctuation make sense; they are based, largely, on a kind of logic—not infallible, not absolute, not over-arching, and certainly not beyond debate—but still the kind that allows the writer to use precision as far as possible to make up for the inability to respond directly, as in spoken conversation, that is: to avoid unintentional ambiguity. One more reason there's no substitute for a good teacher, and why bad ones are such a problem. Then there is the profusion and confusion of grammatical terms.

In his book *Building Great Sentences*, Brooks Landon lauds the power of what he calls "free modifiers" and the "cumulative sentences" built with them. Here's an example given of a sentence so constructed.

> "He drove the car carefully, his shaggy hair whipped by the wind, his eyes hidden behind wraparound mirror shades, his mouth set in a grim smile, a .38 Police Special on the seat beside him, the corpse stuffed in the trunk."[13]

Landon eschews some of the writing instruction in books like Strunk and White's *Elements of Style*—one of the first books on grammar and usage that I read, and still one of my favourites. He deems misguided such advice as "omit needless words," likening this style to "tombstone epitaphs." Yet what Landon calls a "free modifier" does, precisely, omit needless words: it takes an implied clause and turns it into a "modifying" phrase.

Landon's term "cumulative sentences" is in itself a bit confusing. Most reliable North American grammar books use the word "cumulative" to describe adjectives and their use/misuse with commas, not to categorize sentences, which are generally classified by type, according to the number of independent and subordinate clauses they contain (basically as simple, compound, complex, or compound-complex). His method for building great sentences generally eschews subordinate clauses and instead tacks on additional elements as phrases following a main clause. I note that Landon's example of a cumulative sentence remains a simple sentence (with a single independent clause), no matter how many modifying phrases are added on.

What Landon calls a "cumulative sentence" is a kind of loose (as opposed to periodic) sentence. A loose sentence frontloads the main clause, which clause would make a complete sentence on its own, even if subsequent elements were deleted. (He drove the car carefully.) Or, for my own example of a loose sentence: I booked a flight to Paris, my body bone-tired after a long day, my mind glad to cross the item off my to-do list. In both examples, the sentences would be complete if they ended after the opening main clause. (I booked a flight to Paris.)

The periodic sentence, by contrast, completes the main clause at the end, just before the period. (Bone-tired after a long day, glad to cross the item off my to-do list, I booked a flight to Paris.) In my example, choosing a periodic structure seems on balance preferable. On the other hand, the emphasis in Landon's example would lose its punch—in fact it would barely compute—if the very same words were rendered as a periodic sentence (instead of the loose structure that he calls "cumulative"). Check it out: "His shaggy hair whipped by the wind, his eyes hidden behind wraparound mirror shades, his mouth set in a grim smile, a .38 Police Special on the seat beside him, the corpse stuffed in the trunk, he drove the car carefully."

Whether a loose or periodic sentence better serves a given instance depends on what a given writer means to say. Choice of structure may serve meaning but does not create it. Landon's original example sentence is effective not because it avoids subordinate clauses (using instead verbal phrases), but because of the kicker at the end, the last phrase. Everyone who writes already knows or soon learns that the most effective place to position a string of words is at the end: the end of a phrase, a clause, a sentence, a paragraph, or even a whole piece; that's why it's called the kicker. Like other so-called tricks of the writing trade, this one, used without discretion, works about as well as a fish riding a bicycle. It's the writer's intended meaning that guides her choice: structure should serve meaning, not the other way around.

Even academic writers (not generally known for their lively prose) are advised to consider the kicker, to save the best for last, to dispense with the potential opposition by dealing with contrary views early on and reserving the prized place of emphasis for their own viewpoints. In fact, it's standard direction for PhD candidates to deal in their papers with opposing views first ("tipping one's hat to the old guys," the old guys call it), and to augment the candidate's own contribution by putting it last. Because people have short memories, this technique may make easy sense (or not)—but all that has little to do with avoiding subordinate clauses (what amount to ideas embedded in other ideas) by turning them into verbal phrases. I side with the lovely Ursula Le Guin on that score: "To avoid long sentences and the marvellously supple connections of a complex syntax is to deprive your prose of an essential quality."[14]

What's most ironic in debates about grammatical correctness is how clearly the discussion would benefit from more precise grammatical terminology—not in order to be right and someone else (or everyone else) wrong, but in order to make one's meaning clear (that is, to avoid unintentional ambiguity). But experts, being experts, tend to favour their own terms over those of other experts. Even in scientific writing, various experts insist on various terminologies, and it's no secret that scientists would rather share toothbrushes than terminology.[15]

How bad can it get, this bamboozlement by syntax? I believe that abandoning the teaching of reading by traditional phonics and of basic grammar wholesale has contributed mightily to this confusion. Even where grammar is still taught, the teacher usually needs the answer book, meaning that even the teacher isn't really getting it. Of course, I'm not opposed to answer books, only to failing to learn something from them—enough, you could say, to disagree with alacrity. I am eternally opposed, on the other hand, to teachers who insist on rule-bound "correctness" as a mark of their authority or power over students rather than as a matter of meaning clearly expressed.

Punctuation appears to present a perennial stumbling block. Take for example the common habit of putting a comma after an opening "but" in a sentence. It clearly "sounds right" to many, and that's because it reflects a pause in speech. Grammatically speaking, that is in written language, there's no need for a comma after "but"; if there were to be a comma, it would come before the "but" in a compound sentence. When I was working on my grammar book, I had a wonderful editor named Joe, who had excellent suggestions for improving the book (such as adding names from different cultures so it wouldn't read like that familiar and now much-maligned Dick-and-Jane reader), but from "buts" and "commas," he knew not. At one point, I said to him: "Please, Joe, I'm begging you, stop putting commas after the "but" in sentences that begin with "but." Said Joe: "But I see it all time, I see it everywhere." Quite.

According to Ursula Le Guin: "People who say that commas don't matter may be talking about therapy or self-expression or other good things, but they're not talking about writing."[16]

Even for smart and talented editors like Joe, the comma or its absence is strictly optional, and unlike post-modern (nominal) democracies, majorities here really do rule. For some reason, I was never allowed to know Joe's surname and I wondered: Is this something new in publishing, anonymity reserved for the freelance editors that publishers have come to regard as necessary, at cut-rate cost, to their bottom lines? Is this another linguistic revision in the modern era, deemed post-truth, post-modernity, and post-publishing-on-paper?

If I begin to sound carping (and I'm not done yet), there's a reason I'm so bothered by this "sounds-right" school of grammar, which often advises you to trust your uneducated ear: it suggests that understanding grammar is not necessary to writing well, or for that matter reading well—an idea I strongly oppose. Resistance to grammatical understanding is not even about grammar per se but rather about power politics: about who has the right to pronounce, on the basis of presumed personal superiority rather than on that of greater, more thorough understanding. I certainly do not object to breaking rules in the name of artistic freedom, but I maintain that to defy grammatical rules for rhetorical effect (for "art" or "impact" or "style"), you first need to know the rules.

Some of the anti-grammar commentary in books purportedly meant to help students learn to write well reminds me of a phrase Marilynne Robinson used in another context. In a discussion of how time has lowered the value once placed on simplicity, she wrote that back in the day, writers and readers "aspired to an aesthetic of simplicity, of common speech, and of common circumstance." This downgraded evaluation of simplicity, she ventured, "seems to have become entrenched around the time of the Depression, and to have become the condescension that mistakes itself for fellow feeling."[17]

The "sounds-right-feels-right" method often works well, but it's not infallible, because we and our ears are not infallible. Still, better to recognize and rehabilitate the resistant, often arrogant, ear than to cling to a misguided notion of freedom to err freely. When I refer to an educated ear, though, I don't refer to someone who can spout grammatical terms, but rather to someone who understands the grammar underlying the words, most usually from wide reading and much writing, and from serious consideration of meaning in both. I mean grammatical understanding of the operational rather than the descriptive or prescriptive kind. Clearly, many good writers find their way without being able to cite grammatical terms with fluidity. On the other hand, precise grammatical understanding wouldn't hurt anyone's writing style. This much, I promise. What usually serves to cramp style are emotional blockades, and I can testify to that as well.

The trouble with the sounds-right explanation (over grammatical logic) is the lack of precision it can enshrine. If your ear is educated, what sounds right is usually what is right (and if you're not sure, you can look it up—if you can). If your ear is uneducated, and arrogant to boot, what sounds right may amount to a wrong turn and worse, the end of the road. Lack of grammatical precision (again, not necessarily prescriptive) can hurt writing style and tends heavily to verbosity. "Any fool can write long," George Orwell said. It takes thought, often long, to write short. Still, long or short, the choice—and the responsibility—remains the writer's.

> "Most books that purport to teach writing advise you to write as simply as possible. You may be constrained by a formal requirement ... But good standard English isn't more virtuous than any other style. Painters don't paint only in black and white. Different voices, different styles, suit different purposes. The more of them you learn to command, the more resources you bring to writing."[18]

The less operational understanding you possess, the more likely your writing will lack clarity, the more likely that everything you hear will start to feel or sound "right" when in fact it's wrong—wrong not because it breaks "the rules" but because it fails the clarity test. A good example is one book reviewer's assessment of punctuation matters. The reviewer explains that the author in question believes it's more important to follow "your own intuitive sense of punctuation rather than rules handed down from some forensic authority." She quotes the author:

> "I felt I was putting punctuation marks here or there because that's how others were doing it, without comprehending their relation to me: so my marks had only a global meaning but no personal value. And the more faithfully I served this consensually accepted global sense, the more I distanced myself from my personal requirements."[19]

Isn't this truly mystifying? What can the writer possibly mean by a "consensually accepted global sense" of punctuation? (The rules in a grammar text? What people see other people using "everywhere"?) And what are "personal requirements"? (What sounds right?) Of course, not all so-called grammatical rules make sense, and these are properly ignored. But like a broken record with attitude, I will keep insisting on those that do make sense, which are those that make a difference to meaning. You need to understand such rules, and to be able to look them up when in doubt. You need to know what rules you defy and depart from, and why. Once you do, go ahead and defy every rule in the book(s).

How bad does it actually get—this misrepresentation of grammar as some kind of muddled muzzle? Some would-be grammar guides ignore grammatical issues or make fun of them, implying that their authors are members of that elite group of presumably "natural" writers. More interesting than a belligerent resistance to grammatical rules is the unwarranted self-assurance with which such resistance is expressed. For instance, one such book claims that "I feel bad" is correct, and so it is; the writer claims that "I feel badly" is only hypercorrection, when in fact it's also perfectly grammatical—if what you mean is that you do a bad job of feeling.[20]

Some of the most passionate opposition to grammatical rules aims squarely at pronoun use. In her marvellous book *Woe Is I*, Patricia T. O'Conner calls pronouns "among the biggest troublemakers in the language," but she advises us not to despair.

> "You're in good company. Hundreds of years after the first Ophelia cried 'Woe is me,' some pedants would argue that Shakespeare should have written 'Woe is I' or 'Woe is unto me.' (Never mind that the rules of English grammar weren't even formalized in Shakespeare's day.) The point is that no one is exempt from having his pronouns second-guessed."[21]

In that case, I vote for "Woe is [unto] me."

On further matters of pronoun case generally: Should pronouns be in subjective case (for example, *we*) or objective case (*us*)? One author suggests that it depends on personal preference, that one choice or "alternative" is as good as the other:

"They have a bigger house than us. (Alternatively: than we do.)"[22]

The problem here: the two are not equivalent in meaning. Strictly speaking, the first indicates that the house in question is bigger than we are; the "alternative" (correct because it is likely what the writer means) says their house is bigger than our house. In this case, it hardly matters—since readers are unlikely to mistake the speaker or writer's meaning.

Pronoun dread encompasses questions like this one: What is the correct case of pronoun following common prepositions like *between*: should it be *between she and I* or *between her and me*? (Since both pronouns are the objects of the preposition *between*: *between her and me* is correct. In its more usual rendition: *between you and me* (not *between you and I*).

Another perennial pronoun teaser: whether *who* or *whom* is correct. If you understand pronoun case, it's clear that in all circumstances correctness depends on what you mean to say, on whether the pronoun functions as subject or object.

To argue against rules on pronoun case is simply to ignore the logic of case (that is, to assume there is no logic and so no point to the rule). To my mind, there is precious logic to any grammar worth its rules, to any rules that stand to affect meaning, and to any rules that if ignored run the risk of muddling said meaning. And yet, an unmistakable attitude underlies the clued-out, would-be educator's cavalier treatment of grammatical logic. Only the uncool, it implies, need bother with the niceties of pronoun case. I get the objection that "whom" makes you sound like a butler, and I understand if you dislike the very word "whom," in which case, fine, don't use it. But find a way to avoid the word by recasting the sentence, not by ignoring the logic of case—that can only limit you. And if you are applying for a job with your résumé and a cover letter, write "to whom" and not "to who" it may concern. (There's always an off-chance that your prospective employer knows the grammar of pronoun case and doesn't mind butlers.)

One grammarphobe of my acquaintance argues that rule-bound pedants would have you revise the movie title "The King and I" to read "The King and Me"—but that's just plain silly. And rule or no rule, it hardly seems objectionable to suggest that pronouns functioning as objects should be in objective case. Of course pronouns, standing alone or in combination with other pronouns, can function as subjects or objects (of verbs or prepositions). So use subjective case when they are working as subjects and objective case when they are working as objects.

No writer—and none but the most overwrought pedant—would correct dialogue in fiction or song or speech such as "Who do you love," to read "Whom do you love," because nobody talks that way and because the intended meaning of the question is clear. And if no nonfiction writer would engage in such hypercorrection either—who cares? No confusion of meaning ensues in this case by ignoring the rule. Conversely, if there were deemed to be a need to elaborate on "Who do you love?" pedants and normal souls alike would both surely say, sing, and write: "Who do you love, him or me?" (not "he or I").

Issues of pronoun choice are clear—it's just that they don't always matter.

Pedants in particular may regard certain errors (especially the ones that don't matter) as heinous. I regard error, even on a sliding scale from innocuous to unforgiveable, as fairly routine rather than heinous. Initial errors are to be expected. If they weren't, writing would be easy (as would much else in the realms of human endeavour). The point, in any discipline, is to correct errors rather than find a hill to die on for their sake. I do not agree, however, that pronoun case is inevitably a matter only of formal versus informal style; choice of case can indeed make a difference in terms of intended meaning.

For example, some argue that there's nothing wrong (ungrammatical) with sentences like "Rose is smarter than him" or "George went to the same school as me."[23] Purists would argue that the word *than* in such instances should be regarded as a conjunction, and that the use of objective case for the pronoun that follows is a grammatical error (that correct grammar requires subjective case: Rose is smarter than *I*; George went to the same school as *I*).

The Concise Oxford Dictionary (among other standard dictionaries, including Webster's) has long regarded the word *than* as both a conjunction and a preposition; as a conjunction, "introducing the second element in a comparison (*you are older than he is; you are older than he*)." Used as a preposition, the dictionary notes: "The treatment of *than* as a preposition makes it acceptable to say *You are older than him or anyone other than me* in less formal contexts." I agree entirely, but I would argue this point as a matter of intended meaning, and only secondarily as one of formal versus informal contexts.

If constructions such as "Rose is smarter than him," seem or sound right (and indeed cause no confusion of meaning) especially when spoken, and even to highly educated ears,[24] that is only because the example sentences involve only two entities (and so the possibility of misconstruing meaning is slim to non-existent). When a sentence is more complicated, when it refers to more than two entities, it does affect meaning: Isn't there an obvious difference between these two sentences: *He loves the children more than me* (he loves them more than he loves me), and *He loves the children more than I* (he loves them more than I love them)?

I'm all against pedantry and related crackpot theories of correctness. But I am for drawing the line at rules that can make a difference—between clarity and unwitting ambiguity. A grammatical choice may be a matter of preference, but it should never be a choice without regard to intended meaning. A case in point is the grammatical difference between the words *that* and *which*.

> "Most North American writers use *that* and *which* interchangeably, and some contemporary stylists and critics argue there's nothing wrong with so using them. I agree, however, with the authors of the classic

> *Elements of Style*, who insist there remains an important difference between *that* and *which*, one that ought to be preserved."[25]

Some who suggest that the two words are largely interchangeable may dismiss as outdated the idea that they aren't. It's true that in many cases, either word may be used with no impediment to the expression of the writer's intended meaning. But there are other cases in which the choice does affect meaning. Strictly speaking, *which* is for non-restrictive clauses, those not essential to the sentence's meaning (used with commas); *that* is for restrictive clauses (essential and no commas). In the sentences below, the difference is negligible, a matter of nuance, a choice unlikely to mislead. But while both sentences refer to a pair of shoes, only the second identifies the pair of shoes referred to.

Non-restrictive: The shoes, which I ordered online, were too small.

Restrictive: The shoes that I ordered online were too small.)

In other cases, meaning *is* affected. Consider the following two sentences:

The company runs on solar power, which is not cost-effective.

The company runs on solar power that is not cost-effective.

The first sentence suggests that solar power in general is not cost-effective. The second suggests that only a given kind of solar power (the one this company runs on) is not cost-effective. The humble comma or its omission can express an important difference in meaning, one easily grasped when comparing the next two sentences.

The store is run by women, who are disorganized.

The story is run by women who are disorganized.[26]

The first sentence refers to women in general; it's sexist. The second refers to (identifies) a particular group of women (those who run the store). The person speaking or writing this second sentence might be sexist, but the sentence isn't.

To arrive at your own conclusion as to the supposed interchangeability of the words *which* and *that*, try taking a sentence containing both words and see whether you can substitute one for the other and still make sense. Would either *which* or *that* work equally well in the sentence? Are they actually interchangeable, a choice without consequence in terms of meaning?

In Praise of Grammar

Ursula Le Guin wrote about how some people come to fiction writing workshops lacking basic grammatical skills: "They believe that art does not need craft. They are mistaken." She further advised that "the practice of any art is impeded by both egotism and altruism. What's needed is concentration on the work."[27]

The informal context of speech is a lot more forgiving than the formal one of writing, because in conversation any confusion that does arise over meaning may be clarified. But if it were true, in any given instance, that correct grammar doesn't matter to meaning, then why learn the names for prepositions and conjunctions or the differences between them in the first place? And why abide by any grammatical rules whatever, in speaking or writing, in any form of discourse? Because of course it isn't true that grammar doesn't matter; the whole point of grammatical correctness is precision: to say precisely what you mean so others can understand precisely what you are saying—or at least as precisely as reality and our meaning-making capacities will allow. (Take any sentence at all and scramble its syntax, the order of its words, and see for yourself how much sense the so-scrambled sentence makes—or not.)

For those who regard grammar as hindrance, it's really no use saying that grammar is merely conventional (as noted, of course it is). Words themselves are conventional, but to say that they thereby don't matter is like asking someone to pass you the pepper when what you want is the salt. No use arguing that it's a case of formal versus informal; that one is for writing, the other for speaking; that one is for academics and one for presumably more ordinary souls; that one "sounds better" or "classier" than the other. These are not arguments; they are rationalizations.

Finally, if there's nothing inherently wrong or something potentially creative about a supposedly incorrect grammatical structure, then go for it and argue for it. And if there's nothing wrong with it, why not use it in, say, your professional papers? Or reclaim it, say, the way Montreal's francophone writers reclaimed "joual," a dialect that departs from "standard" French, and one deemed not just informal, but more tellingly, one of low prestige. (Though, as it happens, joual is actually closer, linguistically speaking, to Old French than to so-called Parisian or international or "standard" French.) According to Wikipedia, joual:

> "... is an accepted name for the linguistic features of basilectal Quebec French that are associated with the French-speaking working class in Montreal which has become a symbol of national identity for some. Joual is stigmatized by some and celebrated by others."

There are traditional ways and means to reclaim a minority or threatened language: mothers do so by addressing, often in song, their infants in a mother tongue. Montreal's Jewish Public Library maintains its section of Yiddish books and periodicals (though for how much longer is unclear, since languages not spoken are almost by definition already lost). My granddaughter, Clementine, calls me Bubby (instead of Granny, as she calls her gentile grandmother, her father's mother). I called my own grandmother Bubby, just as my mother called hers. I remember a (Jewish) dinner companion asking me, before Clem was born, how I would have her address me. I answered: "As Bubby, of course, what else?" "But it sounds so old," she objected. "I have nothing against old people," I said. "And besides, what's the alternative?" (Is dying young somehow preferable?)

Then again, there's a difference between attempts to reclaim threatened languages, and the later-day status concerns of identity politics. I remember covering in 1990 a Quebec pro-independence rally and saying to another CP reporter also assigned to cover it, that the rally was on St. Joseph Street, pronouncing it in the English fashion (*Saynt Josef*); a passing stranger objected to my English ways and corrected me with his French pronunciation (*Sahn Shosef*), shaking an angry index finger at me for emphasis. I was ready to get into it (in French), but the cooler headed reporter with me prevailed, gently gripping my arm and leading me away from my would-be enlightener. "We really don't have time for this, Max," he said (in English).

What's compelling about anti-grammatical reasoning is how passionate are the attacks, running like arteries through the commentary. As if grammar were a way to shut people up; as if an invisible hand were *trying* to shut them up. Of course, all writers worth their salt rightly resist attempts to muzzle their free expression, but not all disagreement (or editing) amounts to attempted muzzling. If matters of correct grammar (no scare quotes necessary or invoked) are justly and profitably regarded as debatable, and they are, then so are matters of interpretation.

A writer's hyper-vigilant response to attempts at political editing (that aimed at deleting inconvenient facts and "unacceptable" opinions) is well warranted. But good editing (the kind a good writer must do before allowing any editor, however skilled, to chime in) is aimed at communicability: good editing helps a writer to get her meaning across without robbing the work of the writer's voice, and it protects the writer from legal trouble (or it should do) by checking the facts and ensuring precision.

In this respect, I am reminded of the way some inexperienced would-be investigative reporters avoid certain avenues of investigation because they fear someone will try to derail the story before they can tell it. That reaction may be easy to understand and relate to, but it is certainly counter-productive: it has the writer rushing to judgment and print before the facts are fully in hand. My journalism students would sometimes ask me about this when investigating suspected wrongdoing on the part, usually, of local officials: "I can say that?" they would marvel, when I urged them to spit it out rather than hedge their bets and their language. If it's free of malice, if it's relevant and true and you can prove it (to the standard of a court of law), I'd tell them, go right on ahead.

I agree that language evolves to suit speakers, since the point of language is communication, and I applaud any stance against genuine pedants (in all fields, not just language pedants). I regard some of the confusion over grammar, with respect to meaning, as a kind of cop-out. I understand that clumsy usage (throw-away clauses such as "it goes without saying"—then why say it?) may originate in the writer's own self-scouring insecurity (and I say this as one hardly immune). When unsure of one's meaning, the tendency among writers is to splatter text with inchoate attempts at emphasis, hoping that such emphasis will clarify a meaning that the writer doesn't really grasp.

Such re-routing of meaning reminds me of how some journalists use the word "alleged" as if it provides some kind of legal protection with regard to as yet undecided court cases (protection that it does not provide). I get the reasoning behind the use: to show that the journalist is not pre-judging the case and that the public ought not to either, ought not to assume guilt. Ironically, it doesn't work: people do assume guilt; for example, they do assume that to be charged with an offence is to be guilty of it; they bank on the pseudo-wisdom of where there's smoke, there's fire. What does work in the interests of good journalism is to refrain from naming a suspect until that suspect has been arrested and named by police or arraigned (formally charged with an offence). Once that happens (excepting certain circumstances such as crimes committed by young offenders), using the word "alleged" to describe a suspect or an offence is entirely beside the point—which is finally to protect the (alleged) integrity of trials.

I once covered a murder case in which a man, a cult member accused of the ritual murder of a pregnant woman, had his trial declared a mistrial (and was granted a new trial) because of something that happened in the courtroom following his testimony. A few people were still milling around, but the Crown prosecutor had by then retired to his offices upstairs. The defendant was still in the witness chair when a police officer approached and told him within earshot of the several reporters in the room: "You know, Raymond, if you beat this rap, there's a bullet in the head waiting for you." Two of the reporters ran upstairs to tell this to the Crown prosecutor, who asked them—so they told me when they rushed back down again—please to not report this incident, since it would cause a mistrial.

Isn't this what declared mistrials are for?

"I don't work for the Crown prosecutor," I replied. "I work for the Canadian Press and the public's right to know." A little naive, but still nicely put, I thought—though I nevertheless hurried back to my own newsroom to get the story down and out before the discrepancy between my report and those of the other reporters could be noticed and perhaps used as justification by editors to edit out the telling incident.

My story ran as written, but the other two reporters (one newspaper, one television) never forgave me for involving them in this bad business. After a mistrial was duly declared, the print reporter called me at home, to complain: "Because of you, I now have to go to court to testify." (Tough stuff, but justice was still served, sort of: the reporter was subpoenaed to testify, and the accused was ultimately convicted in this new trial, but sentenced to incarceration in a mental institution rather than in a federal jail.)

When it comes to writing well, an uncertain grasp of grammar—of the structure of a language—works against the potential power of words to communicate meaning:

> "Certain constructions attract writers in hiding … to the uncertain stylist, simple declarative sentences sound insufficiently important. … Readers aren't supposed to think anything. It only sounds as if they are. The ghost of logic haunts these constructions. They have been around for a long while, but tradition does not validate them."[28]

I understand the emotional roots of resistance to grammatical understanding (in fact to any approach to language that is aimed at social control, at limiting free speech, at silencing people). But I think that for the currently young generation, the matter of grammar is more mysterious than threatening. When I taught a grammar course under the auspices of the Journalism Department, it wasn't students who objected, but the other professors in the department (none of whom would have passed my entry test, and only one of whom said he ought to and intended to read it). Students loved it—"parts of speech" was a major revelation to them—and some came from other departments to take the course (claiming they hadn't had any grammar instruction previously). Yet while I understand the resistance to grammar, I cannot approve. It's entirely possible to discuss grammar at many levels, without disparaging the whole subject as a culprit, as the root of all evil, rival to money. (If evil there be, I can see tracing its roots to the pornographies of filthy lucre, but I sincerely doubt its origins are to be found in grammatical precision.)

Where I disagree is with the idea that an understanding of grammar is somehow unnecessary to communicate your meaning. Or that grammar has nothing to do with logic. Or, especially, that grammatical correctness is some kind of elitist plot. As long as their motives remain honorable, and as long as they are prepared to defend their positions with reasoned argument (not counting "because I said so"), I say let the sticklers (and even the pedants) have their say. In matters of correct grammar, they are as entitled to their opinions as their rebellious opponents. And as long as she isn't carrying a big stick, I say long live Miss Thistlebottom—and Mr. Thistlebottom, too. May their tribe increase.

One can master grammar from a love of language, rather than from nefarious attempts to shield oneself. I count myself among these former. And I remember a bright student who came to my office after an introductory lecture on grammar and why it matters. He plunked himself down in a chair beside my desk, and (uncharacteristically) almost speechless, stammered before spitting out the revelation: "I mean … I mean … I mean—it makes sense!" "Yes," I was pleased to agree, "that's what I've been trying to tell you!"

Some criticisms of grammar are bona fide: insightful and offered in good humour, usually by wonderful writers. These are markedly devoid of angry dismissals and misplaced resistance. Like William Stafford: "When I write, grammar is my enemy." Good writers acknowledge that grammar is secondary (meaning comes first), but with no attempt to overturn the whole grammatical applecart and quite without smarmy condescension or defensive posturing.[29] Compare the earlier description of the comma (as "global" or "personal") to this one, in Pico Iyer's grand essay, "In Praise of the Humble Comma." Iyer lauds this simple mark of punctuation, so widely ignored and abused. The comma, he writes, "gets no respect."

> "It seems just a slip of a thing, a pedant's tick, a blip on the edge of our consciousness, a kind of printer's smudge almost. Small, we claim, is beautiful (especially in the age of the microchip). Yet what is so often used, and so rarely recalled, as the comma—unless it be breath itself? … By establishing the relations between words, punctuation establishes the relations between the people using words."[30]

Or this bit, from Michael Lydon's *Writing and Life*:

> "To convey thought clearly ... known words need to be used in sequences with recognizable structures. These structures, the architecture of writing, are described by the rules of grammar. ... We may take pride in grammar as one of the great accomplishments of the human brain. Grammar's deepest roots may be biochemical, for it strikes me that grammar links words in sequence much as life combines molecules in strands to make up organic matter. Certainly studying grammar yields useful evidence on how our brains work, how we receive, understand, and use information. I think of grammar as the skeleton of thought; thought lives in grammar as flight lives in the bones of birds. Grammar turns thought into word, logos in ancient Greek. Grammar is logical."[31]

Just so. Grammar goes to accuracy and precision, not just something harder to figure, like style. I remember during my time teaching journalism, noticing at some point a rash of student writing that used the present tense of the attributive verb "say" (she says, instead of she said) at the beginning of the article and then continued with present tense throughout. Of course, this led to serious knots (what some writers call "lumps") in the piece of writing. Apparently, someone had advised them that this tactic would add interest and immediacy to their stories.

I argued against the practice, telling my students that it wasn't just hackneyed (as opposed to enlivening), but more to the point, inaccurate. (Whatever you quote someone as having said, someone must have said it before you could quote it.) Used judiciously, usually at the beginning of a newspaper or magazine story, such usage does work to draw readers in (that's why writers use it), but when it's used indiscriminately, throughout a piece, it amounts to a simple grammatical, logical error, which doesn't mean that it can't or shouldn't be used, just that it doesn't automatically add "immediacy" or any other kind of interest or weight to the writing. What it tends to add are roadblocks.

Writers do often use the present tense of the attributive verb in the opening paragraphs of newspaper and magazine articles, but if the writer were to try to use present tense throughout, the result would be confusing if not nonsensical; it would distract readers rather than interest them. In journalistic and other nonfiction work, attributive phrases as such work best when they are close to invisible, when they allow the reader to concentrate on the content instead of drawing attention to the attributive verbs and their tenses—one reason why in the dialogue of fiction, attributive phrases are often simply omitted (sometimes leading to confusion over who is speaking and sending readers into backtrack mode to figure it out.)

A writer who wants to use only present tense throughout a piece would need to engage throughout in some fancy footwork on the platforms of time and space as represented on a page. This and other kinds of messing with grammatical rules is routinely engaged in by good writers, but for such play to be effective, the messing requires a gifted ear and considerable (operational) familiarity with the rules they defy. For an example of what a master of language can do with time, with mere words on a page, check out this opening line from the 1967 novel *One Hundred Years of Solitude* by Gabriel García Márquez: "Many years later, as he faced the firing squad, Colonel Aureliano Buendia was to remember that distant afternoon when his father took him to discover ice."

Words, *malgré tout*, despite all their problems, are the best we've got. Grammar still matters just as truth does in a supposedly "post-truth" era.

> "All those things for which we have no words are lost. The mind—the culture—has two little tools, grammar and lexicon: a decorated sand bucket and a matching shovel. With these we bluster about the continents and do all the world's work. With these we try to save our very lives."[32]

True, language evolves to suit users, but if all grammatical reasoning caves to what's called "popular usage," the end result is a narrowing of the possibilities of said language, and finally a narrowing of the possibilities of thought and its expression. The issue is always whether or not the writer intends to be ambiguous. If there is more than one possible meaning in a passage of prose, the prose lacks precision, unless that ambiguity, that openness of potential meaning, is intentional. And that is my final stickler point, with which I approach the resting of my case: if there's a potential difference in meaning, potential unintended ambiguity, then the rule that provides for clarity, that accounts for it, is logical and should be observed and maintained. Intentional ambiguity, conversely, *requires* the savvy and precision that grammar affords.

It follows that a mastery of grammar is neither anti-intuitive nor a blind attempt to "overcome" ambiguity: the same mastery of grammar that allows for precision is what helps to make ambiguity possible. Consider the first line from a novel by Joyce Carol Oates, *Expensive People*; it shows how critical is grammatical precision to the expression of meaning. The novel opens with this line: "I was a child murderer." When Oates wrote this opening line, she was not being imprecise, but intentionally ambiguous. The line could mean that "I" was a child who committed murder, or it could mean that "I" was an adult who murdered a child. Both possible meanings put into question who "I" is, and with this mystery, the line snares the reader's attention, just as the writer intended.

At the start of her great book *The Grammar of God*, Aviya Kushner quotes the poet Derek Walcott, saying that grammar "is a form of history." Kushner's book investigates how the various translations of the Bible differ, sometimes radically, from the original Hebrew Bible, and makes an argument for why grammar matters.

> "For those for whom grammar is a list of rules—charting verbs and memorizing exceptions—grammar might sound boring. My mother taught me that grammar is more than that; it is a window into how a group speaks to itself, structures its own thoughts, and defines its world. ... Grammar might seem dull, but it is from the structures of the respective languages that everything else emerges. The differences affect so much, from how law comes across, to how characters are portrayed, to how the music of the Bible does or does not translate. This tends to influence how morality, history, and time are conveyed in each language—all essential stuff. At its base, however, these differences can be encapsulated in one word, 'grammar,' which affects everything."[33]

Some confirmed technophiles say that the new electronic communications are something entirely new, and make a new kind of grammar appropriate, one to suit the technology, one that employs what the technology allows, with developments in digital media of such as hypertext links and mouse-over highlighting (though, to be honest, these latter always remind me of the traffic signs on one-way streets that say WRONG WAY). In an article on how language has changed with the advent of online social media, one fan writes that online communications require a supposedly new disregard of grammar, urging what she describes as flexibility:

> Be flexible ... the language we use online doesn't have to reflect everyday speech. English has always evolved—that's what it means to be a living language—and now the internet plays a pivotal role in driving this evolution. It's where we talk most freely and naturally, and where we generally pay little heed to whether or not our grammar is "correct."

Isn't this strange, to speak of internet communications as "where we talk most freely and naturally"? Is that because there's thought to be little consequence in words online? (A *New Yorker* cartoon has one dog seated at a computer explaining to another dog this apparent advantage: "Online, no one knows you're a dog.") Among humans, too, one needn't identify oneself online (avatars are all the rage, and so are online predators), nor for that matter one's sources or line of reasoning. But when it comes to serious writing, the only way out of the labyrinth is the path of concerted thought, for which rambling online, or for that matter on a printed page, does not and will not substitute or suffice.

One reads text on an electronic screen by scrolling, as opposed to text on a page by turning pages. During my teaching career, I sometimes re-keyed text I wanted my students to read, transforming the staid marks on paper into a sparkling on-screen document. I hoped that by this measure I might better ensure my students' attention. Most went along, perhaps only to please me, but one student, noticing that the text continued for more than a single screen and consulting her computer's word-count function, complained: "Maxine! This document is 2,000 words long!" I had to bite my tongue to keep from saying "And your point is?" Instead, I argued that anyone who intends to write for a living ought not to be discouraged by 2,000 words. I stand by that one.

You might begin to conclude that I am anti-technology, but you would be wrong. Though it's true I began writing in the olden days, with a (manual!) typewriter, I do love my computer, especially its "find" command, especially for when I have to wonder whether I've written exactly the same twenty words somewhere in the previous hundred-or-so pages. And I recognize that electronic writing is evolving and that language in this new and evolving format necessarily contains, as all tools, both potentials and pitfalls. What I reject is the idea of discontinuity. I object only when the new form is treated as a substitute for other kinds of writing, rather than as another tool in the kit. I argue that electronic writing should not be seen or treated as a substitute for previous formats (print or cursive writing on a paper page), but as a different tool and a useful one for writing as self-expression (whether the writing is meant to engage the reader emotionally as in fiction, or, as in nonfiction, to interest the reader with a supposedly disinterested objectivity).

In a brief review of the novel *The Grammarians* (by Cathleen Schine), the reviewer distinguishes in standard fashion between grammar as prescriptivist or descriptivist.[34] The article is interesting (I plan to read the novel because of it), but it strikes me that what this review most clearly exemplifies is a widespread fear of grammar and the almost universal resistance to the idea that there ought to be any sort of rules at all. I think what people are actually responding to when they express this resistance is the idea that the rules exist to censor them—and there is nothing that characterizes the born writer more than this refusal to be censored, a characteristic that helps enable the art of self-expression, that urges on the scribbler when the going gets tough.

The reviewer treats the matter (of grammar, of editing, of linguistic expertise) as one of navigating a route between two poles: grammatical correctness *versus* creative self-expression. She writes that in practice "the principles that govern usage are ever-changing and open to interpretation; the trick is knowing when, and how, they should be broken."

I would certainly agree, but I would also add that in order to break the rules for dramatic or expressive effect, one must actually know the rules. I used to tell my students this: "Go ahead and break the rules, break every rule in the book as often as you like, but break the rules for an intended effect, not because you don't know or understand the rules to begin with." In other words, become so familiar with the rules of usage that they provide an aid (not a barrier) to clarity of expression. The rules exist not to oppose intentional ambiguity (or any other intended effect of prose, fiction or nonfiction), but to strengthen these to powerful effect. Go ahead and create ambiguity on the page, but do it clearly and on purpose.

The reviewer of *The Grammarians* describes "the laws of language" as "cold, hard, and immutable"—but I don't see it that way. I see the rules of grammar as aids to precision: as knowledge that helps writers and editors to express their meaning with blessed clarity. To break the rules without knowing the rules is not creative, it's simple ignorance. That's because the rules don't actually refer to self-expression (which finally remains somehow and gloriously mysterious); they refer to structure (and so, to the conventions that enable communication).

Grammar matters, whether the supposed rules are followed or flouted, even in the generative grammar of linguistics. Consider Noam Chomsky's example of a sentence that is grammatically correct but conventionally nonsensical: "Colorless green ideas sleep furiously."[35] Still, it's structure that allows for interpretation. Poets routinely mess with structure in the service of greater meaning. For example, if I were reading Chomsky's sentence as a line in a poem, I might think it meant something like this: new ideas as yet undefined and uncategorized may yet carry serious import, brewing just below the opaque surface of the words.

In face-to-face communication, in orality, we can know when our meaning isn't getting through by the response of the listener(s), and we can revise our expression in the moment—riding the breath, so to speak—in order to clarify. On the page (in literacy), we enjoy no such opportunity, and so must rely on a deeper understanding of language (grammatical and structural) to convey meaning. As we have seen, words in themselves (that is, without context, without setting, without reference to specifics) have little meaning. On the page or on the screen, in fiction and in nonfiction, meaning is what escapes the text, not what defines it.

Chapter 5

Truth in Literature: Fiction and Nonfiction

Writers of both fiction and nonfiction try to formulate some kind of truth. In fiction, the imagined world can be as bizarre as you like, as long as its characters are believable and act as people do or might. The story's characters must stay in character, not changing without reason or motive. Within the context of the fictional world, then, the made-up narrative must have the ring of truth. In nonfiction, by contrast, the writer makes reality claims; what she proffers or cites as true must be verifiable in the world outside the writing—a fact-check-able truth claim, the touchstone of the form. "Things that are cheap and tawdry in fiction work beautifully in nonfiction because they are true," said the celebrated nonfiction writer and teacher John McPhee.[1]

In the 1990s, a writer at the *New Republic* magazine broke the cardinal faith. Editors discovered that Stephen Glass, who worked for the magazine from 1995 to 1998, had woven out of whole cloth (the emperor's new clothes kind), about half of the fifty or so stories he'd written for them. Glass had quoted sources that didn't exist and described events that never happened. The root of the problem, it turned out, was the magazine editors' very manner of fact-checking. Glass easily evaded the editorial process because the fact checkers checked the facts against Glass's notes, not independently, and Glass's notes referred not to actual facts or events, but to flights of his own fancy. The discovery and subsequent apology to the magazine's readers is said to have changed the way fact-checking is done at many magazines.[2]

Fact checking was always done differently at daily newspapers (than in the longer-form and more opinion friendly magazine article), but newspapers were hardly immune from journalistic transgression, as the scandal of Jayson Blair (among others) showed some five years after the Glass affair. Blair resigned from the *New York Times* in 2003, after editors discovered in his stories both fabrication and plagiarism.

> "Criticism helps keep journalists—like politicians—humble, as we were all reminded in the spring of 2003 when the *New York Times* was convulsed by the Jayson Blair scandal. After the paper published a 7,200-word account of how reporter Blair had stolen the work of others and tricked his editors into printing lies, the staff of the *Times* went into an uproar."[3]

In newspapers, articles are more limited in length and they disallow the expression of opinion (except for the case of columnists, soon to be addressed). Editors at daily news publications do not check facts against a reporter's notes but against external sources, and they automatically blue-pencil-out interpretations, except for those voiced as direct quotations from identified, (almost exclusively) named sources. Newspaper editors check facts—as magazines learned to do—against the real-world events that their reporters describe, usually along with small armies of other reporters also assigned to cover events and report "just the facts." But facts, as we've seen, are also provisional; they require context and interpretation to add up to evidence or meaning. Checking only against newspaper accounts is clearly not fail-proof as method.

The logic of news reports themselves is a little like that of "crowd" sourcing. Daily news reporters may faithfully report only facts, but they may also be easily misled by a kind of employer-sanctioned herd mentality: they may unwittingly collude with each other so as to ensure they quote the same sources and repeat the same facts in order to avoid questioning by their editors, questioning they would certainly face if their "independent" reports differed markedly from those of other reporters. Thus in news reportage, the pressure is toward conformity of reports. Translated into newspaper parlance, that amounts to a kind of methodology: when in doubt, leave it out—or, in a less optimistic or trusting vein: when in doubt about something that cannot be omitted, "fudge" it, meaning write the report so as to side-step possible questions.

The best reporting and the best editing, in any venue, including the writer's own initial revisiting of research and subsequent drafts, do not side-step. In terms of method, they resemble more closely the underlying reasoning of the ancient Jewish court of the Sanhedrin, which regarded easy conformity as inherently questionable. If absolutely everyone initially agreed on a matter under discussion, if no one disagreed even in minor aspects or details, the court reasoned, there must have been something wrong, something missed, in the original discussion. In such cases, the participants would begin the debate anew to flush out whatever it was that no one had yet noticed.

Newspaper columnists (as opposed to newspaper reporters) are not "fact-checked," since they write opinion, but here too the validity of an opinion is based on the facts presumed and/or shown to inform the opinion expressed. The difference is clearly reflected in libel law and in the different defences raised for reportage and for opinion pieces. For reportage, the defendant publication raises the defence of truth (also called the defence of justification). Here, the defendant tries to show the following: that the facts reported are demonstrably true (that the facts are facts and not opinions or innuendo) and that these facts can be proven true (to the standard of evidence required in a court of law); that it is in the public interest to reveal these facts; and finally, that the report is free of malice (evidence of malice being a defect so severe that it can scuttle the defence of truth).

To defend an *opinion* piece, the appropriate defence is not truth, but fair comment, and that defence also depends finally on facts: whether the opinions expressed could be arrived at fairly, that is, on the basis of facts. Whether opinion writing be finally judged fair or unfair does not depend (ideally) on a columnist's strong feeling or strong language (though favourite columnists are indeed valued precisely for their strength of personal expression), but on the basis of the facts whereby the writer reached the published opinion. Thus both truth and valid interpretations are based on the facts relevant to the case at hand.

Many pressures (other than methodological ones) no doubt complicate and sometimes negate the power of truth-telling in journalism. A collection of essays takes up the issue of such pressures on journalism as an ethical pursuit. Its title (*Into the Buzzsaw: Leading Journalists Expose the Myth of a Free Press*) reflects a now generalized disaffection with "the news." The last of the book's essays is more hopeful. Titled "The Light That Won't Go Out," it was written by Brant Houston, executive director of a 4,400-member international organization called Investigative Reporters and Editors.[4]

In terms of creativity, adherence to truth is the defining difference for both fiction and nonfiction. The difference is simply that the reference point in fiction is the fictional world invented by the author; in nonfiction it's the world of facts and recorded history, the world outside the text.

> "Excellence in nonfiction lies in the writer's skills in observing, organising, narrating, and interpreting facts—skills entirely dependent on imagination, used not to invent, but to connect and illuminate observation. Writers of nonfictional narratives who 'create' facts ... aren't using the imagination but betraying it."[5]

In the event, this difference is not always as clear cut as it might appear. Both fiction and nonfiction are structured as narratives; whether presented as imagined or factual accounts, they unfold in some kind of sequence. Even novels that engage in time travel require beginnings and middles and endings. In fact, however, there was a time:

> "… an ancient time when no distinction was possible between fact and fiction, between religious perception and scientific discourse, between utilitarian communication and poetry—when all these functions of language, which we now divide and distinguish according to the situation we're in, were indivisible."[6]

There was a time too when the study of fictional literature was not separate even from the study of grammar; it was part of the latter until at least the fifteenth century.[7] Some say that the modern novel was itself pioneered by one writer's adherence to everyday reality.

> "Fuelled by his passionate belief that a novelist, like God, must 'create and keep quiet,' and be 'present everywhere, yet visible nowhere,' Flaubert became fiction's first master of realism. As Harvard professor James Wood wrote in 2006, 'He is the originator of the modern novel; indeed, you could say that he is the originator of the modern narrative—that the war reporter and the thriller writer owe as much to him as the avant-garde fictionist. The great bear of Croisset … has sired thousands of successors.' "[8]

Still today, many of the boundaries that distinguish fiction from nonfiction are inexact or porous; the two forms borrow liberally from each other. For example, literary nonfiction is defined by its adoption of the techniques of fiction, used to render factual accounts more readable for "the literature of fact." And fiction borrows from the techniques of nonfiction to confer an air of verisimilitude and authority, especially in the form of first-person narratives. In both fiction and nonfiction, the writer must get the reader to imagine, to suspend disbelief, to follow along—to give up her own silent commentary long enough to consider (if not embrace) the writer's.

In many other respects, fictional and nonfictional accounts share basic characteristics. In both kinds, the writing must cohere—its subject matter must hold together, not veer off into unrelated or irrelevant subjects. Just as nonfiction relies on verifiable fact for legitimacy, the characters in a work of fiction must reference consistently their invented biographies. The details of a character's life must not change without reason. A character described as having been born in 1914 on one page cannot then be described in later pages as having been born in 1920. Similarly, in nonfiction, if the author's viewpoint is not concerted, or his reasoning doesn't add up, or if the writer is evasive or dubious in some other way, then readers will not be willing to go along, they will not believe the narrative.

Both fiction and nonfiction have subjects (we call them characters in fiction), and both express themes. In most nonfiction you can assess the subject and themes by the title and introduction and jacket blurbs. In fiction, you have to read the whole story to know what you think it's about. Central to understanding the themes of fiction are what I think of as one-liners, (grand philosophical asides or generalities often expressed pithily enough to quote from). The term "one-liners" may be misleading, since the kind of passage I mean (and the kind I quote throughout this work) may well exceed a single line. In fiction, you can suss out the themes only by reading the whole story, by reflecting on its meaning and the meanings of its one-liners.

One of the most interesting things about the wonderful literary nonfiction writing of John McPhee is that you cannot tell from the titles what the story is all about. And there are no one-liners. You have to, as in fiction, read the whole story to find out, because in his work, it's the whole piece, the whole progression, the whole structure unfolding, the whole narrative that tells the theme and subthemes, and that makes McPhee's work intriguing as the so-called "literature of fact."

The essential ingredient in literature of either form of writing is voice, the ingredient that separates literature from other forms of the written word. When we encounter nonfiction writing with weak voice, we call it "information" (or when that information is utterly voiceless, "data"). Most textbooks and much academic writing seek in fact to excise voice, since a strong voice is evidence of subjectivity rather than the prized objectivity, so-called, of such nonfiction writing. In fact, we have a special term for nonfiction writing that gives free reign to a writer's voice: we call it "creative nonfiction."

The critical importance of voice, the power of voice, is its distinctive individuality, the way its presence affects not just the tone of the narrative but also the telling. Think of voice as the way a person tells a story; think of people around the dinner table and how each would tell the same story quite differently—not just from an individual viewpoint, but in a singular, distinctive voice. Think of how you recognize a friend's voice on the telephone. Or, in wider cultural terms, think of the crusading attempts by writers of all kinds to give voice to the voiceless. We take so for granted the mysteries of communication that we often miss the actual import of voice.

When you read a new work of fiction by an author with whom you are familiar, and when you recognize elements of the writer's style such as rhythm and pacing and level of word-use, you are recognizing distinctive characteristics of the writer's voice, even though that voice remains "off-stage," so to speak. And yet, the fact-based genre of nonfiction also requires a narrator—a voice—to relay the account. Voice, in both fiction and nonfiction, defines who is telling the story. As put by Richard Rhodes, masterful author of both fiction and nonfiction books (including the monumental *The Making of the Atom Bomb*):

> "Voice and its grammatical correlate, point of view, shape the frame through which your reader experiences your story. That necessary frame limits what your reader will know, of course. But its limitations cut both ways. The frame of voice limits what your reader will know because it limits what you can tell him."[9]

For any written work, fiction or nonfiction:

> "... the first paragraph charts a course that may lead the reader—and will restrain the writer—through hundreds and even thousands of pages, to the near or distant end. And first among firsts is voice: who is telling the story? ... Even the you who is telling your first-person story is you but not you, isn't it—is one but not another of your many persona, whichever one you've selected for this particular task. It follows that voice in writing—who is telling the story—is always to some degree made up for the occasion, which is to say, is always fictional, even when you intend to use that voice to convey documented fact."[10]

In the relatively simple, third-person voice of reportage, still someone stands behind the unspoken "I" of the story, and thus even here the writer's choices are not completely straightforward. In fiction, an author's initial decisions on voice are more complex, relentlessly presaging consequences and complications.

> "The best-known American first-person fiction is probably Moby Dick, with its forthright opening sentence, 'Call me Ishmael.' Herman Melville had technical problems with Ishmael's voice as he went along, however; its limitations of range led him to cast several chapters as

> dramatic scenes in play form, and once he required Ishmael to quote himself telling a story at length in 'the style in which I once narrated it at Lima.' "[11]

On a more prosaic level, the main difference between voice in fiction and voice in nonfiction is that in the latter, the first-person or third-person voice (in columns and news reports, respectively) that is adopted to voice an opinion or to tell a true story remains a singular voice; the writer at least purports to be speaking as a single self. In news reportage, any voices other than that third-person voice must be quoted voices, and they are enclosed in quotation marks to indicate the fact. Those quote marks are sacred: they have to be there or it's plagiarism, appropriating and presenting someone else's words as your own. When voices other than that of the singular teller are introduced, they are quoted and sourced, so they can be checked against "reality" or at least against other sources, including previously published references. When we speak of voice in nonfiction, then, we refer to a writer's own characteristic (off-stage) voice, to the opinions and perspectives that inform the writer's account.

In fiction, on the other hand, voice is multi-vocal. Because the writer speaks not only through the voice of the narrator but also through the characters in the fictional work, there are necessarily more voices than the single voice that is de rigueur in nonfiction. Still, the fiction writer's own voice remains central, even when that writer adopts an "omniscient" perspective, that is, with the author able to see and describe the thoughts and feelings of the all the tale's characters.

But then what *is* the relationship in fiction between an author's own views and the views his characters express or espouse? Does the author step out of his characters, so to speak, to reveal a "true" self, even if he puts these revelations in the mouths of invented characters? Is the writer commenting on the views expressed by his fictional characters or expressing his own views through them? Is it what the narrative is talking about (theme) or what it's saying (content)? Is the writer depicting a character with racist views or putting his own racist views in the mouths of his characters? Does an author present a bigoted character who spews hatred in order to vent his own or instead to comment on bigotry?

When Jane Austen wrote the famous opening line of *Pride and Prejudice* ("It is a truth universally acknowledged that a single man in possession of a good fortune must be in want of a wife"), she was clearly not arguing for the stated "truth" but against it, and on at least two levels: first, that a woman is a person, not an object, and ought to be able to seek her fortune independently, not be bought for the proverbial ring of gold. And second, that this and other "universally acknowledged" truths may be based on unexamined, widely held prejudice, on a kind of longstanding wrong-headedness. According to Marilynne Robinson, in a priceless one-liner, human error is after all distinctive: "To err is human," she wrote; "to err catastrophically is definitively human."[12]

In her book, *Reading Lolita in Tehran*, author and professor of literature Azar Nafisi also commented on Jane Austen's fiction to indicate how aspects of social commentary may unfold in a fictional work.

> "It is not accidental that the most unsympathetic characters in Austen's novels are those who are incapable of genuine dialogue with others. They rant. They lecture. They scold. This incapacity for true dialogue implies an incapacity for tolerance, self-reflection and empathy."[13]

Finally, both fiction and nonfiction genres aim to offer some sort of counsel. Decades ago, in a book about American novelists, Alfred Kazin wrote this:

> "The process of self-teaching ... becomes the heart of Bellow's novels, and the key to their instructiveness for others. One could compile ... a whole commonplace book of wisdom in the crisis era that has been Bellow's subject and opportunity."[14]

Addressing a Google generation in his book *The Pleasures of Reading in an Age of Distraction*, Alan Jacobs commented on "the nature of every real story," that it provides counsel, containing "openly or covertly, something useful."

> "But if today 'having counsel' is beginning to have an old-fashioned ring, this is because the communicability of experience is decreasing. In consequence we have no counsel either for ourselves or for others. ... To seek this counsel one would first have to be able to tell the story. ... Counsel woven into the fabric of real life is wisdom."[15]

This "communicability of experience" in multiple voices is the glory of fiction, which can offer love and insight and solace and wisdom, not a single footnote required. So it is in a wonderful book of short stories, *The Heart and Other Strangers*,[16] by the writer Morrie Ruvinsky (in a career replete with wonderful stories, and cards on the table: my much-loved big brother). These stories transcend plot and soar above discursive practice to open the heart and linger there.

In one of my favourites in this collection, a woman named Bess Anderson is being targeted by God for messiah-hood. The story, "Bess Anderson: First Female Messiah," opens with its eponymous heroine going about her daily chores, when God speaks to her in no uncertain terms, and not for the first time: "I want you to save the world," He says. Bess resists, telling the voice in her head that it's only a voice in her head, and pleading for Him to choose someone else. "Why me," she whines, "I'm not even Jewish."

Bess marshals evidence after incident for the argument that she, with a husband and three kids, is the wrong woman for the job. She has just dropped the kids off at school, and now she has to go unpack the groceries, she has to pick up the skates from the repair shop, she has to get the clothes to the dry cleaner ... yadda, yadda. She has no time to save the world. "The world needs saving," God says. "Send Jesus," Bess counters. "I can't," God explains. "Not again. He's still really upset."

Bess resists, reminding God, with evidence galore and gory of his track record: "You have a very bad history with your messiahs." Why would she even want the job? she argues (while her author notes in sympathy, succinctly, that it's true: "None of the prophets seemed to have had a jolly time.") "All you send," Bess tries to get through to God, "are false messiahs." Pissed off now, God corrects: "Failed, not false."

And when Bess complains that God's own opus, the Bible, "as an instruction manual, stinks," God ramps up. "Critics I have enough of," He says, urging "a little sensitivity to the author." Unimpressed, Beth pushes her advantage with a hard-hearted quip: "Self-publishing can be hard." Whereupon God laughs.

So *that's* why God laughs! He finally gets the joke. Which "is a lot," comments the author, "for someone who often doesn't get it." In the end, though, Bess submits to the call. What appears to have decided her is the discourse on who, after all, is to blame for the sad state of this world—if not He Himself? At that, God pulls an ace: "This time, it's not my flood, it's yours."

Perhaps the truth about voice in fiction isn't an either-or choice: either the writer's "own" voice or the voices of the characters he gives voice to, but at the heart of it, a kind of correspondence between the writer and his characters, a "third character," one that remains unnamed and doesn't speak with words. As Eudora Welty put it:

> "... relationship is a pervading and changing mystery; it is not words that make it so in life, but words have to make it so in a story. Brutal or lovely, the mystery waits for people wherever they go, whatever extreme they run to. ... Between the writer and the story he writes, there is the undying third character."[17]

Ultimately, the greatest similarity between fiction and nonfiction remains that both are narrative forms—that is, stories. The essence of narrative form is chronology, an insight as old as Aristotle. First this happened, then the next thing, and the next, and on and on until the last thing. If the interior sequences are jumbled and move freely within time frames, still every story has a beginning, a middle, and an end. Even nonfiction books in the "hard" sciences, for example, don't really make sense (even to insiders) except told as narrative, with precursors and conclusions, that is, by some narrative frame that situates the story in time and space. Randy Olson's book, *Houston, We Have a Narrative: Why Science Needs Story*, makes this point succinctly.[18] Olson argues that narrative is central to all kinds of "telling" and suggests that in the digital age, it's more important than ever to help make sense of the vast increase in knowledge (or at least text). Umberto Eco (an Italian professor of semiotics, better known for his novel *The Name of the Rose*) noted in a similar vein that even the hardest of hard science needs story:

> "Today, those who work in artificial intelligence understand that in order to give a computer the ability to understand words, it's not enough to say 'Man is a rational animal' or 'Water is a transparent liquid.' You have to express it in an elementary narrative way. In this sense, we are narrative animals; we grow up in narrations. … When you are able to tell the story of what happened to you, you have finally understood what did happen."[19]

Sometimes, instead of life imitating art, art makes it into the ranks of real life. I've read that Arthur Conan Doyle's invention of the wily detective Sherlock Holmes, because of the latter's brain-teasing adventures in forensic investigation, is the only fictional character ever to have been made an honorary fellow of the Royal Society of Chemistry.[20] I've also read online that in Conan Doyle's Sherlock Holmes stories, Holmes kept commonplace books and sometimes used them in his research, for example in the story "The Adventure of the Veiled Lodger," for which the detective used newspaper reports of an old murder compiled in a commonplace book. As recounted by his sidekick/straight man, Watson:

> "Sherlock Holmes threw himself with fierce energy upon the pile of commonplace books in a corner. For a few minutes there was a constant swish of the leaves, and then with a grunt of satisfaction he came upon what he sought."[21]

To say that fiction and nonfiction are both narratives suggests that we are influenced by narratives in all forms (including, for instance, by the narratives of television shows or online programs as well as by televised or online advertisements). A major difference between the influences exerted by narratives in fictional versus fact-based forms resides also in the way people read them. Because people love stories, fiction even in low doses has the power to influence thinking. When we read nonfiction, we do it with our "shield up. We are critical and skeptical. But when we are absorbed in a [fictional] story, we drop our intellectual guard."[22]

We may also drop our guard while reading nonfiction, where we assume rigorous adherence to fact, and across the range of nonfiction: from simple newspaper stories to book length biographies and memoirs (and even in crossover forms like the historical novel). Yet it wasn't that long ago that the rules even in journalism allowed for invented quotes to enhance the entertainment value of a report.

> "In spite of occasional journalism scandals that hit the national landscape like plane crashes, our standards are higher than ever. Historical examples of nonfiction contain lots of made-up stuff. It appears as if, 50 years ago, many columnists, sports writers and crime reporters—to name the obvious categories—were licensed to invent. The term piping—making up quotes or inventing sources—came from the idea that the reporter was high from covering the police busts of opium dens."[23]

In book-length nonfiction works like memoirs and biographies, the line between fact and fiction can get blurry. But the line must be drawn somewhere, and today, inventing quotes in news reports is (properly) a firing offence; in memoirs as well, deliberately misrepresenting the facts makes for scandalous headlines and disabused readers. Biographers too come under scrutiny. And it's no wonder, according to Virginia Woolf:

> "If we think of truth as something of granite-like solidity and of personality as something of rainbow-like intangibility and reflect that the aim of biography is to weld these two into one seamless whole, we shall admit that the problem is a stiff one and that we need not wonder if biographers, for the most part failed to solve it."[24]

Woolf regarded fact as a subjective quality, finally inseparable from imagination, but I disagree heartily. Like Roy Peter Clark and like Ursula Le Guan, I see factual integrity as a pillar of journalistic and other nonfiction forms, in which to deviate from fact is to mislead the reader and betray his trust.

When we read or view fictional works, for better or worse, we enter another state of mind, a different world. Some theories say people love stories for precisely this reason: that stories allow us to simulate experience while avoiding consequences in real life, a kind of "ancient virtual reality technology that specializes in simulating human problems." Dreams also engage in this reworking of the dilemmas of daily waking life. Whatever else one might say about narrative, it's clear that stories matter, that they have always been with us and are likely here to stay.

As one bibliophile put it:

> "… the essence of story is not changing. The technology of storytelling has evolved from oral tales, to clay tablets, to hand-lettered manuscripts, to printed books, to movies, televisions, Kindles, and iPhones. This wreaks havoc on business models, but it doesn't fundamentally change story."[25]

On the other hand, this havoc wreaked "on business models"—and by them—is hardly negligible. The fiction industries are undergoing rapid and radical change. In the face of such change, the storyteller is called upon to remember the essence of the art.

> "We need writers who know the difference between production of a market commodity and the practice of an art. Developing written material to suit sales strategies in order to maximise corporate profit and advertising revenue is not the same thing as responsible book publishing or authorship."[26]

That humans everywhere love stories is clear. But why should this be so? Why do stories matter so reliably to the human quest for meaning? Why does storytelling persist as characteristically human across time and cultures? What have stories to do with being human? Storytelling, according to one critic "is not a luxury to humanity; it's almost as necessary as bread. We cannot imagine ourselves without it, because the self is a story."[27]

Why do humans tell and write stories, and why do other humans listen to and read them? Why does storytelling work so fundamentally in cultures and times of radically different hue? Why did writers of ages past and why do writers of today persist in telling stories (even as the prospects dwindle of a living wage thus earned)?

> "Why do you suppose you want to write, to tell stories? For others, of course, for fun, for glory, for the game and the endlessly fascinating puzzle of it, but also always to rewrite and restage your own inner dramas. Any serious writer who denies that aspect of his work is lying to himself. True works of art happen, I suspect, only when inner and outer come together."[28]

Why are stories readily grasped? Why are they easily understood in a way that, for instance, molecular biology and quantum physics are not? E. L. Doctorow commented on this "universal capacity for storytelling," on the idea that stories are an ancient technology of meaning:

> "... whereas an aptitude for mathematics or physics is given to relatively few, narrative seems to be within everyone's grasp, perhaps because it was the very first means people ever had to understand who they were and what was happening to them."[29]

All the preceding speculations on the meaning and importance of storytelling suggest that story is not just a linguistic technology; it is the supreme technology of mind, with ancient origins lost in the prehistory of orality. Storytelling is an activity so central that it acts, despite its lost origins, as evolution per se does, rooting itself in biology. According to one writer, this "confidence of narrative" must be hardwired: "Facts may change, evolve ... but stories find their way to the unchanging core of things."[30]

Because oral language long predates written language, story-telling must have preceded story-writing; literature as such must have begun with people telling stories (not writing them). It's literacy that introduced the possibilities of nonfiction, a different kind of story, with a different kind of voice, one more removed from the teller and from the events told of. Yet both written forms, both fiction and nonfiction, remain forms of story. In this regard, narrative is not a bug but a feature, of evolution.

> "At the most fundamental level, narrative is how we make sense of things. ... narrative is the essential mode of our being in the world, individually and collectively. Narrative is the strategy of the mind for putting things in relation. ... My theory of narrative as a fundamental act of consciousness implies to me that paranoia might be entrapment in a bad narrative, and depression may be the inability to sustain narrative."[31]

When asked by the editors of the *New York Times Magazine* for her choice of the best narrative of the millennium, English novelist A. S. Byatt picked the story of Scheherazade.

> "The stories in 'The Thousand and One Nights' … are stories about storytelling without ever ceasing to be stories about love and life and death and money and food and other human necessities. Narration is as much a part of human nature as breath and the circulation of the blood. Modernist literature tried to do away with storytelling, which it thought vulgar, replacing it with flashbacks, epiphanies, streams of consciousness. But storytelling is intrinsic to biological time, which we cannot escape. Life, Pascal said, is like living in a prison from which every day fellow prisoners are taken away to be executed. We are all, like Scheherazade, under sentences of death, and we all think of our lives as narratives, with beginnings, middles, and ends."[32]

The standard problem structure in fictional narratives, according to one writer, "suggests that the human mind was shaped for story, so that it could be shaped by story."[33] Why is it—how is it—that narrative can shape us even as we shape it? When it comes to language, narrative is more than the sum of the stories we tell ourselves to make sense of our experience—more than the content of our narratives. Narrative is the way we process experience in the retrospective of language; stories are how we think.

> "Our way of facing reality, of understanding things, perceiving things, is narratively structured. To know what a tree is doesn't mean looking in a book to determine its nature. In order for a child to acquire knowledge of what a tree is, he has to learn a story. Once upon a time there was a seed. The seed was put in the earth. And then it grew up into a tree. Once you have the story of that tree, you have understood what a tree is."[34]

Some critics suggest we may be too awash in fiction and using it to avoid certain truths rather than to reveal them. Some suggest that an overabundance of fiction has led us to come to expect that our lives will follow a story line; that stories enable us to get lost in the past or the future, and thus to avoid clear and present dangers. "Do we need novels?" asks Tim Parks, a translator, teacher, and novelist, in his book, *Where I'm Reading From: The Changing World of Books.* Do we "actually need this intensification of self that novels provide?" After all, he argues, as according to Buddhism, the self is an illusion; and this "illusion of self-hood" is what "… makes so many in the West unhappy. We are in thrall to the narrative of selves that do not really exist, a fabrication in which most novel-writing connives."[35]

I'm fairly certain I have a bodily self, and I too love stories. Yet when I read about "narrative selves that do not really exist," about selves that are mere illusions, about the fictional narrative as a "fabrication in which most novel-writing connives," I think first: if novels fabricate selves, then nonfiction does something similar in adopting a voice suitable for the purpose. As for the Buddhist tenet that the self (in real life, outside texts) is also a kind of fiction, I would tend to agree. On the other hand, I think: Fine, there is no self. Now what?

When I say that verifiable truth is the touchstone in nonfiction, I mean only that the statements in nonfiction have to be verifiable in the world outside the text; and certainly not that there is no truth to be found in fiction. But if fiction is a lie that reveals the truth, there remains an essential difference between a fiction and a lie. Fiction may reveal truth, *inter alia*, while a lie is designed only, precisely, to deceive. If the word "truth" is to mean anything at all, it can't have "versions"; to qualify as factual, the roster of facts can't include "alternative" facts. There's a great line in David Mitchell's grand novel *Cloud Atlas*: "Truth is singular. Its 'versions' are mistruths." Mitchell published this book long before the invention of "alternative facts" to suit any occasion, long before the era of truth became supposedly passé. (If we live now in an era of post-truth, mustn't there have been a preceding era of truth?)

The crossover genre of memoir, which partakes of both fictional and nonfictional elements and has gained popularity in recent years, may also lie. No form guarantees that the memoir, or any other genre, contains the truth—the whole truth and nothing but. Memoirs that fabricate are evidence enough that the only way to ensure that what we read is true is to investigate truth claims. "Nothing protects us against practiced liars and hucksters," wrote Mary Karr, adding that "nothing ever will." That no iron-clad guarantees exist of truth in language (as in life), is hardly reason enough to give up on distinguishing truth from lies or to give up on language entire. What rankles, says Karr, is:

> "… a sweeping tendency to deny even the possibility of truth. … In an off-kilter paradox, our strange cynicism about truth as a possibility has permitted us to accept all manner of bullshit on the page. Or maybe our appetite for the fantastic … has eroded all public standards of plausibility, even among perfectly smart people. (Okay, there are

> some dumb bunnies. Walking out of *The Last Temptation of Christ*, a friend overheard someone say, 'I didn't know Jesus was so short.')"[36]

If truth is not the distinguishing feature that separates fiction from nonfiction, it nonetheless remains distinct from lies and from the foundations of meaning.

> "All you want in the finished print is the clear statement of the lens, which is yourself, on the subject that has been absorbing your attention. Sure, it's autobiography. Sure, it's fiction. Either way, if you have done it faithfully, it ought to be true."[37]

Given even the most honorable of intentions (that is, a reverence for truth and a nearly allergic reaction to lies), we still need to master words in order to use them effectively. And to master words, we need to take in a lot of them—but we needn't be taken in *by* them. Humpty Dumpty, in conversation with Alice in Wonderland, had it just right:

> "When I use a word," Humpty Dumpty said rather scornfully, "It means just what I choose it to mean—neither more nor less."
>
> "The question is," said Alice, "whether you can make words mean so many different things."
>
> "The question is," said Humpty Dumpty, "which is to be master—that's all."[38]

In nonfiction as in fiction, the writer must entice the reader to "imagine," not in the sense of drifting out of the narrative into a daydream of her own, but in order to do what I have begun to think of as "internalizing"—to take the words in. When I say that both fiction and nonfiction are narrative forms, I do not mean to imply any sort of relativism: neither to say that all narratives are equally valuable regardless of their truth-value or meaning-value (or lack thereof), nor that truth itself is relative. I mean that while chronology provides the basic structure for narrative, narrative is much more than chronology: it is the way we abstract, the structure that thought itself employs.

What complicates narrative (and it's all narrative from this perspective) is that while stories (fictional or nonfictional) unfold in time and space, time and space are themselves abiding mysteries, even and perhaps especially for scientists who, like writers, work as they must within time and space as the boundaries of perceived reality. Like narrative, time and space refer to basic categories of thought rather than to "things" in reality.

> "Behind even the abstractions of science, there lies narrative of the observations on the basis of which the abstractions have been formulated. … All of this is to say that knowledge and discourse come out of human experience and that the elemental way to process human experience verbally is to give an account of it more less as it really comes into being and exists, embedded in the flow of times. Developing a story line is a way of dealing with this flow."[39]

With no disrespect intended toward science or its narratives, these latter do not compare to what a gifted writer of literary fiction can do with human experience "embedded in the flow of times." We enjoy in everyday life only the limited perspectives of our physical bodies; but our narratives can imagine and encompass much wider views. Take for instance the following samples of some of fiction's great opening lines, and note how they capture space-time in a way that science cannot.

> "The sun shone, having no alternative, on the nothing new." (Samuel Beckett, *Murphy*, 1938)

> "Not the power to remember, but its very opposite, the power to forget, is a necessary condition of our existence." (Sholem Asch, *The Nazarene*, 1939)

> "For many years I claimed I could remember things seen at the time of my own birth." (Yukio Mishima, *Confessions of a Mask*, translated from the Japanese and published in English in 1958)

> "No live organism can continue for long to exist sanely under conditions of absolute reality; even larks and katydids are supposed, by some, to dream." (Shirley Jackson, *The Haunting of Hill House*, 1959)

> "Our eyes register the light of dead stars." (André Schwarz-Bart, *The Last of the Just*, translated from the French, 1960)

> "The drought had lasted now for ten million years, and the reign of the terrible lizards had long since ended." (Arthur C. Clarke, *2001 A Space Odyssey*, 1968)

"Paint me a small railroad station then, ten minutes before dark." (John Cheever, *Bullet Park*, 1969)

"I am not mad, only old." (May Sarton, *As We Are Now*, 1973)

"A screaming comes across the sky." (Thomas Pynchon, *Gravity's Rainbow*, 1973)

"All beginnings are hard." (Chaim Potok, *In the Beginning*, 1975)

"The story so far: In the beginning the Universe was created." (Douglas Adams, *The Restaurant at the End of the Universe*, 1980)

" 'To be born again,' sang Gibreel Farishta tumbling from the heavens, 'first you have to die.' " (Salman Rushdie, *The Satanic Verses*, 1988)

"We started dying before the snow, and like the snow, we continued to fall." (Louise Erdrich, *Tracks*, 1988)

"Now there's no more galloping. Now everything's all right." (Moacyr Scliar, *The Centaur in the Garden*, 1980. Translated from the Portuguese, 1984)

Literature and Morality

Hypocrisy in fiction as in nonfiction is moral travesty, and readers notice. Carl Sagan argued this point in his essay "The Fine Art of Baloney Detection," quoting several august sources:[40]

> David Hume: "Men dare not avow, even to their own hearts, the doubts which they entertain on such subjects [as morality and religion]. They make a merit of implicit faith: and disguise to themselves their real infidelity, by the strongest of asseverations and the most positive bigotry."
>
> Tom Paine: "Infidelity does not consist in believing, or in disbelieving; it consists in professing to believe what one does not believe."

> T. H. Huxley: "The foundation of morality is to … give up pretending to believe that for which there is no evidence, and repeating unintelligible propositions about things beyond the possibilities of knowledge."

While nonfiction tends to put its ethical cards on the table (though some nonfiction writers are cagey about it), fiction is supposed by many to be exempt from morality, to exist in a "higher" realm of art. In fact, though, all forms of writing reveal the writer's character and show where the writer stands on the issues of the day, because literature is intimately entwined with morality, despite what Robert Stone critiqued as:

> "… an old, romantic, antinomian tendency that goes back at least to Nietzsche. It has been argued by people as different as Ortega y Gasset and Oscar Wilde, by Joyce speaking in character as Stephen Dedalus, and by Shaw during the period when he was writing Major Barbara, and, it now appears, attempting to invent fascism. In this antinomian vision, morality and art are independent, and even in opposition."[41]

But Stone flatly rejects the antinomian view.[42] And so do I. Readers of fiction judge the characters in invented tales, and they seek characters with whom they may identify in good conscience. The reader, Stone wrote, is:

> "… always alert to recognition, hoping to see his lonely state reflected across time, space, and circumstance. How then can fiction ever be a process independent of morality? To be so, it would have to be composed of something other than language."[43]

The idea that literacy is a boon to the humanist project, that reading literature will improve human nature (one mind at a time, as the saying goes) is a standard presumption of educational philosophy, and with this idea I have no argument (that is, I believe literacy in its broadest aspect is preferable to illiteracy). But in terms of individual readers, isn't the value of a written work also a question of how and why a given person reads? If people read literature-as-art in order to find meaning or confirmation in only statements that they agree with, those statements will read like truth to them; they will reinforce an existing bias and legitimize its expression (as a justifiable, "just another," point of view). Thus literature may encourage a kind of confirmation bias, with readers choosing and/or understanding only the narratives they already embrace. In plainer terms, as a person unwilling to have his mind or beliefs changed by something he reads might argue: everybody believes what he wants to believe, so one belief, or for that matter, one set of facts or values, is as good as any other. This is the relativist's pseudo-argument.

Clearly, the mere reading of literature doesn't necessarily improve the people who read it (or for that matter, those who write it); it doesn't work to, say, make people more compassionate or humane; it may instead strengthen existing biases and justify cruelty. Case in point:

> "Adolf Hitler is a potent example of the ways that story can shape individuals and histories, sometimes disastrously. The musical stories that Hitler most loved did not make him a better person. They did not humanize him, soften him, or extend his moral sympathies beyond his own in-group. Quite the opposite. Hitler was able to drive the world into a war that cost sixty million lives not in spite of his love of art but at least partly because of it."[44]

Then again, it's not as if Hitler took in a lot of "art" or "story" with the exception of the single narrative he was set on: blood and soil and rage and a superior race.

The practice of writing does not work to oppose hateful attitudes even among writers themselves. As a writer, you could be yourself a bigot, and you could display your tendency, without so much as blushing, through the same literary means. One needn't be a figure of documented historical evil to propagate hateful attitudes in any written form; one might do so as a supposedly harmless—or even "great"—writer of made-up stories. Take the example of Edith Wharton, who, I'm sorry to have to report, "kept a commonplace book and a donnée book all her life and extracted from them some of the more pointed remarks in her novels." In reviewing a biography of Wharton by Hermione Lee, the reviewer noted some "endearing contradictions":

> "Lee is careful to point out that Wharton could be anti-Semitic but in the conventional way characteristic of her class and epoch—and she is less virulent in her novels than in her letters … In a letter to Scott Fitzgerald about *The Great Gatsby* she complimented him for his 'perfect Jew,' Gatsby's crooked friend Meyer Wolfsheim; but she was decidedly for exonerating the Jewish scapegoat Alfred Dreyfus, whereas … most of the French and American members of her Paris circle were violently anti-Dreyfusard. In her pro-Dreyfus sentiments she was like Proust, another anti-Semite (though half-Jewish), but she refused to meet Proust precisely because she'd heard that he was snobbish to a

> fault. (Her social reluctance did not keep her from reading Proust and praising him in print over the years and sending Henry James the first volume of the *Recherche* soon after it was published.)"[45]

According to Proust himself:

> "A book is the product of a different self from the one we manifest in our habits, in society, in our vices. If we mean to try to understand the self it is only in our inmost depths, by endeavoring to reconstruct it there, that the quest can be achieved."[46]

If the reading or writing of literature doesn't necessarily work to improve one's moral character, it may at least mitigate the passion for other kinds of sport. Perhaps it's a blessing that Proust decided to hole up in his room for the reconstruction attempt: before his self-isolation, he'd got up to much less savory stuff in the wider world, where he displayed a different social self from the writer self on whom such exorbitant praise is lavished. As readers of the canon, we are expected to ignore such inconsistencies as the virtues of the text versus the vices of the man. According to one critic:

> "Wherever you look at great lives, you will find areas of almost unspeakable darkness ... I know no way out of the labyrinth. Proust, in his private bordello, the one he partially owned, tortured animals and had young women perform certain acts which he wished to describe exactly in his novel. You and I are forever and overwhelmingly in his debt. I couldn't imagine my life without [Proust's opus, *À la recherche du temps perdu*]."[47]

One may appreciate and admire the linguistic genius demonstrated in Proust's artful *À la recherche du temps perdu*, or in any text, without siphoning off as untouchable or irrelevant the facts of the writer's life. One may appreciate great prose passages without equating these with great lives. I slogged my way through "Swann's Way," the first volume of Proust's famed oeuvre; I found the same compelling artistry and originality so many have noted, but I wasn't inclined to read more volumes. There is clearly art in Proust, but little love. I don't feel in any way indebted.

Does anyone who admires the man's work really admire his life? Do the torture of animals and the degradation of women really rate as other than abominations? After all, many writers of genius produced and still produce great stories without engaging in "real" life in such as these. Instead, they used and use their immense powers of imagination to enter into the minds of such as the torturer and the tortured; if imagination were lacking facts to work with, they could spark it by research. They would find, for example, as regards torture and without engaging in new episodes of torture, that non-human animals when so abused actually squirm, they writhe, in a vain attempt to escape their own skin. When humans are abused, they use their minds to the same end, to disassociate from their bodily selves.

Even Proust's writing method is less than admirable: sequestering himself in a cork-lined room and having his meals abed (served up by his treasured maid and ersatz mama) in an obsession with his own memories (not to say conscience). Do any incline to repeat the experiment? Is this a guy thing? Are there any female readers and writers who feel a debt to the man or his work? Compassion, okay—but a debt? In his biography of Proust, Benjamin Taylor wrote that in 1913, toward the end of his life, Proust fell in love with and lavished money on:

> "... a cunning and ignorant boy with no love to offer in return. But as Proust says in 'Swann in Love,' probity in matters of the heart is '... invariably shown by clever people who, not being in love themselves, feel that a clever man should only be unhappy about a person who is worth his while; which is rather like being astonished that anyone should condescend to die of cholera at the bidding of so insignificant a creature as the common bacillus.' "[48]

Biographer Taylor described Proust, as virtually synonymous with his novel, this way:

> "A man who through his utterly new and personal use of the preterite [simple past] and past indefinite tenses, of the present participle, and certain pronouns and prepositions, has renewed our vision as much as Kant, with his Categories, and his theories of Knowledge and the Reality of the exterior world."[49]

In an interview, Proust said of his own epic (seven-volume) novel:

> "It is the invisible substance of time that I have tried to isolate, and it meant that the experiment had to last over a long period. ... My work is based on the distinction between involuntary and voluntary memory."[50]

A brilliant distinction, yes, and one of many to be noted among the more-than-million-and-a-half words that comprise *Recherche*. The first volume ("Swann's Way") ends like this:

> "The reality that I had known no longer existed. ... The places we have known do not belong only to the world of space on which we map them for our own convenience. They were only a thin slice, held between the contiguous impressions that composed our life at that time; the memory of a particular image is but regret for a particular moment; and houses, roads, avenues are as fugitive, alas, as the years."[51]

It's true that Proust, during his life and his long labour on *Recherche*, and before his death authorized his inclusion in the canon, endured in the wider world his share of non-comprehension: like a woman who wrote to him complaining of the complexity of his analyses and asking why he had to go on at such lengths, why he couldn't just be quick about it; not to mention the hypocrisy of a then-prominent literary critic who first panned the book and then later claimed to have "discovered" Proust.[52]

Such unhappy facts of Proust's writing life spark my sympathy (and they remind me that hypocrisy may be nowhere as blatant and over-the-top as in the "literary" world), but they do not endear me to hateful deeds, nor to the expressions of bigotry all too common among writers of acclaim. Other self-identified and outspoken anti-Semites ("in the conventional way characteristic" of their times—and ours) include Roald Dahl and Louis-Ferdinand Celine. Nobel Prize winner V. S. Naipaul, winner of the 2001 Nobel Prize in Literature, was anti-female and anti-Muslim, denounced by Salman Rushdie as "a fellow traveller of fascism." The racist cartoons of Dr. Seuss "depicted African Americans as savages." Kingsley Amis hated gays almost as much as he hated Jews; his son Martin Amis hated Muslims too and "advocated a restriction on Muslim travel, strip-searching for people who appeared to be Muslim, and even deportation of Muslim people." Being the target of historical persecution doesn't immunize anyone from hateful attitudes. David Mamet espoused anti-gay and anti-Muslim sentiments, and for good measure opposed marriage equality, calling it a "moral affront."[53]

A life is not a text; yet a text is not unrelated to the life of its author. In an essay entitled "Morality and Truth in Literature," Robert Stone engaged this issue without pussy-footing around it or feeling the need to ignore bad behaviour in writers long admired:

> "Evelyn Waugh seems to have been lacking in all the qualities we philanthropists find congenial. A bully, a fascist, a despiser of minorities and the poor, a groveler before the rich and powerful, Waugh was surely one of the worst human beings ever to become a major novelist."[54]

Truth and Consequences

The fruits of publication are uncertain at best. Some of the nastiest of works live on past their royalty claims into the public domain, and some of the loveliest of poetry dies within its own time, or perhaps never makes print at all. To tell unwelcome truth, to confront in print lies and hypocrisy—these are efforts as likely to earn their authors threats to life and limb as accolades. Throughout history, books bearing ideas that threaten established power and the status quo have been dealt with summarily.

> "The first recorded instance of book burning was in 213 BC, when Chinese emperor Qin Shi Huang decided to incinerate any history books that contradicted his version of the past. In addition, he buried more than four hundred scholars alive. … Supposedly, the library contained a half million documents and manuscripts and had a staff of one hundred resident librarians."[55]

Whole libraries have been consigned to the flames ever since the beginning of libraries. Scholars believe that the famous Library of Alexandria in ancient Egypt was burned and rebuilt several times.

> "The last and final burning, which erased it from history forever, occurred in AD 640. By that time, the library was awe-inspiring and a little scary. People had begun to believe it was a living thing—an enormous, infinite communal brain containing all the existing knowledge in the entire world, with the potential for the sort of independent intelligence we now fear in supercomputers. Everything about the Library of Alexandria was enigmatic. To this day, no one is sure whether the stories about it are true."[56]

Religious and cultural differences in written works were also dealt with by fire.

> "In the thirteenth and fourteenth centuries, the pope ordered Jewish books to be collected and 'cremated' (the choice of terms at the time)

> because he believed they spread anti-Catholic thought. The Spanish Inquisition introduced the idea of book-burning festivals, which were community gatherings around bonfires made of 'heretical' books, including any written in Hebrew, especially the Torah. … In the mid-1500s, Hernán Cortés and his soldiers burned scores of Aztec manuscripts on the grounds that they contained black magic."[57]

Modern sensibilities dictate less drastic measures. It's just as Ray Bradbury once noted: you don't have to burn books to destroy a culture: you just have to get people to stop reading them. And that, it turns out, is a tall order, even in the digital age. In his dystopian novel *Fahrenheit 451* (1953), Bradbury depicts a future society where books are prohibited and any that are discovered are burnt. The novel begins with this six-word sentence: "It was a pleasure to burn."

In a talk she gave years ago, Jeanette Winterson said why she thinks books, these bulky, immobile and seemingly powerless things, can arouse such vehement and at times violent opposition.

> "One of the reasons why tyrants hate books, from Hitler to the Ayatollah, is not so much for what they contain, though that is the usual indictment against them, but what they stand for. Church, State, and media have no powers over the private dialogue between a book and its reader. Reading is an act of free will."[58]

Why do writers do it? Why do they persist given the uncertainty of reward and the generally diminishing returns of authorship in a digital age? Why do they risk persecution for thinking wrong thoughts and then having the audacity to speak them aloud or in writing? Gao Xingjian was the first Chinese language author ever to win the Nobel Prize for Literature; he said he wrote for a kind of solace: "Writing eases my suffering. When you use words, you're able to keep your mind alive. Writing is my way of reaffirming my own existence."[59]

The American poet and essayist Mary Jane Oliver loved to take long walks in the woods. In her last essay collection (published in 2016, only several years before she died), she wrote:

> "The world's otherness is an antidote to confusion. Standing within this otherness—the beauty and the mystery of the world, out in the fields or deep inside books—can redignify the worst-stung heart."[60]

Many writers would say they do it simply for the holy curiosity, for the fun of the puzzle, or for the joy of the learning. One thing uniting them all is:

> "... a sense of profound modesty in the face of writing's daily difficulty and mystery, and joyful identification as lifelong students of language, history, and human behavior. Over and over again, they genuflect to writing as the visible struggle of humans engaged in moral reflection—indeed, as the very index of consciousness understanding itself."[61]

Writing is indeed difficult, even if some days go more easily than others. (The late American writer Sidney Sheldon said: "A blank piece of paper is God's way of telling us how hard it is to be God.") In fact, the practice strikes me as a kind of crucible: when you write, you contend with warring impulses with regard to a thousand details, and more scorching, with regard to the truth, with coming to know it. On the one hand, in order to avoid uncomfortable truths, you may enlist every defence mechanism in the book; on the other, you may take off the first layer of skin to get to it. The marvel is double: at the end of the process of writing a book, you find you have somehow retained your skin, and as bonus, that some of your standard defence mechanisms no longer work as they used to: they no longer operate without awareness of previously hidden motives. And thus a spell is broken.

> "Use enough words wantonly and you disappear before your own eyes. Use them well enough and you create yourself. This is why writers must own their language. Own your language or it will own you."[62]

Literature is not life, but it rates a close second. I think I would be unable to live without books, even though I don't love them all (and some of them make me want to scream). But I treasure those that come from compassion, unabashed. I don't think I could live without reading, or without writing, either (though how I sometimes wish I might persist without the latter).

Like so many others, when I write, it's some kind of the truth I'm after. To my mind, it isn't money at the root of all evil—it's lies. I once had an idea for a novel (several chapters of it still gather dust in a drawer somewhere, and pretty bad they were, too). In this novel, to be called "The Muting," I would have some characters capable of compassion and of honest communication, and others not so endowed. A strange virus (imagined long before covid-19) would strike mute the book's characters (in fact, humans worldwide would be stricken, unable to utter a single word). In the end, only those people capable of honest and open dialogue would regain their powers of speech; the others would remain muted for all time. At last, my desire to shut them up forever would be realized in fictional form! Looking back, I have to laugh at myself. The idea for such a narrative reminds me of a T-shirt I couldn't resist buying, though I dislike and rarely don shirts bearing messages. It reads: "Dear Karma: I have a list of people you may have missed."

In reality, there's no such thing as "forever," but then isn't that the beauty of fiction, that it can posit the impossible and run with it? In reality, any life that has a beginning in birth must also have an ending in death, and, insult to injury, life promises us nothing but that first and last breath.[63] In fiction, there's a continuity—beginning, middle, and end—and so the chance of insight that might otherwise elude even the wisest and the longest of tooth. And isn't that the beauty of nonfiction, too? Any writing that lights the sparks of self-understanding and so, compassion, in nonfiction as in fiction, in reader as in writer, goes beyond mere discourse, beyond having your two cents' worth.

> "You can have it if you want. John's story, that is. Do with it what you will. I'd just as soon you forget it, or, at least, not mention my name if you tell it to friends. Just don't say in the years to come that you would have lived your life differently if only you had heard this story. / You've heard it now."[64]

I do believe the world would be a better place if more people wrote for love, for the gifts of insight and insight shared (rather than for dreams of posterity's praise or worse: on command and by committee); not because the world desperately needs more text, but because it desperately needs more love. Only love frees the lonely self from the timid hesitations of discrete individuality; only love emboldens being beyond the self-serving. I've entertained this thought on many occasions: that you write, I write, we write—to avoid being written.

> "Hard times are coming, when we'll be wanting the voices of writers who can see alternatives to how we live now, can see through our fear-stricken society and its obsessive technologies to other ways of being, and even imagine real grounds for hope. We'll need writers who can remember freedom—poets, visionaries—realists of a larger reality."[65]

Note to self: Take courage, go ahead and dream your own metaphor, follow your heart with the work of your hands. Remember that there's nothing you can sing that can't be sung, so go ahead and sing. This single life, so brief, is more than any jumble of words, however artfully arranged, can ever say. It's what moves you to words that matters, words like grains of sand: a small but divine syntax.

Chapter 6

Language Origins and Evolution

"Amoebae leave no fossils," wrote Tom Robbins in the opening line of his 1976 novel *Even Cowgirls Get the Blues*. Like amoebae, words once spoken leave no physical trace. Speech rides the breath and then vanishes into thin air. Of the origins of spoken language, all we know for certain is that speech preceded writing by untold eons.

The Neanderthals (*Homo neanderthalensis*) were a species of archaic humans who lived in Eurasia from 400,000 years ago until about 40,000 years ago. That species, our closest hominid ancestor, was named in 1864. Since then, debate has persisted about who they were, how they lived, and especially when their evolution diverged from that of modern humans. Questionable (and increasingly questioned) is a view of the Neanderthals as primitive and of low intelligence, with only rudimentary tools and incapable of language or symbolic thought. More current and contrary views see the Neanderthals as "highly intelligent, able to adapt to a wide variety of ecological zones, and capable of developing … tools to help them do so."[1]

Like other animals, they vocalized. But did the Neanderthals speak? The evidence is at best inconclusive. No one knows whether or not their anatomy permitted speech. They had a hyoid bone—a U-shaped bone in the neck that supports the tongue. The only bone in the human body that doesn't articulate with another bone, the hyoid attaches instead to muscle, ligament, and cartilage. Without it, we would be unable to articulate speech, and so the hyoid bone figures prominently in the debate.

> "The hyoid bone helps to support the tongue and elevate the larynx when you talk or swallow. … Other animals have versions of the hyoid, but only the human variety is in the right position to work in unison with the larynx and tongue and make us the chatterboxes of the animal world."[2]

The hyoid bone is fragile:

> "...none was found in the vocal tract of a Neanderthal ancestor until 1983, when excavators in Israel discovered a well preserved one." It turned out to be mostly similar to the hyoid bone in modern humans. But this discovery doesn't settle the matter of whether they spoke. In order to speak, they would also have needed a larynx (voice box) in the right (low-lying) position. "In all mammals apart from humans, the larynx is high in the neck ... In humans, the larynx is much lower in the neck, with the consequence that humans cannot drink and breathe simultaneously."[3]

We don't know when archaic humans began speaking words, but we can speculate on how. Did language arise by some kind of divine intervention or did it evolve only gradually over the ages from more earthly origins? Was there some cataclysmic "big bang" that accounts for the fact that while all kinds of animals vocalize, only humans speak words?

> "[In the] big genetic bang scenario for culture ... a sudden alteration in the organization of our brains, probably resulting from a genetic mutation, occurred around fifty thousand years ago. This change was the author of all the cultural innovation that followed, as well as the final successful journey from Africa that left humanity spread across the globe. The saltation gave rise to modern language, words and syntax being the cause and the means by which cultural and technological change spread and evolved."[4]

Others have opposed as untenable the idea of a sudden but momentous change, arguing against the notion:

> "... that spoken language appeared almost out of nowhere in an isolated 'big bang' moment within the past 100,000 years as a result of a chance genetic mutation in a single individual. Evolution tends to inch forward in tiny, incremental steps rather than in huge leaps. Changes build one on top of another over eons like a stalagmite growing on the floor of a cave splashed by countless drops of water."[5]

That makes sense to me. If the big-bang theory were correct, the question would remain: What is it that banged, from where and into what?

In his book *The Descent of Man*, Charles Darwin was unequivocal with regard to the likely origins of spoken language:

> "I cannot doubt that language owes its origins to the imitation and modification of various natural sounds, and man's own distinctive cries, aided by signs and gestures."[6]

I cannot doubt that Darwin got this right.

***

As to why language arose, we can speculate. Was it for the purpose of self-communication or for communication with others?—an "either-or" question that remains as mutely convoluted as it is compelling. Despite the speculations of noted authorities, these are at best chicken-and-egg questions, for without the language of words, we could communicate with words neither internally nor externally. How can you communicate something to yourself verbally without this something having taken some linguistic form within yourself, and how can you communicate with others unless such linguistic forms also arose more or less contemporaneously in these others?

As for beginnings, records of ancestry can reach back only so far. The experience of one's own birth is lost in pre-consciousness; that of one's own death remains beyond commentary. Neither beginnings nor endings can be traced with precision to a single or discrete point. We call this unmapped unknowable "infinity," and measure it with time.

The idea of time as an eternal present is as old as the centuries. The physicist Erwin Schrödinger (1887-1961): "For eternally, and always there is only now, one and the same now; the present is the only thing that never ends."[7] Hundreds of years earlier, in his late-fourth-century Confessions, St. Augustine defined eternity as "supreme over time because it is a never-ending present. … For what is now the future, once it comes, will become the past … Your today is eternity."[8] One contemporary novelist began his tale with this line: "Nothing ever begins."[9] I think I know what he means.

Definitions, predictably, don't help. Consider how adroitly the dictionary sidesteps the matter of origins in its defining of the word "infinity." Typical entries tell us that "infinity" is a noun meaning (in order of appearance): "time or space that has no end; a place that is so far away that it cannot be reached; a number that is larger than all other numbers; an extremely large number of something." The same applies to the word "eternity," defined as "infinite, unending, a very long time." Nothing is said about time or space that has no beginning, about a place so near or a quantity so small as to be undetectable. Even the presumed authority of the Bible's "Genesis," with its "In the beginning God created the heavens and the earth," may amount to a simple misreading of the original idea. So argued Aviya Kushner in her book *The Grammar of God*, citing the authority of Rashi, an eleventh-century rabbi and pre-eminent Talmudic scholar, who suggested that the verb rendered as "created" in English (a language only hundreds of years old) mistranslates the syntax of the original Hebrew (an ancient tongue).

> "In Hebrew, vowels—dots and dashes located above, beneath, and inside letters—frequently determine meaning. And Rashi claims that in Genesis 1:1, the vowels should have been rendered differently. This complaint isn't unreasonable. ... Rashi, in the eleventh century, can argue that the vowels are wrong because he knows that written vowels were added to the text only in the eighth century. ... It's not just recent Jewish translations that are defining the verse in Genesis 1:1 as a phrase, as Rashi did."[10]

The intended meaning was not, as in Genesis, "In the beginning, God created," but rather as per the original Hebrew, "In the beginning of God's creating"—that is, not as a finite verb (created) but as a gerund (God's creating). Kushner concludes that with a period at the end of the sentence, as in the King James version, "God is definitely done with creation, instead of breathlessly rushing on and possibly still continuing."[11]

Definitive answers about how and why language originated continue to elude scientists and philosophers alike. That is the nature of such questions, for the trouble with words—language itself—remains "one of the biggest obstacles to clarity in the study of language evolution."[12] How can one use language to stand outside language, so to speak, in order to view a panorama vast beyond imagination, one that cannot be viewed except by the mind's eye, one that can only be inferred or approximated, that can communicate thought only by translation into words?

> "... the very language used to get at these ideas does not serve it well. Language evolution research has illuminated a complicated geometry of species, traits, and relationships, and in the face of this newly defined space words like 'uniqueness,' innateness,' and 'instinct' have come to mean everything and nothing. Those terms are still bandied about ... but in fact everyone agrees there is linguistic innateness, and everyone agrees there is something unique about language."[13]

The field of genetics had tried for decades to isolate a language gene before it began to accept that no such gene exists. "Why," asked linguist Christine Kenneally, "is the idea of a specific language or grammar gene appealing? Why would isolating a gene that controls language and that controls only language be such a coup?" She offered several reasons: it would allow scientists to track down that elusive point of origin, beefing up the big-bang theory. But most importantly, it would pad the idea of humans as separate from and superior to all other animals: it would provide evidence "for the traditional claim that language is a discrete mental trait unique to our species."[14] The idea of the human genome as a kind of blueprint of the human animal is itself misleading. Genes are not static; they operate dynamically, in response to their environment and changing circumstances, and they can be switched on or off.

***

Questions about the origins of spoken language are so thorny that for a long time they were summarily dismissed as beyond the pale of respectable scholarship. The subject of how language began was actually forbidden, deemed unfit for print. An august scientific body of the nineteenth century (the Société de Linguistique of Paris) declared a moratorium on the topic in 1866.[15] Why speculate on matters to which, the society reasoned, there could never be certain or scientific answers. It wasn't until the latter half of the twentieth century that the linguistic society's ban on publication was breached and the study of language evolution began to gain legitimacy. In our own twenty-first century, the discipline has made up for lost time, with new techniques like computer modeling. As the field of study blossomed, its applications spread to diverse other disciplines, ones previously regarded as discrete, presumably as separate as engineering from philosophy.

To ask how language or consciousness or life itself began are classic questions often posed within a dichotomous frame of either-or—and as such they admit of no solution. But to ask how an individual life began falls nicely outside the either-or conundrum—as for example, when an adopted child seeks out "natural" parents. Though that child may never discover who those parents are, the question and answer is not "either-or" but "who." I believe we seek either-or answers to abstract questions, not only because the perspective is an initial vector of thought, but also because like orphaned children all, we believe (not without reason) that if we know where we came from, we may gain understanding of who we are and where we're headed, as individuals and as a species.

Theories of Evolution

The term "evolution" as applied to change in language use over time is somewhat misleading. Changes in language use may occur in a single generation, over the mere decades that comprise individual lives; evolutionary change proceeds over time immemorial. Though we sometimes speak of language evolution as comparable to biological evolution, the words of a language are a matter of culture, not biology. What evolves in bodies are the biological substrates that make the speaking of words physically possible. These biological substrates of language—vocalizations imbued with meaning—are ancient and common to the entire animal world, by no means unique to humans.

Evolution acts without a master plan, through the life cycles of species, through the very bodies of their members. Biological evolution doesn't act on individuals so much as through them. Parent animals pass on their genetic changes to their offspring; over time genetic variations in a species amount to changes in basic aspects of the species' lifestyle, like diet and habitat. The key idea is that "... evolution consists of changes in the proportion of a population with adaptive traits rather than a transformation of the population so that its traits would be more adaptive."[16] Edward O. Wilson put it this way:

> "The fundamental evolutionary event is a change in the frequency of genes and chromosome configurations in a population. ... But whatever their nature or magnitude, the changes in progress are always expressed in percentages of individuals within or among populations. Evolution is absolutely a phenomenon of populations. Individuals and their descendants do not evolve."[17]

We may naturally hope that individuals and their descendants *do* evolve, but when we speak of individuals evolving we mean something quite different from biological evolution. Shocking as it may seem, there is no proto plan. Not a blueprint but an evolving environment is in charge here. Change is managed moment by moment, and some changes that served species survival at one point can come to threaten it at another. The idea that human-engineered solutions can outdo natural selection over the long term is typically (humanly) short-sighted.

> "Of course, natural selection does not have the foresight of engineers, but that cuts both ways: it does not have their mental blocks, impoverished imagination, or conformity to bourgeois sensibilities and

> ruling-class interests, either. Guided only by what works, selection can home in on brilliant, creative solutions."[18]

The theory of evolution initially proposed by Charles Darwin and Alfred Russel Wallace in the mid-nineteenth century is often misinterpreted to suggest that humans are descended directly from apes.[19] What the theory actually says is that modern humans and modern apes are both descended from an ancient common ancestor.

> "About six million years ago, our common ancestor hit a fork in the tree, and *Pan*, the genus that includes chimpanzees and the bonobo, and the lineage leading to *Homo*, the human line, began separate trajectories. (Gorillas had begun their journey much earlier, about ten million years ago. Orangutans, roughly fifteen.) Various *Homo* species—possibly up to twenty species of humans—evolved and flourished. … Our species, *Homo sapiens*—not gorillas—is the closest living relative of the chimpanzees and the bonobo."[20]

Humans evolved alongside orangutans, chimpanzees, bonobos, and gorillas. All of these shared a common ancestor going back millions of years. Precisely when the first biologically human species is thought to have appeared is unknown, and perhaps unknowable. Consider for example that in 2015, scientists revealed they had unearthed a 2.8-million-year-old specimen of a human jawbone, "400,000 years older than researchers thought that our kind first emerged."[21] Another study suggests that Neanderthals and modern humans diverged nearly a million years ago, much earlier than suggested by previous studies.[22]

Evolutionary biologists have long theorized a "missing link" between humans and the Neanderthals, a "last common ancestor" from which modern humans descended. Despite decades of searching, no such link has been found. What if we modern humans *are* the missing link, I wonder—perhaps a link to a species less self-centered and less destructive than our own, less like chimpanzees and more like bonobos, the so-called hippies of the primate world.

***

The very idea of biological evolution, a landmark theoretical advance, was at first fiercely resisted (and still is by some): it constitutes an unbearable ego wound to the conception of humans as divinely exceptional—a species possessed of a soul and ordained to rule over all. Controversial in its own day, the theory was an upstart in the annals of the scientific literature. Darwin's famed *On the Origin of Species* was published in 1859, to much impassioned resistance. Until 1859 and well into the late nineteenth century, even most scientists refused to accept evolutionary theory. They persisted in believing what they always had: that each species was created in its own form from time immemorial and would retain that form, unchanged and unchanging over time.[23] This belief was abandoned only gradually after Darwin, as taxonomists began to base their systems of classification accordingly, that is, on the basis of evolutionary relationships among all organisms.

The word "evolution" was in use in the early seventeenth century, hundreds of years before its application to Darwin's groundbreaking theory (itself fewer than two hundred years old). In 1622, the word referred to a book (to the process of "unrolling," or "opening up," or "disengaging from an envelope"). By 1700, it was used with reference to geometry ("the unfolding of a curve, so that from it is produced an involute"). It was only in the twentieth century that the term "evolution" began to be used with reference to biology in general (as in "from a simple to a more complex form") and secondarily, in its Darwinian sense (as "a process by which species develop from earlier forms, as an explanation of their origins, etc.").[24]

The theory of evolution is still being elaborated upon, and still evoking contrary interpretations. The earliest objections to Darwinian evolution came (and come still) from the so-called "creationists," who object that the idea of evolution negates the idea of God. Darwin himself anticipated such objections and in *The Descent of Man*, wrote this:

> "I am aware that the conclusions arrived at in this work will be denounced by some as highly irreligious, but he who denounces them is bound to show why it is more irreligious to explain the origin of man as a distinct species by descent [by natural selection] … than to explain the birth of the individual through the laws of ordinary reproduction. The birth both of the species and of the individual are equally part of that grand sequence of events, which our minds refuse to accept as the result of blind chance."[25]

Scholarly disagreement about the meaning of evolution goes far beyond matters of faith to the heart of contemporary science. Take for instance the American microbiologist and geneticist James Shapiro, a kind of renegade among his peers, many of whom, he says, are fundamentally mistaken in their views, peers for whom reigning paradigms have become dogma.

Shapiro holds that every cell of every organism is sentient, that "living cells and organisms are cognitive (sentient) entities that act and interact purposefully to ensure survival, growth, and proliferation." He notes that even bacteria are aware: that they evolve in order to live; that they respond to their environments in ways that can only be described as conscious and intelligent. He argues finally that bacteria should be studied not singly, but as multi-cellular communities.[26] In this less orthodox view, Shapiro is not alone.[27]

A group of scientists and scholars from The Nature Institute (www.nature-institute.org), led by figures like Shapiro and Oxford physiologist Denis Noble, reject what they call Neo-Darwinism and the idea that only small random mutations account for "useful adaptation." They argue against Creationism as overtly anti-scientific, but also against the reigning alternative of Neo-Darwinism, "which is clearly naturalistic science but ignores much contemporary molecular evidence and invokes a set of unsupported assumptions about the accidental nature of hereditary variation." On the home page of the institute's website (www.thethirdwayofevolution.com), the authors explain:

> "We now know that the many different processes of variation involve well regulated cell action on DNA molecules. Genomes merge, shrink and grow, acquire new DNA components, and modify their structures by well-documented cellular and biochemical processes."

In the preamble to an article by Stephen Talbott, a senior researcher for The Nature Institute since 1998, Talbott is described as "… concerned about distortions introduced in biology by technological thinking." To quote Talbott:

> "DNA sequences are appealing as the sole or primary materials of inheritance because they give us conveniently and quantitatively trackable things. But stable things and our own mathematical convenience are not necessarily the best guides for understanding life and change. What if the more pressing need is to learn to track a qualitative and coherent organizing reality we have hardly yet begun to recognize because we haven't yet even thought to look for it?"[28]

Long before molecular biology hit its stride and long before twenty-first-century scientists began questioning fundamental ideas about Darwinian evolution, Arthur Koestler objected in a similar way to the mechanistic stance of behaviourism, writing this:

> "One cannot hope to arrive at a diagnosis of the predicament of man so long as one's image of man is that of a conditioned reflex-automaton produced by chance mutations; one cannot use a stethoscope on a slot machine."[29]

In the twenty-first century, scientists have begun to question the very idea of separate species, or at least of strict boundaries between them. One 2019 article in *New Scientist* notes dozens of competing definitions of the very word "species": "Ecologists tend to categorise based on lifestyle. Paleontologists focus on form. Geneticists sequence genomes and then create family trees based on shared, genetically encoded characteristics."[30] It notes that at some point animals are different enough that we classify them as separate species, but it's not possible to pinpoint when two modern species diverged on the evolutionary tree of life. Yet humans keep trying to place the human animal above the rest of the animal kingdom. The bias is so pervasive as to have become nearly invisible. Frans de Waal made the point, with characteristic aplomb:

> "Humans diverged from the apes about as long ago as African and Asian elephants did from each other, and they are genetically about as close or distant. Yet we freely call both of those species 'elephants' while obsessing over the specific point at which our own lineage moved from being an ape to being human. We even have special words for this process, such as hominization and anthropogenesis. That there was ever such a point in time is a widespread illusion, like trying to find the precise wavelength in the light spectrum at which orange turns into red. Our desire for sharp divisions is at odds with evolution's habit of making extremely smooth transitions."[31]

In the 1960s, that generation of rebellion and cultural upheaval, the discipline of biology, like so many other disciplines of the era, underwent a transformation, one consistent with new discoveries at the molecular level and new technologies like computer modelling to understand the behavior of microscopic entities. The science of evolution inaugurated a paradigm shift that continues to hold sway.

> "Science is undergoing its greatest intellectual revolution since the time of Descartes. The new emphasis is on connections, complexity and the behavior of systems, rather than the inherent properties of the smallest possible units. Living systems are the key to this new approach because well-established biological concepts like homeostatic feedback

> regulation, sensory information processing, behavioral responsiveness, and hierarchical integration are applicable to all complex systems."[32]

To my mind, the most important and interesting thing about evolution is that for better or worse, it never quits. Biologists continue to discover plants and animals "that were thought to be extinct or were never before seen or imagined."

> "Thousands of new species are discovered each year. Most are found in previously inaccessible places, like the high atmosphere, deep in soils, in the ocean and around hot vents on the ocean floors, in the canopies of rain forests, and even within animals themselves. … The Woolemi pine tree was presumed to have gone extinct in its native Australia two million years ago, only to be found still clinging to the planet there in 1994. In 2005, a whole new family of rodents came to light in Laos—the *kha-nyou* … who supposedly had been extinct for eleven million years. A new South American monkey received its binomial moniker in 2005. … [In the same year] a new wild dog species turned up in Borneo—a new fox. … In the following year, 2006, scientists announced the discovery of more than fifty new species of plants and animals in Borneo."[33]

Evolution, it would seem, has its ways, and inexorably outpaces efforts to corral the profusion of life forms into taxonomic boxes.

***

It's obvious that the way people use language changes with time, as for example in the previously noted creativity of generational lingo. From one generation to the next, some words are forged anew and others fall into disuse. In all endeavours and disciplines, word meanings change, with new words invented to coin novel developments as some knowledge grows, and old words losing meaning as other knowledge dims. In other words, language entire does indeed, in these senses, evolve.

So what? Doesn't everything, "in these senses," evolve? Yes, certainly, but biological evolution responds to environmental conditions with the single implicit goal of survival. The evolution of language is a more cerebral affair, and a facility for language may work to oppose species survival as easily as to support it. In short, the meaning of the term "evolution" (whether applied to biology or language) is not synonymous with progress to a better world; it does not necessarily indicate a ranking in terms of value.

> "While it is true that we descend from an apelike ancestor, the ancient species that gave rise to us no longer exists. It dwelled [on] earth about six million years ago, and its descendants went through numerous changes and died out … before giving rise to the survivors around today: the chimpanzee, the bonobo, and our own species. Since these three hominids have equally long histories behind them, they are equally 'evolved.' "[34]

A biologist and anthropologist, Thomas H. Huxley (1825-1895) was a staunch supporter of Charles Darwin when the latter's theory of evolution was new and much opposed. For his advocacy, Huxley was nicknamed "Darwin's Bulldog." Well more than a century ago, Huxley made the very same point about evolution: it is not necessarily a path strictly on the up-and-up.

> "It is an error to imagine that evolution signifies a constant tendency to increased perfection. That process undoubtedly involves a constant remodelling of the organism in adaptation to new conditions; but it depends on the nature of those conditions whether the directions of the modifications effected shall be upward or downward."[35]

We generally think of the evolution of human language (like that of the human species) as synonymous with a kind of general progress, but we may well be missing something here.

> "As much as language allows us to control nature and keep our environments stable, it also makes possible the dramatic altering of our environment in unexpected and dangerous ways. The same language skills that promote technological innovations like water irrigation, road-building, and air-conditioning also produce the ozone-destroying pollution and countless other ecological dangers of the modern age."[36]

Or as Marilynne Robinson put it: "The Neo-Darwinists insist that we, and our behavior, are formed around the project of ensuring our genetic survival. History should be a sufficient rebuttal."[37]

In the expanse of evolutionary time, adaptations include the possibility of species extinction, not just progression to ever higher levels of performance in the interests of individual survival and hence species propagation. In this respect at least, language evolution shares a defining characteristic with biological evolution, and a coordinate threat, as the extinction of languages continues all over the world.

> "The world loses one of its six thousand languages every two weeks, and children have stopped learning half of the languages currently spoken in the world. It's been argued that languages are under greater threat than any endangered bird or mammal. ... When a language dies, we lose the knowledge that was encoded in it."[38]

Like biological evolution, the evolution of human language is a work in progress, based on adaptations to changing environments. Like biology, language as a system evolves not with a master plan, "but through the accumulation over time of a myriad of little adjustments by individuals responding to immediate pressures."[39] Unlike individual living creatures, though, evolution per se does not intend. Although we may see ourselves at the top of some evolutionary hierarchy, as "finished or perfected, we are not in any way intended. There is no blueprint for what humans are meant to be."[40]

> "If there were a moral to the story of evolution, it would be that meaning is something that happens after the fact. There is no rhyme or reason to the mutations that occur over the evolution of a species. ... Evolution is the opposite of destiny, and because we are creatures of both biological and cultural evolution, where we are going is really obvious only in hindsight."[41]

The origin of language, like the origin of life, remains deeply mysterious. No amount of science has been able thus far to nail down an answer. But hope persists in the modern high-tech human heart that more high-tech will settle the matter and dispel the mystery. If the question of origins remains elusive:

> "That is not to say, of course, that it will always be so. Undoubtedly the physical and chemical processes that led to the emergence of life from non-life are immensely complicated, and it is no surprise that we find such processes hard to model mathematically or to duplicate in the laboratory."[42]

At a quick glance, that sounds reasonable. But wait! What on earth might "non-life" be?

Evolution's only motivating force is the propagation of life entire, and life entire is the only abstraction over which death really does have no dominion. Death does not disappear life: a dead organism decomposes, thus feeding the cyclical processes of ongoing life. Matter and energy aren't created or destroyed; they only trade places. Though we humans like to distinguish ourselves from all other animals, especially as honcho primates among the mammals, evolution speaks its own language, one lively and responsive quite beyond the reach of even the best communicators.

Although we know that the human species evolved over millions of years, the different defining characteristics of the species emerged at different times. For instance, the ability to stand upright and walk on two legs (bipedalism) evolved more than four million years ago, while the complex brain that allowed for advanced language traits developed much more recently, by many estimates within the last 100,000 years.[43] Human languages and cultures are all newcomers on the evolutionary stage.

Human primates would appear to be at the top of the food chain, but it's a precarious perch. "Of the entire terrestrial vertebrate biomass on earth, wild animals constitute only about three percent, humans one-quarter, and livestock almost three-quarters!"[44] According to a report already several years old, almost two thirds of primate species are near extinction.[45] The survival (never mind the rehabilitation) of *Homo sapiens* is hardly assured. As Loren Eiseley put it: "Biologists tell us that in the fullness of time more than ninety percent of the world's past species have perished. The mammalian ones in particular are not noted for longevity."[46]

Human civilization as we understand it from the archaeological and anthropological evidence, dates back only a fraction of evolutionary time, about 12,000 years; the earliest written records, a mere 6,000. Modern history (beginning with industrialization in the 1800s) is but a fraction of a blip on the screen of time: barely over 200 years old.

No matter how many times I rehearse these timelines of evolution, I cannot wrap my brain around such expanses of time as millions, or for that matter, mere tens of thousands, of years. Even the 40,000 years that are supposed to separate modern humans from the Neanderthals is a stretch too far (40,000 years: that represents more than 1,300 human generations), a prospect beyond imagining. But perhaps I should say it's a prospect available only to the imagination.

***

For his poetic sensibilities, the anthropologist Loren Eiseley (1907-1977) was considered odd by his colleagues in the scientific community: he went beyond writing poetry on his own time and brought his poetic sensibilities and prose style to his scholarly writing. In one memorable essay, Eiseley described a childhood experience he regarded as seminal to his decision to study anthropology: "not the men of written history but the ancestors beyond, beyond all writing, beyond time as we know it, beyond human form as it is known today."[47]

The story begins when the young Eiseley is out exploring, as youngsters are wont to do. He comes across "a very large, dark mahogany-coloured turtle" that had been killed by someone with a repeating rifle; the killer had, as the evidence revealed, "stitched a row of bullet holes across the turtle's carapace." The young Eiseley remembers how his father once explained to him that "it took a long time to make a big turtle, years really, in the sunlight and the water and the mud." The memory sparks a question that "rose up unbidden. Why did the man have to kill something living that could never be replaced?"[48]

Later at home, Eiseley describes the disturbing incident to his father, who tells the boy an allegorical tale that depicts men as "orphans" and "eternal seekers," forever in search of their roots and ever uncertain of their future. The tale ends with counsel:

> "You will learn in time there is much pain here," he said. "Men will give it to you, time will give it to you, and you must learn to bear it all, not bear it alone, but be better for the wisdom that may come to you if you watch and listen and learn. Do not forget the turtle, nor the ways of men. They are all orphans and they go astray; they do wrong things. Try to see better."

In the course of his studies, Eiseley learns how for a long time, people believed in unchanging life forms created by an almighty deity, believed that life on earth arose only thousands of years ago, with the human species at its centre and pinnacle. It was only in the seventeenth century, with the coming of the scientific revolution, Eiseley wrote, that "thoughts unventured upon since the time of the Greek philosophers began to enter the human consciousness." But these thoughts—this ancient wisdom made new again—wounded humanity's sense of pre-eminence in a universe vast beyond imagination, with a stunning realization.

> "Man had not always been here. He had been preceded, in the 4,000,000,000 years of the planet's history, by floating mollusks, strange fern forests, huge dinosaurs, flying lizards, giant mammals, whose bones lay under the dropped boulders of vanished continental ice sheets."

And so the cosmic orphan, disabused of his sense of supreme importance, cried out in protest, demanding to know "Who am I?"

> "And once more science answered. 'You are a changeling. You are linked by a genetic chain to all the vertebrates. The thing that is you bears the still aching wounds of evolution in body and in brain. Your hands are made-over fins, your lungs come from a creature gasping in a swamp, your femur has been twisted upright. Your foot is a reworked climbing pad. You are a rag doll resewn from the skins of extinct animals. Long ago, 2,000,000 years perhaps, you were smaller, your brain was not so large. We are not confident that you could speak. Seventy million years before that you were an even smaller climbing creature known as a tupaiid."

Despite the differences between biological and linguistic evolution, questions about the latter remain critical, because the answers we find or propose or assume remain consequential. The story of language evolution is "an epic":

> "… about an animal that evolved, started talking, started talking about the fact that it was talking, and then paused briefly before asking itself how it started talking in the first place. … Why does language evolution matter? Because the story of language evolution underlies every other story that has ever existed and every story that ever will."[49]

Among experts in diverse disciplines, the idea is widely shared that no practice has led to more significant outcomes than language itself.

> "In this one species of perpetually hungry, highly social, and highly competitive information processors … selection pressure set off a runaway cascade of trans-generational cultural learning. The still somewhat bewildered beneficiaries of the resulting relentless series of cognitive system upgrades—some genetic, but many more others cultural—now find themselves collectively capable of working miracles, such as killing millions of their conspecifics at the press of a button, saving millions by inventing antibiotics, wrecking their home planet, and landing fancy hardware on other planets."[50]

The Advent of Writing and Evolution of Scripts

Spoken language is as old as the species, but writing is radically new. Even the word literacy is new (coined in 1883, in an article in the *New England Journal of Education*).[51] Compared to orality, literacy is a project barely begun, but a project with momentous consequence. Before the advent of writing, people could communicate only with those within hearing distance. With literacy came the ability to record the products of human thought and the stories of human experience, to preserve these through time and disseminate them across space. Though literacy is an evolutionary fledgling, no development has proven as critical. Thanks to literacy, we have history, the ability to record the words of times and minds gone by, and so to preserve knowledge.

> "When the first words were written down in what is now southern Iraq in the late fourth millennium BCE, history was made in more senses than one, for it is writing that separates history from prehistory, the time that can be studied through written records from the time that can be studied only through archaeology."[52]

Writing, as a system of graphic marks, is said to have been invented independently in the Near East, China, and Mesoamerica. Some of the earliest known scripts are the Sumerian cuneiform and the Egyptian hieroglyphics, created in Mesopotamia (an area of Iraq, today) about 5,000 years ago (3300-3200 BCE).

In tracing the history of literacy, however, much depends on how words are defined. How old is writing? That depends on what you mean by "writing." If you mean the making of marks on a surface to represent and communicate something, a set of symbols to represent things in reality, then human technologies of writing have been evolving for tens of thousands of years, from the drawings on cave walls through the earliest scripts to words and images glittering on electronic screens. The very earliest writing consisted of graphic markings that referred not to spoken words but to numbers used for commerce, for the keeping of accounts. Some of the earliest markings were made on clay tokens (as early as 8000 BCE); other early writing systems took various forms.

> "Little tokens in hardened clay envelopes, intricate dyed knots of twine in Incan quipus … graceful designs scratched on the surface of turtle shells: the origins of writing took wondrously various shapes and forms for the last 10,000 years, all over the earth. Crosshatched lines on stones thought to be 77,000 years old were found recently under layers of earth in the Blomos Cave in South Africa and may prove to be still earlier signs of the first human efforts to 'read'."[53]

The initial impetus for early writing systems, whatever their particular origins in a given population, were less poetic than political: writing was used to record the details of ownership and status, "to make laundry lists, to keep track of cows and slaves and household goods,"[54] and especially, "to keep tax records for kings."[55]

Ideas about the origins of writing, though more amenable to historical tracing than spoken language, must remain speculative. Consider for instance that modern "archaeologists have yet to fully decipher" some of the earliest scripts, including the quipus used by pre-colonial cultures in the mountains of western South America.[56] Consider that while most agree writing began in Sumer (an ancient nation of Mesopotamia), Sumer itself, though a staple of standard language histories, is hardly a closed case. [57]

> "It is the oldest civilization known in the Near East, but its origins are still a mystery. Its language is neither Semitic nor Indo-European. It dominated most of Mesopotamia during the fourth millennium before Jesus. … The Sumerian language continued as the hieratic language of Babylonia and Assyria for many centuries after the Sumerians themselves had disappeared and were forgotten. The very existence of Sumer was unknown until the relatively recent decipherment of ancient tablets bearing the cuneiform writing that was probably the invention of the Sumerians and the ancestor of Phoenician script."[58]

Before literacy, oral cultures used narrative to record even numbers: if there were lists or numbers of things to be communicated, these were embedded in stories. For example, "as in the catalogue of the ships and captains in the *Iliad*—not an objective tally but an operational display in a story about a war."[59] Like orality before it, literacy has always been political.

> "The kings and priests of ancient Sumer wanted writing to be used by professional scribes to record numbers of sheep owed in taxes, not by the masses to write poetry and hatch plots. As the anthropologist Claude Lévi-Strauss put it, ancient writing's main function was 'to facilitate the enslavement of other human beings.' Personal uses of writing by nonprofessionals came only much later, as writing systems grew simpler and more expressive."[60]

What made writing systems "simpler and more expressive," what constituted a critical advance in literacy, was the invention of a special code called the alphabet, in which each letter symbol represented a sound of spoken language. Alphabetic writing moved literacy beyond pictographic representations and numerical accounting.

> "Quite suddenly, around 1400 B.C., an entirely new kind of script made its appearance on the border between the Egyptian hieroglyphic tradition and the cuneiform of Mesopotamia. This North Semitic alphabet was the first to have signs for sounds only, and only one sign for each group of sounds."[61]

This letter-based alphabet is thought to have been invented by "Semitic peoples," about two thousand years after the earliest of scripts. The question of which Semitic peoples invented the alphabet is debatable; most sources trace the invention to the Phoenicians. But peoples and languages in the ancient world were closely related and virtually overlapping culturally. Who, precisely, were the Phoenicians? Oxford defines a Phoenician as "a member of a Semitic people of ancient Phoenicia in southern Syria or of its colonies"; it defines a "Semite" as "a member of any of the peoples supposed to be descended from Shem, son of Noah, including especially the Jews, Arabs, Assyrians, Babylonians, and Phoenicians."

The original alphabet had no vowels, only consonants; it was the ancient Greeks, centuries later, who added vowels. But debate is entertained as well about the relationship between Hebrew and Greek civilizations.

> "Archaeological discoveries at sites like Ugarit prevent us from regarding Greece as the hermetically sealed Olympian miracle, or Israel as the vacuum-packed miracle from Sinai. The thesis of this book is simply that Greek and Hebrew civilisations are parallel structures built upon the same East Mediterranean foundation. … For centuries scholars have been forced to grapple with the problem of accounting for the parallels between Greek literatures and the Bible. Did Greece borrow from Israel? Or did Israel borrow from Greece? Can the parallels be accidental? … Already in pre-Christian Alexandria, pagan critics had begun to invoke Greek myths to discredit the Bible of their Jewish neighbours."[62]

Disagreements about who authored the alphabet (especially those that insist it was anyone but the Hebrews) always remind me of that great line from *Fiddler on the Roof*, when a wise town elder named Tevya, in response to a threatened pogrom, pleads with God: "I know we're the chosen people," he says, "but once in a while couldn't you choose someone else?"

In any case, with thanks to the Arabs, Assyrians, Babylonians, Jews, and Phoenicians, we have the alphabetic principle, which constituted a profound insight and advance over earlier forms of symbolization. The earliest (pictographic) systems needed only object recognition. Alphabetic scripts require the reader to use a code to translate the marks on a page or other surface into the sounds of speech. Because alphabetic writing recorded speech sounds by means of a code, speech could now be represented by a finite group of letters (26 in the English alphabet). The hieroglyphics of ancient Egypt, by contrast, required an estimated 700 symbols or marks. With alphabetic writing, you could now write anything you could say or think, with words.

> "If alphabetic writing can be spoken of as bringing the human race into existence, it is only because this kind of writing is unique ... The alphabet records only sounds, and it is only through sounds that it provides meaning."[63]

Learning the alphabetic code made new demands on the human brain. Reading requires several areas of the brain to connect: "specifically, visual with auditory, linguistic, and conceptual areas."[64] The learning didn't come easily, and still doesn't among contemporary children, many of whom experience their share of difficulty in learning to read. This "meta-awareness of individual speech sounds didn't just magically appear in the history of writing; nor does it appear magically in the child. When asked by the reading expert Marilyn Adams what the 'first sound' in 'cat' was, one child promptly replied, 'Meow'!"[65]

Not a bad guess, and the point stands.

Some scholars contend that alphabetic writing enabled certain kinds of thought, leading to "literate-style" thinking, made possible by the "interiorization of the alphabet in the Greek psyche."[66] Once the code has been mastered, written letters and words become automatically associated, effectively synonymous, with their speech sounds. In literacy, when we read, we "see" with the mind's ear. The alphabet made spoken language visible.

It took hundreds of years, however, for the original alphabet to develop into a system that fully represented the sounds of speech. The accepted account says the first great leap forward occurred between 800 and 750 BCE, when the Greeks re-designed the original alphabet to include vowels (the Phoenician alphabet, like the Hebrew, consisted of consonants only).

> "To do this, the Greeks systematically analyzed each of the phonemes of the Phoenician and the Greek languages. Then, using the Phoenician consonant-based system as a base, they created their own symbols for vowels, doggedly perfecting the correspondence between letters and all

known sounds. On this basis, the Greek alphabet became the progenitor of most Indo-European alphabets and systems, from Etruscan to Turkish."[68]

Further innovation was necessary. It wasn't until the second century CE, with a shift from the volumen to the codex, "that people no longer had to unroll books to read them. Instead, they could jump around in a book by 'leafing' backward and forward."[69] It wasn't until the ninth century that some of the graphic conventions we take for granted today were adopted. It took several centuries, beginning in the late seventh century, for spaces between words to become common practice. Techniques of reference (such as summaries and chapter headings and the Bible's divisions into verses) took hundreds of years to develop. It was only at the end of the twelfth century, for example, that references were compiled into indexes.[70]

It took centuries more for literacy to spread widely, and even by the early Middle Ages, to write still meant to dictate to a scribe, not to hold a pen or pencil or other writing implement; "the usual method of writing, both for copying and for originals, was and remained dictation."[71] It took technical innovations—such as pencil and paper—for the "author" of a document to become the actual writer.

In the early stages, special mechanical skills were needed to deal with writing materials. By the thirteenth century there was parchment (the writer no longer had to use hard leather which needed to be scraped smooth with the point of a knife). Now the writer could do the writing, using a quill on parchment. The advent of paper made writing easier, but paper (invented by the Chinese in the second century) was diffused by the Arabs to the Middle East only in the eighth century; it wasn't manufactured in Europe until the twelfth century. Our contemporary version of paper didn't become widely available until the nineteenth century, with the advent of steam powered machines.

By the late Middle Ages, from about 1150 to 1300, writing began to be more widely disseminated and "letters ushered in a new type of society," as written words began to get "under a culture's skin," effecting changes in consciousness.[72] This evolution of writing from the earliest forms of symbolization to alphabetic writing, with each advance making more arduous demands on the brain, took thousands of years. But what took literacy viral, so to speak, was the invention of alphabetic letterpress printing (aka: movable type) in mid-fifteenth-century Europe, an invention generally attributed to Johannes Gutenberg (a German goldsmith, printer, and inventor). But again, when printing began depends on how you define the word "printing." Like the earliest systems of symbolization called writing, printing as such long preceded Gutenberg's press.

> "For thousands of years human beings have been printing designs from variously carved surfaces, and since the seventh or eighth century, Chinese, Koreans and Japanese have been printing verbal texts, at first from wood blocks engraved in relief. But the crucial development in the global history of printing was the invention of alphabetic letterpress print in fifteenth-century Europe."[73]

Although the art of printing designs had been known long before, it was only with the advent of movable type that printing was used to convey information, and that print itself began to transform consciousness.

> "Alphabet letterpress printing, in which each letter was cast on a separate piece of metal, or type, marked a psychological breakthrough of the first order. It embedded the word itself deeply in the manufacturing process and made it into a kind of commodity. The first assembly line ... was not one which produced stoves or shoes or weaponry but one which produced the printed book. In the late 1700s, the industrial revolution applied to other manufacturing the replaceable-parts techniques which printers had worked with for three hundred years."[74]

Letterpress printing meant that identical copies could be produced mechanically in quantity, instead of having to be hand-copied by professional scribes, one copy and one scribe at a time. The template for printed matter was the handwritten manuscript, and the idea of an original that could be copied long preceded the invention of movable type. But the advent of printing made more than a technological advance. "The transformation of the manuscript page during the eight hundred years that precede Gutenberg," wrote Walter J. Ong, "illustrates the steps through which the mind of the West has come into being."[75] According to another scholar:

> "One consequence of the new exactly repeatable visual statement was modern science. Exact observation does not begin with modern science. For ages, it has always been essential for survival among, for example, hunters and craftsmen of many sorts. What is distinctive of modern science is the conjuncture of exact observation and exact verbalization: exactly worded descriptions of carefully observed complex objects and processes. ... Eisenstein suggests how difficult it is today

> to imagine earlier cultures where relatively few persons had ever seen a physically accurate picture of anything."[76]

The printing press transformed the very nature of literacy.

> "Between Chaucer [in the fourteenth century] and Defoe [in the eighteenth], the printing press has intervened, and it turns out that Defoe's real subject is the bureaucratization of the word, authenticated through the reality of type, and spread like contagion, in hundreds and hundreds of copies, directly from the platen of the press. The printed word impresses its own version of reality."[77]

With the discovery of electricity in the seventeenth century, print helped spur more new technologies of the word. By the industrialized nineteenth century, new technologies further powered the dissemination of written words and printed images, with inventions like the telegraph (1837), the typewriter (1867), the (now practically antique land-line) telephone (1876), and the camera (1888). By 1900, all kinds of writing (fiction and nonfiction, novels and newspapers) were gradually disseminated. Writing was democratized, its once special status rendered less elite. "Cheap wood-based paper … meant that keeping personal diaries or writing letters became possible and so, by 1850, the clerk, or writer, ceased to be a high-status job."[78]

And so it was in the nineteenth century that critics began to worry about machines in general; the nineteenth century when "for the first time ever, wrenching technical and social change was felt within a single lifetime."

> "In 1800, the cities had been small, the air and water relatively clean—which is to say that it would give you cholera, not cancer. Nothing moved faster than by wind or limb. The sound of machinery was almost unknown. A person from 1600 transported to 1800 could have made his way around quite easily. But by 1900, there were motor cars on the streets and electric trains beneath them; movies were flickering on screens; earth's age was reckoned in millions of years, and Albert Einstein was writing his Special Theory of Relativity."[79]

In much the same way that print altered the mindset of literacy, the technology of the clock transformed awareness of time. Clocks first took form in the thirteenth century, about the same time that literacy began transforming social relations.

> "The technology of clocks, and machines in general, provided an immensely influential model for modern thinking about reality in general. Long before Newton's scientific depiction of the astronomical and physical order as a great machine, the regular motions of the moon and planets had been modeled in clockworks. ... With Galileo and the stress on the language of mathematics as the key to 'reading the book of nature,' with Descartes and the integration of the geometry of space with the algebra of thought, and with Newton's triumphant equations, the model of the clock-machine could be articulated in detail by the powerful mechanistic theory of the world."[80]

Like print, the mechanical clock changed the way we see ourselves and the way we think. In our own contemporary high-technology culture "everyone lives each day in a frame of abstract computed time enforced by millions of printed calendars, clocks, and watches."[81]

Before "writing was deeply interiorized by print," most people would not be aware of this kind of accounting for time and didn't need to be. From the thirteenth to the twentieth century, human ideas about time and space were transformed. Quantitative methods of studying nature began with the regular measurement of time and led to this "new mechanical conception of time"—one we take as much for granted (for reality) as the air we breathe.

> "The profound breakthrough that the seventeenth century brought to science was the understanding of motion. ... Part of the reason for this was an absence of any sufficiently accurate means of keeping time, i.e., of a reasonably good 'clock.' ... Thus, Galileo's observations in 1583 that a pendulum could be used as a reliable means of keeping time had a far-reaching importance for him (and for the development of science as a whole) since the timing of motion could then be made precise."[82]

This "new" conception of time—time that ticks along a one-way track, time whose progress may be measured (today to the nanosecond)—is now centuries old and so thoroughly embedded in human culture that we no longer question the idea of time as something other than something measurable. All our science and technology, all our society and culture, depend irrevocably on this notion of time.

> "Abstract time became the new medium of existence. ... A general time-consciousness accompanied the wider use of clocks: dissociating

> time from organic sequences. ... The gain in mechanical efficiency through co-ordination and through the closer articulation of the day's events cannot be over-estimated. ... The modern industrial regime could do without coal and iron and steam easier than it could do without the clock."[83]

Much as print, the mechanical version of writing, changed our awareness of language, the mechanical clock changed our conception of time. For technologies "are not mere exterior aids, but also interior transformations of consciousness, and never more than when they affect the word."[84] A given language technology imposes a sort of world view, a set of assumptions, a frame. In the galloping technical advances of recent decades, the technological frame basically says our science and technology—all our apps, not all our relations—will save us. I would that it be so, but I'm hardly reassured. Perhaps technologies are bound to fail. I worry, along with others, that "noise crowds out the signal," that the "systems we have built to collapse time and space are being attacked by space and time."[85]

Technologies of the Word

The big picture of language evolution beyond the earliest writing is generally construed in terms of three technological advances: alphabetic writing (c1500-1400 BCE); letterpress printing (mid-fifteenth century); and electronic communications (beginning in the twentieth century and moving right along as I write in the twenty-first).

Scholars speak of the "invention" of writing, but perhaps "invention" is the wrong word. To trace the history of writing and writing systems remains a complex affair (little admitting of any one original inventor). Most societies with writing didn't create a script out of whole cloth or adopt it in a vacuum; most societies borrowed, adopted, and adapted a writing system rather than inventing a completely new one. Some advanced societies that existed before modern times proceeded without benefit of writing (as do some contemporary societies).[86] While virtually all human societies have spoken language, not all have writing.

The development of various scripts illustrates how closely tied all human inventions are to the environments of the societies in which they arise.[87] For any technology to be invented and its use disseminated, there has to have been, along with enabling environmental factors, some social need or use for it, and then there had to evolve specialists well versed in the application of the technology. On the other hand, if a technology was limited to a specialist class, its progress was limited as well. For example, one of the earliest forms of writing and printing (by means of pre-made printing blocks on disks) occurred in ancient Crete, but because few people could read the printed marks, the invention didn't spread.

> "... printing in ancient Crete died out after 1700 BC and didn't come back until it was reinvented in China and then mass-produced by Gutenberg. ... So Cretan printing died out, as did writing itself in Crete and Greece, around 1200 BC. Writing came back to Greece about 800 BC, but it wasn't until the population increase in China and then in Europe that there were enough princes and bureaucrats—and enough people ready to read—that there was a demand for printing."[87]

According to geographer Jared Diamond, this is how inventions generally arise: they are made initially by a sort of accident, by people who like to "tinker," and "eventually somebody else figured out what it was good for." Diamond turns on its head the idea of necessity as the mother of invention. For him, the reverse is true: invention spawns necessity. (Modern day advertising would no doubt agree.) From a wider perspective, it seems to me that both aphorisms are true—necessity as the mother of invention, and invention as the mother of necessity—and equally true, because neither could obtain without the other. Causes create effects, but effects also become causes. Language-based knowledge, like all human endeavour, builds on or negates or supersedes or in some other way references previous work. And every technology, by the very parameters of its design, imposes a mindset. As language moved from oral to written, and writing produced an "inward turning of the psyche," consciousness evolved to emphasize interiority.

> "The evolution of consciousness through human history is marked by growth in articulate attention to the interior of the individual person as distanced—though not necessarily separated—from the communal structure in which each person is necessarily enveloped."[88]

If the nineteenth century initiated concern about machines per se, these worries were mild compared to those that arose in the twentieth century, with technological advances of stunning ingenuity, scope, and impact. Scientists discovered how to split the atom; they revealed the shape of DNA and mapped the human genome. Space ships were launched into the far reaches of the universe. Alan Turing built the first computer (which British intelligence used to break the German code of the Second World War). The changes that ensued from the first computer to today's Internet-connected globe ought not to be under-estimated. On the other hand, there was also a "great contradiction" at the heart of the nineteenth century's scientific progress, for example in medicine, with the development of organic chemistry, anesthetics, bacteriology, and sepsis. Yet "while the science of medicine advanced, the art of medicine dragged."[89] Truly novel ideas, in all fields, including medicine, often gain a foothold only after decades of resistance.

In the 1840s, a Hungarian doctor named Ignaz Semmelweis was ridiculed and ostracized for advising his colleagues to wash their hands before examining pregnant women. At the time, it was common medical practice to move without hand-washing from the morgue, where doctors did their research, to the obstetrics ward, where they examined pregnant women, with the result that many women died in childbirth. Ironically, poorer women did better because they had midwives. Midwives of the mid-nineteenth century, like physicians of the day, didn't know about germs either. But they also weren't coming from their morgue research covered in blood and gore.

> "It wasn't until the advent of germ theory, based on the research of Louis Pasteur and the urgings of Joseph Lister, that finally, in the 1880s, the reluctant doctors were forced to comply with new rules of cleanliness and antiseptic conditions."[90]

Medical malpractice didn't begin or end with the revelation of sepsis.

> "As late as the 1950s, there were still some professors teaching medical students that syphilis could be cured by giving patients the poison arsenic, a turn-of-the-century belief that had long since gone the way of blood-letting."[91]

Ignorance is everywhere a level playing field; and new knowledge, a threat to standing hierarchies. In order to overcome ignorance and the reign of dogma, knowledge must be considered basically provisional. Alexander Fleming's discovery of penicillin in 1928 led to the introduction of life-saving antibiotics against bacterial infections that were once tantamount to death sentences. The discovery of antibiotics saved lives, but nearly a hundred years later, antibiotics present new problems. No longer is arsenic or blood-letting used to treat syphilis, but the syphilis bacterium itself has mutated and become increasingly resistant to antibiotics. Since its decline in the mid-1990s, syphilis has returned with renewed vigor in the twenty-first century. What was once miraculous new knowledge changes with time and social context.

> "Over time, and after repeated exposure to penicillin, bacteria can develop resistance to the drug. This means it stops working. New antibiotics are needed to replace penicillin, but few are being developed. This is because research and development costs greatly surpass the profit generated by them. It is estimated that for each new pharmaceutical company entering the antibiotic development field, three exit. Those withdrawing are mostly major companies."[93]

Despite its failures, medicine has of course also made laudable advances, and the dangers of myopia, of a failure to consider social contexts in the pursuit of knowledge, is hardly limited to medical progress. Such dangers apply across the board, including to the electronic technologies of the word in a new millennium. Perhaps not ironically, the advent of electronic communications has apparently brought us back to the future.

> "... with telephone, radio, television and various kinds of sound tape, electronic technology has brought us into the age of 'secondary orality.' This new orality has striking resemblances to the old in its participatory mystique, its fostering of a communal sense, its concentration on the present moment, and even its use of formulas. But it is essentially a more deliberate and self-conscious orality, based permanently on the use of writing and print, which are essential for the manufacture and operation of the equipment and for its use as well."[93]

I believe human beings are still psychically reeling from this accelerated pace of technological change and its much discussed severing of language from its origins in orality—ideas I address in the next chapter.

Chapter 7

Literacy and Its Discontents

It took thousands of years to get from the clay tablets of the ancient Greek academies to the era of the printing press, and it took several more centuries for literacy to spread. Then, within a single generation, humans went from the expanse of print culture to the heights of e-literacy. The Internet, an emblem of the digital age, is a marvel of invention, an evolutionary leap beyond print. It allows for centralized control of infrastructure systems almost as easily as it does communication among people over great distances in "real" time. But the age of e-literacy is not without its critics. And even confirmed technophiles sense that amid the gains, something has been lost.

Orality Versus Literacy

Before the advent of writing, language required a speaker. Spoken words rode on the speaker's breath, the very vehicle of communication. "Proverbs from all over the world are rich with observations about this overwhelmingly human phenomenon of speech in its native oral form, about its powers, its beauties, its dangers," wrote Walter J. Ong, adding that for people in early oral cultures, air itself was "the archetype of all that is ineffable, unknowable, yet undeniably real and efficacious."[1] David Abram made a similar point in his book *The Spell of the Sensuous*:

> "Its obvious ties to speech—the sense that spoken words are structured breath (try speaking a word without exhaling at the same time) ... —lends the air a deep association with linguistic meaning and with thought. Indeed, the ineffability of the air seems akin to the ineffability of awareness itself, and we should not be surprised that many indigenous peoples construe awareness, or 'mind,' not as a power that resides inside their heads, but rather as a quality that they themselves are inside of, along with the other animals and the plants, the mountains and the clouds."[2]

Orality is primary phylogenetically (in the history of the species) and also ontogenetically (in the language development of individuals). Children learn to speak a mother tongue, without formal instruction, long before they learn to read and write in the more structured setting of school. Even before birth, hearing takes precedence over sight in fetal development. Myelin, the fatty substance that sheathes nerve fibres and promotes the exchange of signals between them, develops in the auditory nerves six months before birth; in the visual nerves, six months after birth. The primacy of hearing remains a consequential fact of human evolution. "Human hearing is most acute at around 2,000Hz, which is the frequency of most human speech—spoken language playing perhaps the key role in the evolution of modern human beings."[3]

Children acquire spoken language by imitating what they hear and absorbing the sense of syntax. They learn to read only later (and to write, along with the rules of grammar, later still). The experiential primacy of orality persists in language acquisition and use, as it does in powerful writing and oratory. This is why prosody (the patterns of sound, rhythm, and intonation inherent in speech) is important to meaning and to a child's acquisition of language. For example, it's easier to learn and remember the alphabet in sequence when you sing the classic primary school song devised for the purpose—a tune based, like a dozen other popular tunes (for instance, "Twinkle, Twinkle, Little Star" or "Baa Black Sheep"), on a melody by Mozart. Try singing or playing this alphabet song in triple time (three beats per measure) rather than in common time (four beats per measure, as per the original), and see how readily this widely familiar tune becomes instantly unrecognizable.

I've read that inside the womb, the fetus recognizes the voices of Mom and Dad; if so, fetal consciousness is detecting prosody, not the alphabet. Neither speech nor text can do without syntax. But prosody, the music in language, may well be lacking in both. We even have names for such inadequacy in texts: we call them "leaden" or "flat" or "turgid"—among other terms of non-endearment. In his book *When Breath Becomes Air*, Paul Kalanithi describes one of his patients, a man with a brain tumor, who had suffered damage to the parts of the brain that affect language: "The tumor had interrupted his speech circuitry, so he could speak only in streams of numbers, but he still had prosody, he could still emote: smile, scowl, sigh."[4]

Plus, he could swear like a trooper. During an operation, this patient had to remain conscious, so that doctors could judge the effect of sensors touching specific places in his brain. Kalanithi reported that the patient swore vehemently throughout the procedure, and he concluded: "Profanity supposedly ran on a slightly different circuit from the rest of language."[5] This makes sense to me: profanities are after all rarely uttered without high prosody, even in people not suffering from brain tumors. Prosody, like profanity, is heartfelt. It is rooted in orality, and only further articulated in text (more or less faithfully or effectively as according to the purpose and skill of the writer and reader).

Hearing takes precedence over sight. To see something, we need to focus our eyes on it, but sound surrounds. We don't have to direct our ears; we respond to sounds we can hear (especially sudden unexpected ones) even if our eyes and our attention are at the moment directed elsewhere. Hearing represents an automatic sense connection to the world outside one's skin. Seeing requires looking at something—an automatic sense separation.

> "Sight isolates, sound incorporates. Whereas sight situates the observer outside what he views, at a distance, sound pours into the hearer. … You can immerse yourself in hearing, in sound. There is no way to immerse yourself similarly in sight."[6]

What we see is partially determined by our language. Annie Dillard made the connection:

> "Seeing is of course very much a matter of verbalization. Unless I call my attention to what passes before my eyes, I simply won't see it. … Like a blind man at the ball game, I need a radio."[7]

Though I can consciously direct my attention, I can't separate what I see, hear, or feel at any given moment *without* re-directing my focus: raw experience is not actually separable into sequential aspects of awareness. Sound surrounds, but we don't focus on ambient sounds unless the sound alarms or otherwise interrupts. Imagine reading in a quiet room and then hearing a sudden loud noise: the whole body clenches in preparation for fight or flight—or paralysis.

Thought itself "is nested in speech, not in texts," wrote one expert. Text may appear more reliable than speech, but finally, "no text can stand by itself independent of the extratextual world. Every text builds on pretext."[8] Given its ancient origins, it's unsurprising that the spoken word remains powerful. "The interaction between the orality that all human beings are born into and the technology of writing, which no one is born into, touches the depths of the psyche."[9]

The coming of literacy heightened the ability to think in abstractions and sparked stunning advances in both traditional and newly named disciplines. But literacy also led to a deepened sense of human separateness from the rest of nature, especially from the rest of the animal kingdom, and critically, from the untutored orality of mother tongues. Literacy spawned critical advances in human culture and technology, but along with these advances came a tendency to dismiss orality as an evolutionary appendage, a leftover from a lower form of mind.

With the advent of print and the availability of printed matter, orality was devalued. One scholar cites Daniel Defoe's *A Journal of the Plague Year* (published in 1722) as a kind of signpost in the ascendancy of the written word over spoken ones. Set in the London of 1665, the novel employs a now-familiar technique of fiction.[10]

> "Defoe needs to establish the veracity of a new form [the novel] ... Defoe wants his story to be taken as true, and so he needs to fabricate a believable lie, which he does by presenting his narrative as a journal kept by one H.F., who purportedly lived during the plague year of 1665."[11]

Defoe's *Journal* partakes in an early re-set of the reading mind: the idea that mere talk can't tell the whole truth, that oral discourse lacks analytical power. "For that, one must have writing, or better yet, the authority of print."[12] The assumed authority of print made the text a kind of bully. Words on a page do not broach any back-talk; their author is out of reach and cannot, in the moment, be rebutted or otherwise engaged.

> "There is no way directly to refute a text. After absolutely total and devastating refutation, it says exactly the same thing as before. ... A text stating what the whole world knows is false will state falsehood forever, so long as the text exists. Texts are inherently contumacious."[13]

As the printed word spread, the bully became inescapable.

> "In the society that has come into existence since the Middle Ages, one can always avoid picking up a pen, but one cannot avoid being described, identified, certified, and handled—like a text. Even in reaching out to become one's own 'self,' one reaches out for a text."[14]

Literacy has always been recognized as consequential. Rulers everywhere have sought to control its spread, managing the "narrative" to gain and maintain power. With print, certification by the word became an instrument of state, through which the state managed to ensure and augment its hold on power.

It's often assumed that "illiterate" is tantamount to "uncivilized." But in fact the majority of human societies develop without written language, and illiteracy remains the norm in much of the world. Most dialects have never been "translated" into writing, and while all human societies have spoken language, most lack writing (and hence a body of literature). According to one source, "no more than a hundred languages have produced a significant literary tradition."[15]

Before writing became widespread, different spoken languages existed on a spectrum, not as the discrete entities of completely separate tongues. The earliest grammar books weren't penned until late in the fifteenth century; the first in any modern European language was published in 1492 (the same year Columbus sailed out in search of a trade route to the east, and bumped into America instead). This first European grammar was the project of a Spaniard named Elio Antonio de Nebrija, who tried to "reduce a vernacular tongue to the rules of grammar."[16]

Nebrija wanted to standardize the Spanish language in order to unify Spain, by "gathering and joining the scattered pieces of Spain into a single absolute kingdom." In his pitch to the queen of Spain for support in the project, he argued that "the unbound and ungoverned speech in which people actually live and manage their lives" had become a challenge to royal rule. The people, he warned, "had become the victims of a reading epidemic." Shameless in their choice of reading materials, they displayed a wanton tendency to "waste their time on novels and fancy stories full of lies."[17] In other words, books were circulating outside the Crown's bureaucratic ability to control their influence.

The record shows that the queen praised Nebrija "for having provided the Castilian tongue with what had been reserved to the languages of Scripture, Hebrew, Greek, and Latin." But she regarded grammar itself as a matter for teachers; she believed that people mastered their own vernaculars on their own, without formal instruction. She conceded that spoken language was thus "beyond the reach of the ruler's authority."[18] While written language is obviously more permanent than spoken language, it is not through written language that cultures actually develop:

> "Writing, printing, and the Internet give a false sense of security about the permanence of culture. Most of the million details of complex, living culture are transmitted neither in writing nor pictorially. Instead, cultures of all kinds live mainly through word of mouth and the example of elders."[19]

Although speech long precedes writing in human history, linguists virtually ignored speech until the 1960s. In early linguistic study, speech got short shrift. The "talker" was considered, if at all, separately from the talk, as if talk were text.

> "In the middle of the twentieth century, linguistics was dominated by the theories of Noam Chomsky, which considered language in its most perfect and ideal state—perfectly fluent, grammatical, uninterrupted sentences, as if all communication were written text. But starting in the 1960s and '70s, a surge of interest in the practical aspects of spoken language revealed just how elaborate and subtle the processes are that govern turn-taking, interruption, and composing a sentence or story on the fly while being attuned to a listener's reactions every step of the way."[20]

Speech, it turns out, is a more complex achievement than we usually allow, much more complex than the vaunted digital language of computers. "No computer program has even approached the speech ability of the average person."[21]

Earlier times did not assume that writing was superior to or more reliably true than oral accounts. In fact, the opposite belief prevailed. Laws in medieval Europe were memorized rather than written down, and the spoken word was considered more reliable even in legal matters. The written word then was still suspect, considered less trustworthy than the spoken word. During the Middle Ages, important communications, including oaths, were delivered orally.

> "An oath is a ceremonial giving of one's word, a spoken promise. This kind of emphatic utterance seems to occur among all peoples. An oath swears to a given word. The truth or intention of the thing sworn to is reinforced by a ritual association between word and gesture, both traditional in form. ... In the context of orality, truth is inseparable from veracity. The oath reveals an epiphany of this unity of form and content that captures the essence of the oral mentality."[22]

Today as well, oaths are made orally. In contemporary society, though, the custom of spoken oaths is more a matter of ritual significance than of "emphatic utterance." We still pay lip service to lip service, but we don't believe, as earlier cultures did, that "the seat of the soul was in the tongue," that the tongue "was a rudder or steering-oar" with which to steer one's "course through the world."[23]

Orality is the very foundation of literacy and rests like groundwater beneath the written word. Language, "the gift of tongues … has a rebellious and wayward vitality compared to which the foundations of the Pyramid are as dust."[24] Orality persists.

> "Though Renaissance humanism invented modern textual scholarship … it also harkened back to antiquity and thereby gave new life to orality. English style in the Tudor period and even much later carried heavy oral residue in its use of epithets, balance, antithesis, formulary structures, and commonplace materials."[25]

Student testing was traditionally oral; written exams became common only centuries after the invention of writing, and in most of the world, oral testing remains the norm. In many universities, the awarding of a doctorate still requires an oral defence of the written dissertation, presented before a panel of scholars. (The way the word "dissertation" is understood in contemporary parlance largely overlooks or obscures the root differences between speaking and writing, and to privilege the latter—despite that the word itself comes from the Latin dissertare, meaning "to discuss.") In the England of the eleventh and twelfth centuries, the spoken prevailed over the written, even for administrative purposes.[26]

> "Written material was subsidiary to hearing in ways which strike us today as bizarre. At least as late as the twelfth century in England, checking even written financial accounts was still done aurally, by having them read aloud. [One scholar] describes the practice and draws attention to the fact that it still registers in our vocabulary: even today, we speak of 'auditing,' that is, 'hearing' account books, though what an accountant actually does today is examine them by sight. Earlier, residually oral folk could understand even figures better by listening than by looking."[27]

Hundreds of years after the advent of writing, the spoken word prevailed and persisted. The power and traditions of orality are reflected in contemporary letters; oral discourse in effect provided the template for written work. But the written word also represented a break in tradition. For example, the Learned Latin taught in the all-male schools of the ancient world was primarily a written language: "Of the millions who spoke it … everyone was able also to write it. There were no purely oral users." And yet:

> "Paradoxically, the textuality that kept Latin rooted in classical antiquity thereby kept it rooted also in orality, for the classical ideal of education had been to produce not the effective writer but the *rhetor*, the *orator*, the public speaker. The grammar of Learned Latin came from this old oral world. So did its basic vocabulary, although, like all languages actually in use, it incorporated thousands of new words over the centuries."[28]

The essence of orality persists in the process of writing, as most professional writers are aware, and as most aspiring writers may learn. One writer took this fact seriously when he revised his working method to enlist the innate power of the spoken word. In his book *Page Fright*, Harry Bruce quoted writer Richard Powers, who at one point decided to write by speaking his narrative into a recording device on his tablet. It took him weeks to get used to this manner of writing, Powers said, but once he did, he never missed the old way and "no longer had any use for 'straightjacketing keyboards.' "

> "What could be less conducive to thought's cadences than stopping every time your short-term memory fills to pass those large-scale musical phrases through your fingers, one tedious letter at a time? You'd be hard-pressed to invent a greater barrier to cognitive flow."[29]

Bruce concluded with his assessment of the writer's talk-it technique:

> "Having worked as a computer programmer and data processor, Powers was better prepared than most writers to use the newest electronic gadgetry to discover the forgotten virtues of the oldest way on Earth of telling stories."[30]

With the evolutionary embedding of literacy in humans comes a tendency to overlook the powers of speech. Yet in many ways, and despite the contemporary explosion of electronic communication media and devices, orality remains not only primary but also powerful, often more powerful than words on a page. For many if not most of us, the primacy of orality helps explain why writing is so much more difficult than speaking. Perhaps this is why aspiring writers are often advised to write as they speak and when revising, to read their work aloud. One of the easiest, surest ways for writing to go astray in the genuine expression of meaning is the failure of this bond between orality and literacy, the failure to hear the intonations, the emphases, the subtext, that occur "naturally" in speech (and that practised liars learn only to imitate).

Yet in comparisons of orality and literacy, it's never a matter of orality good, literacy bad (or vice versa). Literacy is after all but an iteration of orality in the evolution of language. What matters is the relationship between them, something easy to forget in our cyber-solitudes. Crucial in both speaking and writing is the expression of meaning, rather than that of subservience to higher powers, whether of God or State or Science or Nature or Favourite Figurehead. All human societal progress and individual intellectual progress rest ultimately on this radical freedom of thought. Much depends, however, on what you mean by grand words like "thought" and "freedom." Are thoughts truly free, as per the old German song "*Die Gedanken Sind Frie*" (Thoughts Are Free)? Or is freedom "just another word for nothing left to lose," as per Janis Joplin's "Me and Bobby McGee"? I would have to answer: "Yes."

The Age of Information

With writing, language was mediated, and with the printing press, further mediated. Now, in the age of e-literacy, we can communicate across the globe. Anyone with a computer and Internet access may publish online, broadcasting personal expression, and others may read and respond. Online communities develop without the need for presence in the flesh. Masses of Facebook friends can be had with minimal reciprocity: just a few words and click SEND. The only breath required is the breath that keeps the creature alive, fingers clicking.

The Age of Information is aptly named. An online computer provides practically inexhaustible founts of information at the touch of a keyboard. Basic computer science has advanced every other branch of science since Alan Turing invented the first universal computing machine.[31] The capabilities of the electronic brain allow calculations that not long ago were too complex to figure with pen and paper. In both the arts and humanities, computers and the vectors that connect them across the globe have transformed in mere decades the literacy that took centuries to develop. The Internet, sending words and images around the globe, is more than the emblem of a digital age; it is the engine of its progress. Despite its limits and its critics, e-literacy actually addresses and overcomes the one-way, bully aspect of the text. It allows for real-time inter-communication by means of text and image.

> "Good things come about with the new technologies. ... Tiananmen Square was the fax revolution. Email helped organize the WTO shutdown in 1999; Facebook was instrumental in the Arab Spring's initial phase in 2011; Occupy Wall Street was originally a Twitter hashtag."[32]

And then there are the images, like the smart-phone video of the murder of George Floyd by former police officer Derek Chauvin on May 25, 2020. The video showed how the white officer murdered the black George Floyd by kneeling on Floyd's neck for the torturous nearly ten minutes it took to choke the life from the man, who was handcuffed and prone on the pavement. The video was taken by a teenaged woman; she was among a small group of bystanders who tried to intervene by means of words, to no immediate avail. But as the video made its way around the world, it sparked mass protests and initiated a change of consequence: Chauvin's conviction on three counts of murder. It marked the first time in U.S. history that the so-called blue wall of silence was broken, with police officers in the courtroom called as witnesses for the prosecution. Televised testimony at the trial cut through mountains of legal jargon to open awareness of the scourge of systemic racism. The video images of Floyd's murder are seared into memory in a way that no number of words, however informative or eloquent, could equal. Ultimately though, it wasn't the high-tech transmission of words or images but the humanity of individuals who tried to intervene that made the difference.

No one speaks any more about "computer literacy," so integrated is the technology in the infrastructure of everyday life. Jeremiads like the following barely compute.

> "By 1885 [just two years after it had coined the term "literacy"] the *New England Journal of Education* was already conducting surveys to determine levels of literacy in Cambridge, Massachusetts. ... No one would have thought in the nineteenth century that we would be hanging fast to literacy, as we see it too vanishing: People now becoming enslaved to the power of a machine in their pursuit of computer literacy."[33]

The calculating power of computers is not to be discounted or under-valued. Yet basking in its penumbra, we may fail to notice that computers represent (and can represent) only a small slice of human experience.

> "Only one narrow band of our experience is represented in the computer: logical reason. Sensual contact, intuition, inarticulated common sense judgments, aesthetic taste have been largely, if not wholly, left out. We do not bring the full resources of the self to the computer."[34]

Because we do not bring the "full resources of the self to the computer," the fount of potential meaning that is the stuff of language is attenuated. As we've seen, this result has been a long time coming in the history of developing literacy. In the digital age, some critics allege, language is being reduced to a sort of code.

> "When George Orwell wrote about Newspeak, no computer language had as yet been named or published. … In this age of computers, which Orwell did not live to see, his Newspeak is an ominous parody of the intent to use English as a 'medium of communication.' "[35]

In the early 1980s, many believed that computers would drive great progress in education. But by 1990, the hope was already fading. Research had begun to show the cognitive downside of the Internet's hypertext links as artificial connections that deter us from forming our own. The Net defines intelligence on its own terms, favoring the superficial over the deep, the fast over the slow. Computers don't help us learn, said the critics; they actually weaken comprehension and retention.

But perhaps the hopes for e-literacy as an educational boon were unrealistic to begin with. And on the other hand, why couldn't computers with their hyperlinks be fashioned and employed in order to realize the hope, to aid and extend learning? The calculator, when new, was also promoted—and worked—as an aid to memory, and as a faster, more efficient way to answer mathematical questions. But could a calculator fortify memory for people who hadn't already memorized their multiplication tables and internalized mathematical concepts? Many of the students I taught in the early decades of the twenty-first century relied entirely on calculators; that is to say they could not figure simple sums or percentages with low-tech pen and paper.

In his book *The Shallows: What the Internet Is Doing to Our Brains*, Nicholas Carr argued that except for alphabets and number systems, the Internet is the most important mind-altering technology in the history of cogitation. But he also pointed out the downsides, arguing that over-dependence on the Internet flattens the ability to think, to remember, and to imagine; that it alters not just the content of our thoughts but the very neuronal circuitry of our brains. Thus, despite the prowess of e-literacy, not everyone regards the advent of electronic communications as an unalloyed blessing. Garbage in, garbage out, say the critics.

> "Technology, our servant, has also become our master, as the information highway—potentially the greatest tool for the diffusion of learning ever devised—has, for too many, become a highway to the far-flung regions of junk thought."[36]

A litany of complaints about e-literacy has attended its progress from the start. The Internet distracts us, because distraction is the essence of its business model. Web content steals our attention instead of focusing it; it "seizes our attention only to scatter it."[37] On the Net, everything moves and changes too quickly for time to weed out the bad ideas from the brilliant ones. Internet culture induces a quantitative mentality and, like Mother Science, discounts what it cannot measure. The *New York Times*:

> "... recently profiled a Silicon Valley entrepreneur who had this to say about the secret of his success: 'If you can't measure it, you're asking the wrong questions.' Such is the metric-based mentality that dominates our world and shapes our post-literary future."[38]

More approving assessments of electronic media note that the Internet has increased dramatically the number of books published. American journalist and author Anna Quindlen argued that despite what the "prophets of doom and gloom" say about book publishing in the electronic era, many more books are published now than were published in a pre-electronic age.

> "More than 350,000 new books were added to the Library of Congress in 1995 alone; that institution, founded with funding of $5000 two centuries ago, now has 200 times the number of items once found in the legendary library in Alexandria. ... And if some new books only manage to make their way onto the Internet, isn't that better than losing them entirely?"[39]

Alberto Manguel, another erudite book lover, made the same point, noting for example, that "359,437 new books (not counting pamphlets, magazines and periodicals) were added in 1995 to the already vast collections of the Library of Congress." He added: "Those who see computer development as the devil incarnate (as Sven Birkerts portrays it in his dramatically titled Gutenberg Elegies) allow nostalgia to hold sway over experience."[40]

I'm obliged to point out here (respectfully): that's not actually what Birkerts said. This is:

> "I am not going to argue against the power and usefulness of electronic technologies. Nor am I going to suggest that we try to turn back or dismantle what we have wrought in the interests of an intensified relation to meaning. But I would urge that we not fall all over ourselves in our haste to filter all of our experience through circuitries. We are in

> some danger of believing that the speed and wizardry of our gadgets have freed us from the sometimes arduous work of turning pages in silence."[41]

Birkerts admirably makes the point missed by both Quindlen and Manguel in their citing of increased numbers of books published. After all, quantity in itself is clearly no guarantee of quality, let alone some kind of sign of literary progress. The advance of electronic media has allowed for people to communicate more quickly and more widely, but it has often also seemed to leave us as individuals with little to say. The hyper-digital, screen-sogged culture of e-literacy (metrics aside), may threaten rather than enhance book culture and the future of reading.

> "... the question I would put to ... celebrants of the connected life is this: in the late modern Western world today, which is in greater danger, the social aspect of our lives or the solitary one? Which suffers from undercultivation? Which is being drowned out by the other?"[42]

While it's true of course that the digital revolution has widened access (especially the access of writers to readers through the ease of self-publishing), much of the citizen writing that appears online (and that was supposed to democratize access by extending it to many non-traditional commentators) is curiously anonymous, even when the writer is named. Somehow the ubiquity of online text makes it seem superfluous, at best. The sheer volume of online text tends to devalue content, even content that appeared previously in "hard copy" through traditional publishing.

Though plenty of inane writing appeared in print long before the reign of the Internet, electronic communication devices devalue the very features of human interaction that the devices were invented to mimic, amplify, and extend. Such devices allow people to communicate over vast distances but, at the same time, to avoid the intimacy and risks of face-to-face relationship. In fact, says one astute analyst, the reason for the popularity of e-communication devices is precisely that they allow us to avoid one another, to substitute emoticons for feelings.

> "Technology is seductive when what it offers meets our human vulnerabilities. And as it turns out, we are very vulnerable indeed. We are lonely but fearful of intimacy. Digital connections and the sociable robot may offer the illusion of companionship without the demands of

> friendship. Our networked life allows us to hide from each other, even as we are tethered to each other. We'd rather text than talk."[43]

Socrates' Lament

Centuries ago, the Dutch humanist and Renaissance scholar Desiderius Erasmus (1466-1536), wrote a best-selling textbook called *De Copia*. Published in 1512, the book stressed the connection between memory and learning. Erasmus urged his students to keep commonplace books, arranged by subject, to transcribe the excerpts in their own hand, and then to rehearse them regularly to fix them in memory. But Erasmus wasn't advising memorization for its own rote sake. "To him, memorizing was far more than a means of storage. It was the first step in a process of synthesis, a process that led to a deeper and more personal understanding of one's reading."[44]

More than a millennium before Erasmus penned *De Copia*, the first-century Roman philosopher Seneca also insisted on the critical role of memory in matters of mind. Seneca warned that the technology of writing would interfere with genuine learning. Memory for him was much more than a storage receptacle for words.

> "Memory, for Seneca as for Erasmus, was as much a crucible as a container. It was more than the sum of things remembered. It was something newly made, the essence of a unique self."[45]

The concern that writing would injure memory and thus learning began even earlier, in ancient Greece. Before the beginnings of literacy in the fifth century BCE, schooling in Athens was purely oral, musical, and gymnastic. When writing was new and began to be taught and to replace orality as the way to transmit knowledge, some among the ancients decried the original communications technology. They feared that in coming to rely on written words, students would cease to recall from memory. They would depend more on written sources, calling things to remember "no longer from within themselves, but by means of external marks."[46]

Plato stood at the crossroads of orality and literacy. In the ancient Greece of Plato's day, "people had already been reciting Homer from the text for centuries," but the art of writing was still primarily a handicraft, and literacy meant "craft literacy": the ability to read and write was restricted to professional scribes. Most people couldn't read or write, and so would hire scribes to write a letter or other document, dictating to the scribe, in much the same way people today would hire carpenters or electricians or other professionals with specialized expertise (like those who design and repair computers and computerized systems).

The iconic Socrates wrote nothing; we know of his philosophy through Plato, his most famous student. Plato himself was ambivalent about literacy and quoted Socrates' objections: changing the method of instruction from oral to literate, from talk to text, would produce an over-reliance on written words and give students "only a semblance of truth, not the truth itself." It would finally "train ignorant know-alls, nosey know-nothings, boring wiseacres."[47] The rise of the written word, he warned, would end by diminishing the capacity for independent thought, turning out graduates with a "false conceit of wisdom."[48] Literacy was firmly established in education only with Plato's student Aristotle, who wrote volumes. "It is not too much to say that with Aristotle the Greek world passed through oral instruction to the habit of reading."[49]

Socrates had decried the spread of writing and famously favored the teaching method that bears his name. Only through dialogue, the Socratic method says, can we learn to examine the word (not just regurgitate it), and only through such examination can real virtue be had. In Socrates' day, memorization was at the heart of education. The point, however, was again not simply to hone the skills of memorization. In the era before writing, memorization was the way (the only way) to preserve sayings and stories for future generations. Put to death by authorities for his "corruption" of the youth of Athens, Socrates is famously known for this charge that writing would injure memory. His ultimate concern, however, was not the loss of the capacity to memorize, but the loss of the capacity to think independently and critically.

Yet memory as sole method wasn't failsafe either. Before writing, students were taught to memorize the epics—but not necessarily to question them. One could, then as now, memorize words with little understanding or appreciation of their meaning. Socrates knew that rote memorization doesn't produce knowledge, much less wisdom. He knew that no volume of memorized recitation could ensure comprehension. But he also knew the value of speech and discourse, and, it seems to me, the simple if limited advantage of memorization: it requires the mind to internalize, so that in the eventual act of recalling, the mind is forced to consult itself. The act of memorization creates distance in the form of self-awareness, and so an opportunity to change the angle of attention. What would happen to awareness without memory? How could real learning occur?

It seems Socrates was right to worry.

Contemporary pro-technologists argue there's no point to memorization when we can store practically endless amounts of information on computers—vaunting the idea that a computer database far exceeds the power of personal memory. This conception of memory is misconstrued in two ways. First, there's a big difference between "storing" information and remembering it; and second, this idea assumes that learning is tantamount to storing—in other words, that as long as we can store and manipulate endless amounts of information, nobody needs to learn anything.

***

By the mid-fifteenth century, with the advent of print and the more rapid spread of literacy, the loss of rhetoric as the curricular mainstay of earlier centuries was sealed. One complaint about this loss—echoed through the centuries since—is that the omission has led to lessened literacy and even lower intelligence in successive generations. By the mid-twentieth century, educators had begun to openly mourn the perceived deficits. In 1947, in an address delivered at Oxford University, Dorothy Sayers said that students had become "a prey to words in their emotions instead of being the masters of them in their intellects."[50] (She would address the problem, she added, by reinstating the trivium.)[51]

Today when you sign up for a course in rhetoric, you get a writing class. The original subject called "rhetoric," however, was about speech making, and speech making remained the paradigm for written work. In the ancient Greco-Roman world, the whole point of the education system was rhetorical proficiency, meaning effective public speaking, since this was essential to careers in law and government. Today, we commit almost nothing to memory. Instead, we consign memory to machines. And machines, as W. H. Auden noted, "are beneficial to the degree that they eliminate the need for labor, harmful to the degree that they eliminate the need for skill."[52]

As late as my own generation, students took for granted the necessity to memorize at least some materials (for example, the letters of the alphabet or times tables in math). But the generations that have grown up in digital culture disparage memorization. Why bother, they figure, since you can always "google" the facts. Maybe so, but there's dis- and mis-information and hate literature and pornography online too—not just "facts." You can find billions of facts online, of course—facts galore, facts to fit whatever stance you favour. But even actual facts are pointless without the capacity for independent thought and the ability to distinguish fact from opinion and the true from the false.

True literacy depends on the ability to think for oneself, not just the ability to decode letters into the sounds they represent. And by many estimates, true literacy is threatened in the digital age. Critics who say e-literacy tried to turn "the English language into no more than a code"[52] were making the point that to decode is not necessarily to understand.

> "I fear that many of our children are in danger of becoming just what Socrates warned us against—a society of decoders of information, whose false sense of knowing distracts them from a deeper development of their intellectual potential. It does not need to be so, if we teach them well …"[53]

Critics of the new technology, like critics of the old, are calling attention not to the mechanics of the technology but to the broader social context of its use.

> "John Locke stressed the same point three centuries ago, when he observed that the Bible would read very differently if it were printed as a continuous narrative instead of being sliced into tiny fragments suitable for quoting as chapter and verse. Drawing on Locke and a wide range of English literature, the greatest bibliographer of our time, Donald F. McKenzie, has argued that bibliography must expand into a "sociology of texts," that is, a study of literature which will relate texts to their total environment, one that extends beyond printing shops and bookstores to the entire range of media and mentalities in a given society."[54]

New technologies come from older technologies, and some technologies are better than others for specific purposes. If writing, printing, and texting are all technologies of the word, then they are all capable of serving purposes both noble and nefarious: technologies amplify without regard to motives or consequences.

> "Technological change is neither additive nor subtractive. It is ecological. … One significant change generates total change. Surrounding every technology are institutions whose organization—not to mention their reason for being—reflects the world-view promoted by the technology. Therefore, when an old technology is assaulted by a new one, institutions are threatened. When institutions are threatened, a culture finds itself in crisis."[55]

The advantages of electronic messaging (over messaging on paper) are much quoted and touted, but they don't invariably apply. Electronic messages (including those in electronic voting machines) are easily hacked. When whistle-blower Edward Snowden revealed to journalist Glenn Greenwald "the extent of the surveillance on the public" by the U.S. National Security Agency, the two men devised an old-fashioned method to avoid NSA scrutiny: they communicated by sitting together and passing each other notes handwritten on paper, later tearing up or burning the paper.[56]

The first computer (ENIAC) was launched in 1946 but people are still trying to figure out how best to integrate the potentials of e-literacy with that of society and the public good, not always with great success. Magnificent as inventions go, the Internet has nevertheless "unleashed an unprecedented amount of fraud and a network of lies that move so fast that the rule of law can hardly keep up."[57]

> "Thus far, we've managed to use digital technology to increase economic inequality in the United States, facilitate illegal drug abuse, undermine the economic sustainability of the free press, cause a 'fake news' crisis, roll back voting rights and fair labor protection, surveil citizens, spread junk science, harass and stalk people (primarily women and people of color) online ... This is not the better world that the early tech evangelists promised. It's the same world with the same types of human problems that have always existed. The problems are hidden inside code and data, which makes them harder to see and easier to ignore."[58]

When all is said about e-literacy, a computerized device remains a machine, not an additional organ or a new life form recently discovered in the wilds of civilization.

> "Technology begins not with the tool, but with the human imagination, and the acts of imagining, inventing, and using tools and machines are human acts. So, while technology is certainly artificial, it is also eminently natural. ... The auxiliary 'organs' that extend our sight, our hearing, and our thinking really are an extension of our physical bodies. When we are able to accept this, we shall discover that the struggle to control technology has all along been a struggle to control ourselves."[59]

The question, then, is not whether technology is good or bad, but what a given technology is good *for*.

Is Literacy Maladaptive?

Some critics believe the newest technologies of the word have moved human societies, in a "nightmarish scene," ever closer to a "new dark age."

> "Our vision is increasingly universal, but our agency is ever more reduced. We know more and more about the world, while being less and less able to do anything about it. The resulting sense of helplessness, rather than giving us pause to reconsider our assumptions, seems to be driving us deeper into paranoia and social disintegration: more surveillance, more distrust, an ever-greater insistence on the power of images and computation to rectify a situation that is produced by our unquestioning belief in their authority."[60]

As people grow ever more comfortable with their electronic devices and ever more accepting of their presumed authority, the tendency also grows to consolidate the blind assumptions and enshrine the inequities of an earlier era (call it Error 1.0). "If machine-learning models simply replicate the world as it is now, we won't move toward a more just society."[61]

> "The allure of the technology is clear—the ancient aspiration to predict the future, tempered with a modern twist of statistical sobriety. Yet in a climate of secrecy, bad information is as likely to endure as good, and to result in unfair and even disastrous predictions."[62]

If it's true that communication devices have reduced a sense of human agency and fed abject unfairness, it's the human users and not their devices that are to be held responsible. From Gutenberg's movable type to desktop publishing and cloud computing, technologies of the word have promised large, and for a time, they've delivered. Initially they empowered individuals in newly decentralized power structures. But the pendulum, even in the rapid ascent in the digital age of the self-publishing movement, always seems to swing back to centralized control. As for the traditional publishing industry, it too, in the age of Amazon.com, is more centralized than ever before, with trade concentrated in large cities, sales monopolized, and profits concentrated among the major players.

And yet, despite its limitations and its complications, literacy "is still the only bulwark against the dissolution of language into 'information systems.'"[64] In formal communications theory, meaning is often reduced to the idea of "messages" as things that can be relayed from senders to receivers, across some kind of gap, the space that separates them. Human brain function is also conceived of as the movement of "information" from one neuron or group of neurons to another, across the synapses that separate them. Walt Whitman's praise of the body electric, which long predates the era of high-tech neuroscience, paints a more accurate (and not just a more poetic) view of how embodied brains actually work. (Electrical impulses travel throughout the body, after all, not just in the organ of the brain.) Debates about technologies of the word may seem irrelevant to us in contemporary society; they are not.

> "We take books and mass literacy for granted, but in reality, they are a recent iteration, going back not even a millennium. Less than four hundred years ago—barely a century and a half after Gutenberg—John Milton could still pride himself without exaggeration on having read every book then available, the entire history of written thought accessible to a single mind."[65]

The Internet increases the mass of written words available to be taken in, but not the individual capacity to process that mass. Despite the original vision of its founders, the Internet is not a grand, all-embracing library (*tant pis*!). No matter how many books and other reading materials are made available by electronic means, the rate at which people can read them, though variable, is limited. And yet the sheer profusion of e-text leads many to assume that screen text is superior to hard copy—and worse, to expect that there are technological solutions for every problem. The Canadian experimental physicist Ursula Franklin compared the changing social patterns brought by the machines of the Industrial Revolution to the changes occurring today in our own Age of Information.

> "Both ages had irrationally high expectations of the beneficial effects of science and technology voiced by their respective proponents. Machines—or today, electronic devices—were soon to overcome the physical and mental shortcomings of mere humans. Machines, after all, did not drink; they did not require moral guidance of the kind Victorians lavished on the working class."[66]

I think the critical effect of advancing technologies, from writing through print and now e-media, is a largely unmarked change in the networking and mediation of social control.

> "While I was writing this book, the world changed. The digital revolution had been under way for some time, of course, but the aggressive marketing of hand-held electronic readers had not begun in earnest. Consumers in the West who had been groomed to form emotional attachments with their phones and cameras responded eagerly to the idea of a device that could galvanize the outmoded pastime of reading."[67]

Human travesties long preceded writing, of course, and human-perpetrated horrors long pre-date high technology. Writing in its advent did not invent lies or betrayals; it only codified them.

> "The Old Testament knows of infidelity, broken promises, betrayals, and perjury. It knows of slander, false witness, and, what is worse, false prophecy and the abominable service of false gods."[68]

The idea that a new technology necessarily makes for positive political change goes by the name of the "technological fallacy"; this notion—that more egalitarian access to information can undo political oppression—goes back to the Industrial Revolution, and what one writer calls that revolution's first book: Diderot's eighteenth-century *Encyclopédie.* Diderot was inspired by the same kind of idealism that moved the creators of the Internet. He hoped "science and technology would free society from the shackles of an outmoded order," that it would "replace the oppression of the church and the reigning aristocracy," and even that the encyclopedia would begin to change "the general way of thinking."[69] But it didn't pan out that way; the famous encyclopedia did not overthrow oppression. And neither will the Internet.

The printing press was implicated in many of history's movements for social change, from Martin Luther's manifesto and the Protestant Reformation in the sixteenth century to the French and American revolutions in the eighteenth. But printing did not cause these movements, contrary to the belief of many historians. The idea that it did is a "classic example of the technological fallacy at work," wrote Mark Kurlansky. Instead of the printing press siring the Reformation: "It would be closer to the truth to say that the printing press was the child of the Reformation."[70] Many historians do credit a rise in reading at the start of the nineteenth century to the advance of the printing press and related technologies.

> "But others, not succumbing to the [technological] fallacy, correctly point out that this dramatic growth in reading began before any of these advances in technology. Cambridge professor William St. Clair

> observed, 'The technological changes, the evidence suggests, came after the expansion of reading was well under way, and were more a result than a cause.'"[71]

Neither the word nor technologies of word can explain, much less reverse or repair, the dysfunctions of civilization. To blame words for lies and bigotry would be like blaming money for poverty. It's not words that are to blame, but the liars and bigots who wield them like weapons. Blame instead the pornographies of power; blame severe and widespread inequity and injustice.

Is literacy maladaptive? No, but social arrangements may well be.

> "Where justice is denied, where poverty is enforced, where ignorance prevails, and where any one class is made to feel that society is in an organized conspiracy to oppress, rob, and degrade them, neither persons nor property will be safe."[72]

Whether or not literacy proves maladaptive must depend on the uses to which is it put, given all the potential goods and ills to which the literate mind is heir. There's a lovely Native American story, attributed to the Cherokee nation. An elder is telling his grandson a parable about the meaning of life. He says that there live inside every human being two powerful wolves engaged in a fierce fight. One wolf is evil, full of anger and greed and lies; the other is good, full of love and kindness and truth. "Which wolf wins?" the boy wants to know. Answers grandfather: "The one you feed."

Not for a moment do I believe that the current generation of the young is any less intelligent than its forbears. Neither do I believe that the link between language and meaning is broken (though it is clearly often beleaguered), nor that the ancient connection is beyond retrieving. At the same time, as a Chinese proverb has it: "Unless we change direction, we are likely to end up where we are headed." Or as per Seneca: "If one does not know to which port one is sailing, no wind is favorable."

As my generation passes on, and future generations know only reading on screens and know writing only as typing (or more likely, as "cutting and pasting"), the transition to everything-online culture means a dismissal not just of prior technologies but of the past per se.

> "Facebook, with its flow of useless particularity, makes it impossible to forget, thus impossible to remember. Memory is really the story left behind by forgetting—the essence that remains when the years have stripped away all that useless particularity. You remember as much by

> forgetting as you do by remembering. But on Facebook the past becomes the wound that is never allowed to heal so never scars into deep experience."[73]

My journalism students didn't believe they needed to be able to take notes in longhand. They thought all they needed was their digital recorders, so that they, as print reporters, could take what they heard and saw and turn it back into something to be read. In the longer term, in historical research: if future generations can't read longhand, any history recorded in handwritten documentation is lost. Further into the future, research would require specialists in the new "classics" to break the code. How strange that the roots of written language are becoming, like those of ancient orality, lost in time. And all of that is quite aside from the fact that when the power source fails, so does the software, however impressive. That's when the owners of the power supply (governments and other global corporations) get worried and the law gets ready. Or not.

Will the easy availability of information (and disinformation) cause the brain to devolve, to implode or self-destruct, with a whimper or a bang? Will the futurists' dreams of a gleaming world just ahead—not only computer-enhanced communication, but also computer-enhanced humans—only bring *Homo sapiens* rushing to the cliff? Will we get even dumber? Is the Internet *making* us dumber? Are we really in danger of becoming Socrates' numbskulls? If so, it would be hard to make a case for technology as the culprit author of our devolution.

How the digital environment affects oral, face-to-face communication remains a matter of debate, especially among educators (who compete for attention in the classroom with a variety of handheld devices). But whether or not personal relations are enhanced in the new electronic landscape is a question apparently only for those who were not born into it. Those who grew up with e-literacy don't question the high-tech gadgets of their world any more than I question the use of my (land-line) telephone, or the cell phone I vowed never to own, and finally reconciled myself to—no more than a fish questions the reality of water. "Reality, as Nabokov never got tired of reminding us, is the one word that is meaningless without quotation marks."[74]

You have to be of a certain age to find at all strange or disconcerting this common sight: a lovely young couple at dinner, sitting across from each other, within touching distance—both individuals deeply engaged with their cell phones and its many attractions, as if shielded by magic screens from eye contact.

The merits and demerits of the frame may be debatable; what's clear is that with the progress to electronic communications has come an important change in the locus of control: if young people no longer learn to write or even read longhand, and no longer exercise their own memories, they become entirely dependent on outside sources—ultimately the owners of the power supply. Thus they come increasingly to depend on external and denotative meanings (just as Socrates had predicted). Meaning is externalized: you don't create it or sense it even dimly; you just look it up (if you still know how) and accept a dictionary or other authority's denuded meaning as your own.

Still, language is disconnected from its source in meaning and intent only when the language user is. To trash the potential of literacy because not everyone notices or engages that potential is like trashing poetry as maladaptive because it isn't mathematics, or for that matter, mathematics as maladaptive because it isn't poetry. Robert Graves got it exactly right: "There's no money in poetry," he said, "but then there's no poetry in money either."[75]

With more automaticity in language use, words are treated more as numbers, as close-ended systems. This allows, in science as in any kind of formal inquiry and analysis, for greater precision. But when language use across the board becomes more automatic, words may also lose meaning, resonance and impact. We adopt the frame suggested by the technology and forget it's a frame (a map, not the territory).

Thus not everyone is convinced that although words may incite violence, words themselves are not bombs. Once, overseeing the production of a student newspaper, I authorized the final send-to-print, including a cover that bore an anarchist symbol. A (male) student from outside the (female-led) production group complained to me about the symbol and asked me to intervene to disallow its appearance in print. I declined. "Words and symbols are not bombs," I said, "and in this case, the symbol was not intended to and did not promote or incite violence." Unimpressed, the student took his complaint to the dean of arts, who (sigh of relief) also refused to interfere.

But words are surely consequential. And doing away with unauthorized words or views and their authors is a favourite tool of tyrants everywhere. In fact, the repression with which authorities tried to stem the tide of literacy indicates just how powerful literacy could be for the common good. Printing had helped spread literacy to wider and wider circles of readers and writers (let's not forget that before printing, authors had to rely on the patronage of the rich for monetary support).

In eighteenth-century England, as newspapers grew in numbers and circulations, the government tried to suppress their advance by taxing the papers into submission. It wasn't until 1771 that the British government gave in to pressure, and "finally granted the press the right to report on parliamentary debate." Newspapers tried to keep their prices low, and the government tried to keep them "out of the hands of the working class." In France too, during the French Revolution, the monarchy "felt threatened by all the reading going on. … An estimated 40 percent of the prisoners in the infamous Bastille were involved in the business of books."[76]

Literacy both threatened and emboldened ruling powers.

"This fear of reading was connected with the desire to oppress, as is evident in the many arguments over time that reading was not good for the working class or for women or for slaves."[77] As reading materials became readily available, widespread literacy engendered a growing political awareness—a fact of which aspiring autocrats everywhere were (and remain) acutely aware.

> "The Big Lies of demagoguery required more stealth and cleverness, for careful reading of books and newspapers could reveal their flaws to ordinary people. Not for nothing did the Nazis light up the night skies in their cities with the burning of books. Not for nothing were free white folks in America prohibited from teaching slaves to read, and slaves in South Carolina threatened with the loss of the first joint of their forefingers if they were caught looking at a book."[78]

Books became "the greatest purveyors of truth"—the truth that is supposed to set you free. But first, as that poster popular in the 1960s claimed, it will make you miserable.

George Orwell once called book burning the most characteristic Nazi activity, and he was right. The Nazis did take the title for torching text.

> "World War II destroyed more books and libraries than any event in human history. The Nazis alone destroyed an estimated hundred million books during their twelve years in power."[79]

But they didn't invent the practice; book-burning traces its origins to the earliest days of literacy.

If, as consistently argued, literacy transforms consciousness, why doesn't it transform real, power politics? Why are there still the equivalents of castles (extreme wealth) and dungeons (extreme poverty), and why are these deemed necessary to assess an individual human's place in a social hierarchy, awarding for each a specified rung on the seemingly invisible ladder? A long-touted ideal says competition for status produces excellence: applying the screws enhances performance. May the best white man win and all that. So wrong: "... competition does not produce better people (a myth we have swallowed whole); it does not even produce better candidates; it simply produces more desperately grasping competitors."[80]

Hierarchical structure is a social feature of all social animals and among most contributes to the general peace. Among humans, though, complex competition for top spots has led to inequities of all sorts and these are now endemic to socio-economic systems. Within countries and among countries, the wealth gap widens. Gross inequities are the root cause of systemic poverty, and systemic poverty is the sign of an economic system gone badly wrong. Not language or literacy or e-literacy but organized inequity and injustice: these are the maladapts.

> "If there are people starving in the world—and there are—it is not caused by insufficient information. If crime is rampant in the streets, it is not caused by insufficient information. If children are abused and wives are battered, that has nothing to do with insufficient information. If our schools are not working and democratic principles are losing their force, that too has nothing to do with insufficient information. If we are plagued by such problems, it is because something else is missing."[81]

In Praise of Literacy

When I speak, it feels completely natural, as if my thinking something and saying it are virtually simultaneous. It feels as if there's no gap between thinking words and speaking them, no sequence of plan and execution. When I try to locate the source of words in my mind, I find I cannot. Is it the case that I cannot find the place within me where language originates because there is no such place (spoken language is integrated, evolutionarily embedded, without a single source or origin)? Or is it (or is it also) that even if I could locate a discrete internal point of origin, I still couldn't be aware of my thinking in words at the same time as speaking those words, including "speaking" them internally, that is, hearing words in my head?

Similarly, when I read, I don't consciously hear the words in my head as if I were reading them aloud; I engage in the silent intake of the words (their meaning) as I read. The exception is when I've lost the light of focus, and purposely hear the words (sound them out internally), as if I were reading aloud, in an attempt to regain focus, to re-engage in the silent intake of words. When I ask other people whether they hear words when they read, most say they don't know and are as baffled by the question as I am when I pose it to myself. But finally, the explanation is simple: we can be aware of words as sounds and we can be aware of words as meaning, but we cannot be aware of both at the same time.

This is how Ray Jackendoff explains it in his book, *A User's Guide to Thought and Meaning*, where he advances his "unconscious meaning hypothesis," which basically says that:

> "... we can only be aware of the content of our thoughts if they're linked with pronunciation," that is, if they are verbalized/vocalized, externally or internally. Before that, we may be aware of some process (thinking) going on, but "not of exactly what the thought is."[82]

Other scholars have noted this phenomenon:

> "... as you read, you are not conscious of the letters or even of the words or even of the syntax or the sentences and punctuation, but only of their meaning. As you listen to an address, phonemes disappear into words and words into sentences and sentences disappear into what they are trying to say, into meaning. To be conscious of the elements of speech is to destroy the intention of the speech. ... Try speaking with a full consciousness of your articulation as you do it. You will simply stop speaking."[83]

Still, silent reading is no passive process. When we read, something quite extraordinary occurs. Studies into what happens in our brains when we read narrative have shown that we often simulate as we read. The same brain regions are activated as would be activated if we were actually living the scenes we imagine. Our bodies experience what words evoke. Imagine running up stairs, for instance, and your heartbeat increases while your breathing quickens. When I am completely involved in what I'm reading, it's soundless, and I take in words and patterns of words as meaning rather than as individual letter sounds. Absorbed in reading, I become lost in the text, enveloped by the text.

Ah, but when I write, then I must hear words to reproduce them. Writing elicits the self-communication that some linguists believe was the very origin of language. Speech can express thought, certainly, but writing can extend and articulate it, drawing from the dark a faintly dawning insight.

For when we write (at least if we're intent on meaning), there's no recourse but to search within for words and some orderly connection between them, albeit with varying degrees of success. In all kinds of writing, even supposedly "objective" expository writing, external texts alone won't do. More important is to consult an inner voice (not invariably small or still, let alone wise), a voice that persists in questioning: Is this true? Is this really what I think and believe? Coming up with answers is harder than it looks. But if something extraordinary happens in your brain when you read, something even more extraordinary happens when you write.

> "Writing introduces division and alienation, but a higher unity as well. It intensifies the sense of self and fosters more conscious interaction between persons. Writing is consciousness-raising."[84]

Here's the catch: speaking may be easy, but writing is hard. Ernest Hemingway made an oft-quoted comment about the difficulty of writing and how to respond to mock-aspiring writers, people who commit no words to paper but believe nonetheless that they could do a fine job of it, usually if they only had the time. "Tell them it's easy," he said. (He is also reported to have said this: "It's none of their business that you have to learn to write. Let them think you were born that way."[85])

Although a given technology may aid or support a given purpose, it's not the technology of transmission as such that advances intellect, but the very act of committing words to a page (though the page be other than paper and the instrument other than pen).

> "... we can see that what promotes the development of intellectual thought in human history is not the first alphabet or even the best iteration of an alphabet but writing itself. ... [The Greek alphabet provides] one of the best examples of the creative reciprocity between writing and thinking."[86]

Book readers know this:

> "Reading is an act of interiority, pure and simple. Its object is not the mere consumption of information. ... Rather, reading is the occasion

> of the encounter with the self. … The book is the best thing human beings have done yet."[87]

Book writers know this too, and more:

> "Even the oddest, most particular book was written with that kind of crazy courage—the writer's belief that someone would find his or her book important to read. I was struck by how precious and foolish and brave that belief is, and how necessary, and how full of hope it is to collect these books and manuscripts and preserve them. It declares that all these stories matter, and so does every effort to create something that connects us to one another, and to our past and to what is still to come. … All the things that are wrong in the world seem conquered by a library's simple unspoken promise: Here I am, please tell me your story; here is my story, please listen."[88]

Despite nineteenth-century predictions of the book's demise (with critics arguing long ago that books would be displaced by newspapers), books remain, and people keep writing and reading them. For devotees of the word, there is no argument between the old technology and the new, and no need to choose between them. A writer as admired as Douglas Adams gracefully embraced both.

> "He was delighted with the new possibilities it offered him and writers like him; equally, he never under-estimated the centuries-old power of words on a page, arranged in set, unchanging lines. He was a man who loved Wodehouse, Dickens and Austen. He never lost his faith in the realignment of the synapses that occurs every time we pick up a good book and start reading, find something that interests us or makes us turn to the next page, so much so that when we look up, the world has changed. / This is the abiding miracle of the book. We choose what happens next."[89]

Words—spoken, written, glittering onscreen—may open windows to insight. But words can't act on their own (they need agents to voice them), and so facts never actually do speak for themselves. And if technological advances don't necessarily advance social justice, that's only because "change and resistance to change always work hand in hand."[90] If time be granted, we humans are bound to change our ways for the wiser. These still early decades of the twenty-first millennium are clearly no time for a loss of nerve. The great Jon Stewart said humanity's biggest problem "is ignorance, not malevolence."

> "Ignorance is an entirely curable disease. ... Ignorance is often cured by experience, by spending time with what you don't understand. In the same way that [Donald] Trump's recklessness is born out of experience, so is my optimism, because good people outweigh [expletive] people. By a long shot."[91]

Ignorance may be addressed and even "cured," but as William James noted so long ago, pessimism has more staying power of the grasping kind.

> "For a philosophy to succeed on a universal scale it must define the future congruously with our spontaneous powers. ... a pessimistic principle like Schopenhauer's incurably vicious Will-substance, or Hartmann's wicked jack-of-all-trades the Unconscious, will perpetually call forth essays at other philosophies. ... Witness the attempts to overcome the 'problem of evil,' the 'mystery of pain.' There is no 'problem of good.' "[92]

A cynically pessimistic attitude is more than counter-productive; it's destructive, especially when it comes to the potentials of literacy.

> "The humanities have yet to recover from the disaster of postmodernism, with its defiant obscurantism, self-refuting relativism, and suffocating political correctness. Many of its luminaries—Nietzsche, Heidegger, Foucault, Lacan, Derrida, the Critical Theorists—are morose cultural pessimists who declare that modernity is odious, all statements are paradoxical, works of art are tools of oppression, liberal democracy is the same as fascism, and Western civilization is circling the drain."[93]

Biologist Peter Brian Medawar said that to "deride the hopes of progress is the ultimate fatuity, the last word in poverty of spirit and meanness of mind."[94] I agree. Optimism (at least the eyes-open kind) really is the true moral courage.[95] E-literacy really could ease the way to a promised land of freer communication in a more humane world.

But if it does, love and not power will have been the answer.

Chapter 8

Naming, Identity, and Crucibles of Individuality

The most basic operation of language is naming, and names do more than identify; they also indicate status. As a matter of survival, status concerns all social animals, but status among humans is routinely confused with survival. Using names as labels to jockey for status is considered normal in human societies (especially "advanced" ones). Rank rules where credentials are the name of the game and where some labels are decidedly more prestigious than others. So, for instance: "You always know when a person has been to Oxford or Cambridge … because they always tell you."[1]

According to some critical views, the common people lack the wherewithal to appreciate the deemed heights of high culture. This idea says more about the critics than it does about the commoners, and it's been roundly debunked, especially among artists and writers not intimidated by normalized narratives of class and value. Antonin Artaud:

> "It is idiotic to reproach the masses for having no sense of the sublime, when the sublime is confused with one or another of its formal manifestations, which are moreover always defunct manifestations. And if for example a contemporary public does not understand *Oedipus Rex*, I shall make bold to say that it is the fault of *Oedipus Rex* and not of the public."[2]

No doubt, I too make bold to agree.

In the face of global unrest and a widening gap between rich and poor, battles for status may seem unimportant; everyday games of status mongering may seem harmless compared to the ravages of world hunger. But of course discrimination exists on a spectrum: food insecurity and access to elite education rarely go hand in hand.

It wasn't until I happened on Andy Miller's book *The Year of Reading Dangerously* that I understood precisely why it is I don't like to read Virginia Woolf.

> "Happy medium, middle England, middlebrow: all names for the same unfortunate tendency. 'The middlebrow,' wrote Virginia Woolf, 'is the man, or woman, of middlebred intelligence who ambles and saunters, now on this side of the hedge, now on that, in pursuit of no single object, neither art itself or life itself, but both mixed indistinguishably, and rather nastily, with money, fame, power, or prestige.' She must be turning in her family plot. … By sheer weight of numbers, the plebs appear to have gained the upper hand at last. And nothing exemplifies their triumph more than the irresistible rise of the reading group."[3]

In matters of social relations, I take solace in a great line originated by a South African humorist and quoted by Desmond Tutu: "Love your enemy, it will ruin his reputation."

***

Language, said Neil Postman, is "pure ideology": "It instructs us not only in the names of things, but, more important, in what things can be named."[4]

Abstract names—names for groups of people, for countries on a map, for philosophies, for virtually any abstraction, especially in education—also carry connotations that can become fixtures of thought.

> "… we absorb attitudes as well as subject matter in the learning process. Moreover, the attitudes tend to determine what we see, and what we fail to see, in the subject matter. This is why attitude is just as important as content in the educational process."[5]

In short, names are symbols, and symbols are variously interpreted by different individuals. Thus names may mislead.

> "Scientists have found that the very symbols which crowd our brains may possess their own dangers. It is convenient for the thinker to classify an idea with a word. This can sometimes lead to a process called hypostatization or reification. Take the word 'Man,' for example. … if we are not careful of our meanings, it becomes easy to speak of all men as though they were one person. In reality men have been seeking this unreal man for thousands of years. … In reality he has never been found at all."[6]

You get a family name and a first name, and as you grow up you realize you have other names too, ones that identify you as a member of a given religious, ethnic, or other group. Group names characterize; they suggest "appropriate" (condoned) attitudes toward the group named. Every name, said E. L. Doctorow, carries "an injunction and so, if coordinate enough with other circumstances of life, a fate."[7]

Seemingly innocuous, group names may entail drastic consequences for individual members. For example, the first step in the Nazi genocidal project of the Second World War was to identify and thus locate the Jews of Europe. They couldn't have done that without the help of IBM and its punch-card technology, a basic precursor to computers.[8]

In fact, to identify and locate their targets is the first step of all hate campaigns. You might say white supremacists are targeting people they can identify by colour (rather than by name), but that would miss the point of the Black Lives Matter movement, a contemporary American epic in the centuries-old battle for civil rights. It would discount Canada's Truth and Reconciliation Commission, on behalf of the thousands of native Canadian children abused in the country's residential schools system and the tens of thousands of indigenous adults still widely discriminated against in everyday life. In point of fact, people come in all grades of colour (not black or red or white); without the labels as hateful words that seek to sanction violence, skin colour would be a characteristic almost imperceptible in binary terms.

In the world as we find it, though, violence recurs with numbing regularity. The blood eventually dries, but the bias remains. Each time history finishes repeating itself, it lurches forward to repeat itself and, like a natural law, creates a kind of propaganda by the fact. The belief "that's just the way it is" preaches powerlessness. Naming has always been a political as well as a personal matter. And whether or not we understand it:

> "All flourishing is mutual. … Such communal generosity might seem incompatible with the process of evolution, which invokes the imperative of individual survival. But we make a grave error if we try to separate individual well-being from the health of the whole."[9]

Identity: Jewish Female

As a Jewish woman, I've seen anti-Semitism right up close and sometimes in unexpected ways. I once had a student complain to the dean of arts at my university that "Maxine's ideas are too Jewish." Naturally, I took this as high praise, though the comment was clearly not so intended. "What's a Jewish idea?" said the dean and several liberal friends, meaning to be supportive.

And yet, as it happens, I do think that the need to engage intellect, to argue positions, is characteristically Jewish. There are, I think, typically Jewish themes, themes about wholeness and making whole, that resonate through the history of Jewish culture (and more than the obvious ones: Marx's workers of the world unite; or Freud's where id was there shall ego be; or, my personal favourite, Einstein's dream of a unified field).

The neurologist Oliver Sacks made a related point in an interview, when he said that although he doesn't believe in a personal God, "a law-giving God in the sky," he is nonetheless "very conscious of coming from a Jewish culture, from a culture of curiosity and questioning and debate, which is characteristically Jewish."

> "I sometimes wonder whether my love of footnotes has something to do with the Talmud ... which consists of a central text with commentaries on it and then commentaries on the commentaries and commentaries on the secondary commentaries. The idea of the Law is very central in Jewish religion and sometimes takes on an almost mystical form, where the Law is seen as a beautiful woman who will perhaps reveal a tiny bit of herself to the student."[10]

It's ironic that virtually all cultures and subcultures profess the same basic values (I don't know of any that give merit points for in-group murder, though history's strongmen are often widely admired), but alas, they profess in mutually foreign tongues: an e-model Tower of Babel.

This reminds me of a discussion in the late 1970s with a long-time friend named Nathan and his southern belle wife, Nanette. Nathan and I were arguing about Israeli politics. Nanette had begun backing away from us, but we didn't notice until we were surprised to hear her blurt out her alarm: "Stop fighting!"

"We're not fighting, that's just the way we talk," said Nathan, trying to reassure her that we two old friends were not about to come to blows (we weren't). I consider this incident evidential backup for my counterpoint claim to my mother's theory about language. Mom had uncanny insight into human emotion, even that of total strangers. She used to say that if only people couldn't talk, the world would be a better place. Instead of talking, people would have to emote, she reasoned. I disagreed. Yes, without language, it would be harder by means of words to lie to and gaslight others (or to be lied to or misled by others). But it would also be harder to sustain control over murderous impulses.

The very first step in any genocidal project is to define the target group as Other. People defined as the ever-handy Other must be distinct minorities and at the same time must be seen as holding mysterious powers, in order for this kind of narrative to prove useful politically. Jews, for example, comprise less than one half of one per cent of the world's human population, yet are still by some supposed to control the world's banks along with the (so-called) liberal media.

Anti-Semitism remains a kind of template for the expression and political uses of "racial" hatred. Jews make a model target: identifiable as a group, small enough to be isolated and managed, different enough to be suspect, but also old enough and socially integrated enough to serve as plausible scapegoats long-term (the eternal bogeyman enemy within). Even today, when Muslim minorities in the West are rabidly discriminated against on the basis of their religion, when breathing while black or Asian incurs daily dangers, and when indigenous Canadians face ubiquitous discrimination, Jews retain the top spot as avowed targets of hatred. Nothing like a more-than-two-thousand-year-old familiar to pull off that trick. Or is there?

***

The older the bias, the more effectively it operates behind the scenes to perpetuate hateful ideas. No bias is older than that against females. And unlike the "minorities" that make up most racist targets, females comprise no kind of minority but fully half the herd, and the locus of procreation besides.

Violence against females is a global scourge, but a normalized one. A reporter I knew years ago was finishing a story about a man who had threatened numerous times to kill his wife; the news was that he'd finally carried out the act. Told to slot the story for that day's Lifestyles Section, the reporter objected (Brava!). "Murder is a crime," she said, "not a lifestyle."

In the face of such physical violence, it might seem petty to complain about the mere downgrading of female intelligence, but of course the words used to "mansplain" female inferiority and acts of violence against women are two aspects of the same scourge, intimately related and mutually reinforcing. This bias precedes every other in the history of bigotry.

When I refer to "God" as "She," as I often do (just to be a pest in the purview of patriarchy), almost everyone laughs; almost everyone gets the primordial joke even if it isn't all that funny. Violent men are different from your average dinosaur, who is merely blind to the personhood of females. The predator takes advantage of this cultural blindness to operate in open secret and power-clad immunity from his own wrongdoing. From Greek mythology, comes:

> "… a series of unforgettable women: Medea, Clytemnestra and Antigone among many others. They are not, however, role models. For the most part, they are portrayed as abusers rather than users of power."[11]

The story of a powerful race of warrior women did not originate in admiration for them:

> "The hard truth is that the Amazons were a Greek male myth. The basic message was that the only good Amazon was a dead one. … The underlying point was that it was the duty of men to save civilization from the rule of women."[12]

The power of female intellect was widely regarded, if at all, as suspect. In the fifth century, a woman named Hypatia (c370-415) made good use of the famed sanctuary of knowledge in Alexandria's libraries to become an esteemed philosopher in her own age. Erudition doesn't automatically translate into political power, however, and Hypatia's professional status didn't protect her from adversaries suspicious of any claim to authority outside that of the church's—especially those issuing from an uppity female.

> "… to the religious zealots of the day, such pagan learning represented a threat. Not enough is known about Hypatia's efforts to establish a harmonious relationship with the early Christian church—but we do know that she was brutally murdered, and the libraries destroyed."[13]

Centuries before Hypatia was the ancient Greek poet Sappho. Born circa 630 BCE, Sappho was esteemed for her verses and for her teaching. She lived in the city of Mytilene on the Greek island of Lesbos, where she ran an academy for unmarried young women. Little is known about her life, but one legend from Ovid says she committed suicide after an unhappy love affair with a soldier. I don't buy it. Her feminist insights and inclinations ring so strong in her poetry (which sounds strikingly contemporary) that it's hard to imagine Sappho giving up the ghost on account of disappointed love. As for love-and-marriage-go-together-like-a-horse-and-carriage, I'm with Emma Goldman: "If the world is ever to give birth to true companionship and oneness, not marriage but love will be the parent."[14]

Despite Sappho's status as one of the best poets of her day, only fragments survive of the volumes she wrote. Here's one:

> Sleep, darling
>
> I have a small daughter called Cleis,
>
> who is like a golden
>
> flower
>
> I wouldn't take all Croesus'
>
> kingdom with love
>
> thrown in, for her

***

It's mid-February of 2019, and I'm in Toronto, looking after granddaughter Clementine while her folks are at their annual video conference in Miami. We're in bed, reading "just one more" story, when Clem says, OK now make up a story for me, a request with which I usually comply. But on this night, I'm so exhausted, I say that I'm too tired to make one up, why don't you tell me a story. You don't have to make it up, I add; you can just tell one of the old standbys, like Cinderella or Sleeping Beauty. So she tells me a story that's kind of an amalgam of the two mentioned, plus bits of Snow White. When she's done (like all good fairy tales, this one ends happily ever after), I point out that she has mixed up several stories. She says it's OK because "it's always the same prince."

I say, "But if it's always the same prince, doesn't that mean that the prince is two-timing, telling more than one damsel at a time that she is his one true love?"

Clem is not sure about that, but she's positive it's always the same prince.

"How can you be so sure?" I ask.

"Morrie said so."

"Whaddaya mean?"

Clem tells me that Alicia (loving wife of brother Morrie) asked about it, and Clem concluded: "Morrie said, yes, it's always the same prince. And Morrie is very old, so he must know everything."

The following morning, when my daughter Lienne calls, I ask her about this, and she explains: In a recent visit to Los Angeles, Clementine heard Morrie raving about a great script one of his students had written. It told the stories of the unhappy love affairs of a series of different women all seeking their Prince Charming. The scenes change along with the female characters but—you guessed it—"it's always the same prince." Clementine had taken this idea to heart. I emailed Morrie right away; he loves these stories about Clementine. "I thought you ought to know," I signalled, "since she's apparently relying on you, who must know everything, to set certain records straight."

In a Different Voice

The idea of females as intellectually inferior persists; it is not a remnant from supposedly less enlightened times and ancient authorities. It was only late in the twentieth century that substantial numbers of women gained admission to universities, previously bastions of male dominance. Since then, females have made up for lost time (for instance growing to comprise half the student population at Harvard within a decade after being admitted in 1982). In his book *Bobos in Paradise*, David Denby says the strong presence now of women in the academy shows that Aristotle was wrong about the presumed inferiority of female intellect. (I wonder what the wage gap shows.)

In history, too, women tend to be dis-included, especially from the aerial heights of human thought. In tomes on the history of ideas (at least those before the surge of feminist scholarship in the late twentieth century)—the kind I love and have retrieved from second-hand bookstores across this country—I've tried quantifying the number of times a female voice appears: rarely, and on those rare occasions, usually only as the lover or other sidekick of a presumably important male.

Take, for example, the 502-page *The Western Intellectual Tradition: From Leonardo to Hegel.* I found the book strangely unimpressive (despite my undying gravitation to such books, books that attempt to make sense of wide swaths of intellectual history). In this tome, like many of its type, women may as well not exist. They are conspicuous mainly by their absence. The book raises all the usual great names—at least those promised in its title, from the original Renaissance man, Leonardo da Vinci (1452-1519), to the German philosopher Georg Wilhelm Friedrich Hegel (1770-1831). But in its index of some 600-plus names, fewer than 20 are those of women. Most females mentioned get one or two pages, occasionally three or four. Queen Elizabeth I (with numerous references, 29 pages worth to be precise) is the sole exception to that rule. The exception is telling. The authors note, as to the queen's professional role: "The circumstances surrounding Elizabeth's refusal to marry are difficult to fathom."

Apparently also difficult for the authors to fathom were some of Elizabeth's more personal attributes, such as her fondness for glitter and the potentially dire consequences of this preference for matters of state. The queen, the authors write:

> "... liked to bedeck herself with jewels and decorations of all sorts. In fact, some historians claim that her taste for jewels had state repercussions; Elizabeth spent so much money on them that little was left over to pay for ships."[15]

She was, the authors tell us, needy in the extreme:

> "Elizabeth insisted on getting adulation from everyone, particularly from her court favorites, and had a tendency to take strong likes and dislikes to various members of the court. All this behavior was undoubtedly rooted in a wish for a kind of adoration which, without being physical in character, had a deep sexual undertone."[16]

Taking the trouble to note at further length these "baffling" aspects of the queen's personhood, the authors proceed to give fulsome licence to their inborn bias.

> "In spite of the fact that she did not fulfill the natural functions of marriage and may even have had deep masculine traits, Elizabeth certainly affected an intense femininity. She wore feminine dress in an excessive way ... [a Spanish ambassador, called to an interview with her, complained that] she was so indecently dressed that he ... really did not know where to look."[17]

Now this is funny—not strange-funny, just side-splitting funny: it reminds me of Elizabeth Renzetti writing in *Shrewed* about how if she were able to tone down her tendency to express herself assertively, things might go differently; and then again, if she didn't have such big breasts, maybe men would stop talking to them.

Sexless or over-sexed, either way, Queen Elizabeth is, QED, convicted.

There are a few positive remarks about females mentioned in *The Western Intellectual Tradition*, but even these are laced with killing assumptions about intellect and what it means to be female. Marie Antoinette, for an instance of positive review, gets a glowing footnote, a quotation from Edmund Burke's

Reflections on the Revolution in France. Burke admired Marie and wrote that with her execution, "the age of chivalry is gone."

> "That of sophisters, economists, and calculators has succeeded; and the glory of Europe is extinguished forever. Never, never more, shall we behold that generous loyalty to rank and sex, that proud submission, that dignified obedience, that subordination of the heart, which kept alive, even in servitude itself, the spirit of an exalted freedom!"[18]

Borrowing from *Charlotte's Web*, I must object: Some exalted! Some freedom!

More recent anthologies evaluating many of the same great men of intellectual history take a more critical view. Rosalind Miles's *The Women's History of the World* (published in 1988), for one example among many, goes the distance, rewriting well-worn historical themes as if women really did exist and as if they mattered.

Kenneth Patchen wrote somewhere that when you kill a person (he wrote when you kill a man, but I'm updating), you destroy a way of life. In a writing seminar that I attended long ago, a panelist raised the once-hot issue of sexist language, and wondered aloud what to do about the nearly ubiquitous use of the male pronoun "he" to refer to all people, including women.

I couldn't help myself (a long-time family friend says it's a family trait). I blurted out: "Here's a possible solution, instead of using 'he' to mean to include 'she,' let's use 'she' instead of 'he,' since speaking linguistically, the latter 'she' does actually include the former 'he.' (I got a couple of chuckles, but mostly, stunned silence. Who *is* this woman?) Yet the use of 'he' to refer to humans generally is invisible because it's culturally syntonic. Pronoun substitutions won't redress the imbalance (trust me, I've tried). Were a writer to try to replace the "he's" with "she's" (or even with "s/he's") throughout a text, readers would notice. They would lose the drift of the narrative (not to mention that the writer would have to pseudo-falsify any references to the events and persons of history, where women exist in a separate sphere if at all).

Despite the pronoun issue, women have indeed come a long way, and once they gained admission to universities, they flourished there and blazed trails for other women. Feminist scholarship flowered; no need for weapons of destruction, no hard decisions to make between costume jewelry and ships of war. Would the (theoretically at least) grand history and evolution of human intellect make more sense if female intellect were not cut out of it? Maybe, and maybe not—but it's doubtless worth the old college try that many female historians have given it, especially in the rise in recent decades of feminist scholarship. You don't need to be female to harbour feminist convictions, I've always thought. You just need to be fair-minded. (And conversely, being female, *malheureusement*, doesn't guarantee fair-mindedness. But let's hope it helps.)

***

On the first of December, 2015, I went to hear Gloria Steinem speak at Montreal's historic Rialto theatre. During questions after Steinem's talk, a native woman in the audience rose and sang a song in her own native Canadian tongue. Then, in further tribute to the woman whose work has touched so many, and because neither Steinem nor the bulk of the audience could understand the woman's mother tongue, she gave further praise by offering to play a short piece on her drum. This she did, to a rapt audience. When the woman was done, Steinem, with her hand on her heart, thanked the drummer and said her performance had "changed the molecules in the room." It was only then I noticed the many women around me who also cried. Truly:

> "There is no law of complex systems that says that intelligent agents must turn into ruthless conquistadors. Indeed, we know of one highly advanced form of intelligence that evolved without this defect. They're called women."[19]

In social life generally, the idea has been widely internalized that there is some essential difference between how males and females think, and that males are more seriously to be taken. Even the great Charles Darwin "was after all a man of his time, class, and society."

> "True, he was committed to a monogenic, rather than the prevailing polygenic, view of human origins, but he still divided humanity into distinct races according to differences in skin, eye or hair color. He was also convinced that evolution was progressive, and that the white races—especially the Europeans—were evolutionarily more advanced than the black races, thus establishing race differences and a racial hierarchy. Darwin's views on gender, too, were utterly conventional. He stated that the result of sexual selection is for men to be, 'more courageous, pugnacious and energetic than woman … [with] a more inventive genius.' … Such nineteenth century differentiation between the sexes was crucial in providing an alleged biological basis for the superiority of the male."[20]

In the more than century-and-a-half since Darwin wrote his opus, such views, far from being antiquated, persist. (We refer to "social Darwinism," as if to absolve Darwin from the full title of his famous 1859 book: *On the Origin of Species by Means of Natural Selection, or the Preservation of Favoured Races in the Struggle for Life.*) Even in disciplines we like to regard as antiseptically objective, such outdated views retain their apparently irresistible allure.

> "The biological sciences are becoming re-racialized and re-sexed. Distinct population groups—not races in the biological sense—do, after all, show reliable variations in gene frequencies, some of which are associated with known disorders such as Tay–Sachs disease or cystic fibrosis. And there are small but robust differences, chemically and anatomically, between the brains of men and women, although nobody has any real idea what the implications might be. A recent essay in *Nature* even argues that it is time to re-open the 'untouchable' question of racial and gender differences in intelligence—or rather, its ostensible surrogate measure, IQ (Ceci & Williams, 2009)."[21]

There may well be some biologically based differences in the way males and females think, and there are clearly (and clearly defined) cultural differences, but as usual in diametrically opposed, either-or, them-or-us classifications, the differences *within* each group are far more numerous than those *between* them.

> "Eighty-five percent of human genetic variation consists of the differences between one person and another within the same ethnic group, tribe, or nation. ... In other words, the genetic difference [between any two individuals of the same group] is about twelve times as large as the genetic difference [between groups of people]. ... Race is, quite literally, skin-deep, but to the extent that perceivers generalize from external to internal differences, nature has duped them into thinking that race is important. The X-ray vision of the molecular geneticist reveals the unity of our species. And so does the X-ray vision of the cognitive scientist."[22]

Alas, not all cognitive scientists possess this X-ray vision. And it's a reliable assumption that for all kinds of people, the politics of personal identity tend to align with the political interests of a given class. People who don't "believe in" climate change, for instance, tend not to believe in a living minimum wage either.

Denied the educational opportunities open to males, females were left to their own devices, and so they came to speak (and write) "in a different voice," one less restrained than that employed in the all-male schools of old. Woman-write was flush with orality.

> "One of the loveliest ironies in the world's great mix of writing systems involves a very old Chinese writing system used only by women. Unlike the rest of Chinese writing, which is logographic, this system was completely based on phonetic translation of the sounds of Chinese words."[23]

In ancient Sumer, too, where women in royal houses did learn to read, they employed a separate dialect. Called Emesal, it was similar to Emegir, the standard dialogue for males, but with words pronounced slightly differently.[24]

Even in the seventeenth century, when girls did begin to be admitted to schools in larger numbers, they attended the "newer vernacular schools," where they were taught to run households, not curricula. In the academic schools for boys, all subjects, including rhetoric, were taught in Latin. Thus female authors who published (from the seventeenth century and well into the nineteenth) wrote in a language uninfluenced by Latin or by traditional rhetoric.

> "For well over a thousand years, [Latin] was sex-linked, a language written and spoken only by males, learned outside the home in a tribal setting, which was in effect a male puberty rite setting ... It had no direct connection with anyone's unconscious of the sort that mother tongues, learned in infancy, always have."[25]

Learned Latin—about as far from mother tongue as it gets—has been associated with objectivity itself, and even credited with the birth of scientific thinking.

> "Writing ... serves to separate and distance the knower and the known and thus to establish objectivity. It has been suggested that Learned Latin effects even greater objectivity by establishing knowledge in a medium insulated from the emotion-charged depths of one's mother tongue, thus reducing interference from the human lifeworld and making possible the exquisitely abstract world of medieval scholasticism and of the new mathematical modern science which followed on the scholastic experience. Without Learned Latin, it appears that modern

> science would have got under way with greater difficulty, if it had got under way at all."[26]

Whether the advance of "modern science" indicates an arc of the moral universe toward justice is hard to say. So much depends on what you mean by words like "science" and "justice." Especially "science." James Bridle wrote of:

> "... a growing awareness across the sciences that something is deeply and widely wrong with scientific research. The number of new results is not only falling, but those results are becoming less trustworthy, thanks to a combination of different mechanisms."[27]

Bridle notes these mechanisms: a rise in number of retractions of scientific findings; misconduct rather than error by researchers (including failure to retract); fraud by scientists, including fabrication of results; and the most controversial: failure to replicate a study's findings. He concludes: "Across the board, from medicine to psychology, biology to environmental sciences, researchers are coming to the realisation that many of the foundations of their research may be flawed."[28] Such concerns led the editor of a leading medical journal "to publish an editorial attacking statistical methods entitled 'Why most published research finds are false.' "[29]

The Language of Science

Crises of faith across the lacunae of C. P. Snow's two cultures persist—in science and in the humanities; both are marked by mutual suspicion and both long predate the age of Big Data.

> "A good many times I have been present at gatherings of people who, by the standards of the traditional culture, are thought highly educated and who have with considerable gusto been expressing their incredulity at the illiteracy of scientists. Once or twice I have been provoked and have asked the company how many of them could describe the Second Law of Thermodynamics. The response was cold: it was also negative. Yet I was asking something which is the scientific equivalent of: Have you read a work of Shakespeare's?"[30]

The language of science is mathematics; numbers and the relationships between them allow for a kind of precision not possible with words. On the other hand, if words lack the precision of numbers, numbers also lack the nuance of words. Though both require context, numbers have no synonyms; by themselves, they are meaningful only as adjectives. Names are based in orality; mathematics, in a specialized form of text.

> "When we talk about mathematics, we may be discussing a secondary language, built on the primary language truly used by our central nervous system. … [Whatever that primary language may be] it cannot fail to differ considerably from what we consciously and explicitly consider as mathematics."[31]

Math can express concepts beyond words. But even numbers need names, and names as we've seen are consequential. In his *Corfu Trilogy*, Gerald Durrell tells a story about how the collared dove got its Greek name.

> "In Greek … the name for collared dove is *dekaoctur*—'eighteener' … The story goes that when Christ was carrying the cross to Calvary, a Roman soldier, seeing that He was exhausted, took pity on Him. By the side of the road there was an old woman selling … milk, and so the Roman soldier went to her and asked her how much a cupful would cost. She replied that it would cost eighteen coins. But the soldier had only seventeen. He … pleaded with the woman to let him have a cupful of milk for Christ for seventeen coins, but the woman avariciously held out for eighteen. So, when Christ was crucified, the old woman was turned into a turtle dove and condemned to go about for the rest of her days repeating *dekaocto*, *dekaocto*—'eighteen, eighteen.' If ever she agrees to say *deka-epta*, seventeen, she will regain her human form. If, out of obstinacy, she says *deka-ennaea*, nineteen, the world will come to an end."[32]

The presumably hard-core measurements of modern physics bear their share of paradox. Take for instance Werner Heisenberg's uncertainty principle, which says you can't measure a particle's speed and its position at the same time. The principle threw a philosophical wrench into the materialist works. According to one explainer, the theory "in plain language, says that the more we know about half of the subatomic world, the less we can know about the other half."[33]

I must be missing something here, because "in plain language," it seems obvious that of course you can't measure the speed of a moving particle and at the same time measure its position. One viewpoint precludes the other. It's impossible to know a particle's speed of movement if it's not moving; and equally impossible to pinpoint a particle's location if it is moving. Then again, that *is* the point of the uncertainty principle—and of the quantum theory in which the principle finds its real-world meaning.

> "As strange as it is, quantum theory has become the most successful, powerful, and accurately tested scientific theory of all time. Although its rules would never have been discovered without many clues from experiment, quantum theory represents a triumph of abstract, mathematical reasoning. … Before we observe it, the world is in an abstract, nebulous, undecided state. It follows beautiful mathematical laws but cannot be described in everyday language. According to quantum theory, the very act of our observing the world forces it into terms we can relate to, describable with ordinary numbers."[34]

In 1865, long before Werner Heisenberg's 1927 paper on the uncertainty principle, James Clerk Maxwell formulated a complete theory of electromagnetism: of electric forces and magnetic forces as two manifestations of the very same force.

> "The most spectacular outcome of Maxwell's unified theory of electricity and magnetism had been its prediction of the speed light. This prediction raised a paradox so deep and far-reaching in its implications that it took physicists decades to resolve. The paradox may be summarized in the simplest of questions: the speed of light relative to what? According to Newton, and to everyday intuition, if you see something moving away and chase after it, it will recede more slowly. If you move fast enough, you can catch up with it or overtake it. An absolute speed is meaningless."[35]

Just so. An absolute anything is meaningless.

The uncertainty principle is as much a linguistic conundrum as it is a "real" problem in physics. As narrative, the theory (like others written in the language of mathematics) confounds the algorithms of measurement, but also can transcend the limits of measurement the way that in language, poetry can transcend syntax. Such narratives and their suppositions are not pointless to entertain; they drive both linguistic and scientific enquiry.

> "Subatomic particles cannot be precisely measured without making quantifiable sacrifices. If you measure precisely what a particle is doing, you cannot at the same time measure precisely where it is. If you measure precisely how much energy it has, you lose all information about

> time. / Subatomic physics gives some people the willies because of this inherent uncertainty. But knowledge is also lost with the most mundane measurements of everyday life. You cannot chemically analyze your dinner and eat it (or at least the very same bit), too. You cannot dissect the mathematics underlying Mozart and at the same time feel the emotional impact. A Picasso, viewed through a powerful microscope, dissolves into a grainy pattern of dots. … Something is lost for every measure that's gained."[36]

Numbers may mislead in science, just as words may mislead in sentences. From Einstein's relativity to the quandaries of quantum entanglement, even the closed system of mathematics posits intents. Even physics has a God particle.

Is the universe really expanding, as science claims to have shown? If so, into what does the universe expand—a non-universe? Something separate from Walter Ong's "human lifeworld"? The universe, as I imagine it, doesn't expand or contract; instead, it does both: it breathes.

Over and over again I'm struck by the trouble with words, with stories "that fundamentally cannot be reduced to verbal description."

> "This disjunction between thought and language is not a new problem in science. The physicists who developed the quantum theory early in the [twentieth] century were well aware of this difficulty. For example, it began to be appreciated that the very attempt to conjure a mental picture of an individual electron automatically involved one in error. For an electron was quintessentially not something discrete and individual, since it demonstrated properties that showed that it was connected to all other existing particles. This interconnectedness was such a prominent feature that the very meaning of the word 'particle' was in doubt. How could one describe this quality? The problems of language here were profound, and Niels Bohr suggested that many of the new concepts could best be described metaphorically and in the language of poetry."[37]

What about molecules? Are they "real"? In her book *Molecules of Emotion*, Candace Pert tells a story relayed to her by Deepak Chopra when he was introducing her for a talk she gave at his institute. The story is about some wise men ("the rishis, or sages, who are the spiritual leaders") whom he met while visiting India.

> "In the course of conversation, he attempted to explain my work to them, the idea that neuropeptides and receptors communicate as information molecules. But they could only shake their heads and give him very quizzical looks. Finally, the oldest and wisest appeared to suddenly get it. He sat up straight and, with an expression of great surprise, said. 'Oh, I understand. She thinks these molecules are real!' "[38]

Whether molecules or atoms or subatomic particles are real entities or linguistic fictions depends on what it is you want to do with or about them. Discussion of C. P. Snow's two cultures doesn't have to degenerate into one-versus-the-other. In reality, there is no Other.

> "Of course, there is only one. Of course, the natural sciences are just as humane as letters. There are, however, two languages, the spoken verbal language of literature, and the written sign language of mathematics, which is the language of science. This puts the scientist at a great advantage, for, since like all of us he has learned to read and write, he can understand a poem or a novel, whereas there are very few men of letters who can understand a scientific paper once they come to the mathematical parts."[39]

Despite the difficulties of the "mathematical parts," there's really no need to choose between science and the humanities. The best of both tend to converge. "We cannot live or think at all without some degree of faith," wrote William James. "Faith is synonymous with working hypothesis."[40] Thus there is no need to be intimidated by scientific thinking, much less to genuflect before its language of numbers. According to one non-scientist:

> "Physicists and astronomers see their own implications in the world being round, but to me it means that only one-third of the world is asleep at any given time and the other two-thirds is up to something."[41]

Scientists and mathematicians are after all humans, as prone to experiment as to err.

> "According to one popular conception of science that goes all the way back to Francis Bacon's invention of it in 1620, scientific endeavour is all about getting answers from nature. That said, given that the quality of answers one gets depends conspicuously on the quality of questions one asks, scientific enquiries lacking in intrepidity, imagination, and insight are likely to yield little more than scientifically validated tedium."[42]

Literacy is new in human evolution, but science is even newer, and its achievements are massive. More than a century ago, William James wrote this:

> "Few of us realize how short the career of what we know as 'science' has been. Three hundred and fifty years ago hardly any one believed in the Copernican planetary theory. Optical combinations were not discovered. The circulation of the blood, the weight of air, the conduction of heat, the laws of motion were unknown; the common pump was inexplicable; there were no clocks; no thermometers; no general gravitation; the world was five thousand years old; spirits moved the planets; alchemy, magic, astrology, imposed on every one's belief. … The men who began this work of emancipation were philosophers in the original sense of the word, universal sages. Galileo said that he had spent more years on philosophy than months on mathematics."[43]

> "Are names or numbers more objective?" asks Carl Safina in his wonderful book *Beyond Words*, and answers with an anecdote:

> "Jane Goodall's first scientific paper on chimpanzees was returned by the Annals of the New York Academy of Sciences because she'd named, rather than numbered, them. The editor also insisted that she refer to a chimpanzee as an 'it' rather than 'he' or 'she.' Goodall refused. Her study got published anyway. Do names or numbers bias us, or do they help us see?"[44]

Once again: Yes.

I like the solidity of numbers and the pristine logic of equations. I like the idea that everything in the universe follows the same mathematical laws. But after all, numbers are like the symbols that name them: they cannot deliver the certainty that both the sciences and the humanities seem to crave. Heraclitus was right: change is the only constant. So was Einstein, when in 1921 he said this: "As far as the laws of mathematics refer to reality, they are not certain; and as far as they are certain, they do not refer to reality."[45]

The laws of mathematics, like the rules of syntax, nevertheless remain useful as hypotheses. Even though I don't live my life by mathematical reckonings (I obsess instead over words), I view with great respect the reasoning of science and I embrace its progress with an enquiring mind and an open heart.

> "The incredible reliability of physical laws is what allows us to build computers, smartphones, the internet, and all the rest of modern technology. But the universe is not like a machine or a digital computer. It operates on quantum laws whose full meaning and implications we are still discovering. According to these laws, we are not irrelevant bystanders. On the contrary, what we see depends on what we decide to observe. Unlike classical physics, quantum physics allows for, but does not yet explain, an element of free will."[46]

Even if quantum physics can't explain free will, and even if there is nothing at all that ever can, I stand solidly on that score with William James, who said that the first act of free will should be to affirm free will.

The Language of Money and the Persistence of Inequity

It may seem strange to think of money as a language. But like music and like mathematics, which are more commonly considered languages, money also employs a basic symbolic code to convey meaning (the plus sign in math, for instance, or the key signature in music, are like the dollar sign in money). Of the three languages, money is most commonly consequential. Most people like music, but not everyone makes music; some people enjoy mathematics, but few can speak higher mathematics. On the third hand, everyone needs money: everyone understands money as the currency that can make the difference between survival and starvation. Money is real politic, and if you don't recognize its worth, you are likely to be deemed and treated as one dealing without a full deck.

In his book on the origins of consciousness, Julian Jaynes argued that consciousness arose in "the breakdown of the bicameral mind"—when, according to his thesis, people realized that the voices they heard were internal, spoken not by God but by one hemisphere of the brain to the other. He wrote that consciousness emerged "as something genuinely new at a critical stage of evolutionary advance."[47] Despite the erudition of Jaynes's book, modern neuroscience has rendered moot some of its speculations about the bicameral brain. Yet the idea unwittingly persists that some inner voices (our own "self-talk") come from somewhere or someone outside ourselves.

Take a walk down any major street in any large city—especially ones where institutions for the mentally ill or disabled have been shut for lack of funds—and you are likely before long to see people who clearly believe the voices they hear come from somewhere outside their own heads, or minds, or brains, or any other labels for any other forms of isolate consciousness. Yet those of us labelled normal also believe in voices that originate outside our selves, beyond our control. What the economy "dictates": a perfect example.

The forms and meanings of money, like those of words, comprise a symbolic language. Cultures and social stratification systems are affected by changing forms of language and money, as by other symbolic operatives. There is a little noted connection, however, between language and money, and a hypothesized broken link: between substance and inscription, between the form of money and its meaning (its value). Both money and words are mediums of exchange that enable communication. But what we think of as money changes as the forms of exchange do (from the earliest tokens to the latest Internet currencies). The institution of money changed the way people did business, but people engaged in trade and commerce long before bitcoin.

> "The idea of exchange, the basis of economics, is nearly as old as man, and deal-making has been the stuff of legend since the Levantine kings and the pharaohs traded gold and chariots for weapons and slaves."[48]

The invention and development of money evolved along with that of literacy. As writing reified the language of words, the inscriptions on paper money reified exchange values. Like written words, paper monies got confused with the values they were meant to represent and serve in economic exchange.

In the beginning of money, an ingot (a piece of cast metal, usually gold, silver, or electrum, an alloy of silver and gold) was literally worth its weight. The first important change in the form of money was the institution of coinage, about 500 BCE. With coinage, the material form of money was still a chunk of metal, but the value of the coin was not its weight (not a measure of its substance); it was the information the coin bore, the inscription stamped onto the metal.

In his book, *Money, Language, and Thought*, Marc Shell argues that the changing forms of money are closely linked to intellectual developments, that is, to stages of literacy. He sees evolving literacy in broad stages, each with its own culture-changing implications. With the institution of coinage and then paper money and finally electronic funds, came revolutionary changes in human intellect:

> "The eventual development of coins whose politically authorized inscriptions were inadequate to the weights and purities of the ingots into which the inscriptions were stamped precipitated awareness of

> quandaries about the relationship between face value (intellectual currency) and substantial value (material currency). This difference between inscription and thing grew greater with the introduction of paper moneys. Paper, the material substance on which the inscriptions were printed, was supposed to make no difference in exchange … [but] the material substance to which the inscriptions referred was connected with those inscriptions in increasingly abstract ways. With the advent of electronic fund-transfers the link between inscription and substance was broken. The matter of electronic money does not matter."[49]

Changes in the forms of money, and especially the broken link that Shell posits "between inscription and substance" had social consequences. Some "came to recognize interactions between economic and intellectual exchange, or money and language."[50]

In his book *The History of Money*, Jack Weatherford traced the evolution of currency. He too described the history of money in a wide narrative sweep of three revolutionary generations. The first generation was the invention in the ancient world of coinage, and its dissemination created the "classical civilizations of the Mediterranean," gradually destroying "the great tributary empires of history."

The second generation came with the invention of paper money (the value of which is decreed symbolically, determined almost solely by the inscription it bears rather than the paper on which the inscription is written). Paper money and its related global banking systems reigned from the Renaissance through the Industrial Revolution.[51] This regime of paper money lasted until the twenty-first century consolidated the reign of electronic communications and electronic "cash":

> "The invention of banking and the paper money system destroyed feudalism, changed the basis of organization from heredity to money, and it changed the basis of economic power from owning land to owning stocks, bonds, and corporations. … Now, at the opening of the twenty-first century, the world is entering the third stage of its monetary history—the era of electronic money and the virtual economy. The rise of electronic money will produce changes in society as radical and far-reaching as the two earlier monetary revolutions caused in their own eras. The new money will make sweeping changes in the political systems, in the organization of commercial enterprises, and in the

> nature of class organization. Virtual money promises to make its own version of civilization that will be as different from the modern world as from the world of the Aztecs or the Vikings."[52]

In the contemporary monetary system, money moves faster than ever and speaks with more clout than ever ("it doesn't talk, it swears," sang Bob Dylan). Opinions about money, from lucre itself as the root of evil, to capitalism as a form of forward-thinking, have occupied critics in various disciplines. And yet money as material is complicated in the digital age: it has become almost entirely immaterial. Weatherford writes that not only the dollar bill but all national currencies around the globe are threatened with extinction in the age of electronic funds. While money dominates in social systems, it also "faces some strange and ominous challenges. In the last decades of the twentieth century, the global money system began to cough and sputter, to jerk and stumble."

> "The dollar is dying. So too are the yen, the mark, and the other national currencies of the modern world. Our global money system is infected with a deadly virus, and, already severely weakened, it is now only a matter of time before it succumbs. The dollar, mark and yen will join the ducat, cowrie shells, and the guinea in the scrap box of history, as items of interest primarily to antiquarians and eccentrics."[53]

As the twentieth century drew to a close, this "extinction" was already in evidence, not with the disappearance of dollars, but with runaway inflation, erratic exchange rates, and the demise of banks that had ruled since the Renaissance as they "teetered and fell under billion-dollar losses that seemed to occur inexplicably overnight."

> "Despite rather awkward but extensive intervention at many levels, no government seems able to control its own currency, and new financial institutions now stretch across the globe in a network of interconnected businesses with a power never before known in history. Supposedly global agencies such as the International Monetary Fund, the United Nations, and the World Bank seem largely irrelevant to the finances of any but the weakest players already on the international dole."[54]

Weatherford speaks of the extinction of earlier forms of money, but perhaps "extinction" is the wrong word. After all, though money may mean figures glittering on a high-tech screen rather than figures engraved in some harder form (on coins, paper, plastic cards), global economies still require the coordination of exchange rates for different national currencies. Weatherford and others argue that although the old monetary system is bound to fall, a new form of money and the cyber-sphere institutions to support it will arise in the lurching progress of electronic communications.

> "In the realms of cyberspace, money is now being reinvented as a free-floating force that can appear instantaneously anywhere in the world in any amount. No longer tethered to the fortunes of one government or a single country, the new money is emerging in a large variety of new forms. The new money is raw power."[55]

According to some, the new technologies of money will continue to transform commerce and civic life; they will "create a whole new class system of rich and poor." This new monetary system (in full force today but described as only "emerging" when Weatherford's book was published in 1997) "will change the very meaning of money."

In fact, electronic funds and fund transfers have already changed the way people use money, just as electronic communications have changed literacy and language use. But I don't believe that electronic funds represent a revolutionary change in "the very meaning of money." At least, I'm not holding my breath.

The changing forms of money do not appear to make any essential difference to the sociology of money—to the meaning of money for individuals and groups of individuals. Thus, I do not believe that changes in the form of money do or can amount to revolutionary developments in human society (though they may intensify trends already long under way). A revolution of any kind (with regard to language, to money, or to any arena that claims to have been affected in a transformative way by a new form or a new theory) would have to mean a change in significance, not one in mere form. It would have to entail a momentous reversal in the direction of change, not just a cultural game of ladders in which individuals at the top and bottom of a social structure from time to time change places, only in order to finally eliminate players until a single player remains, a winner to take all. A true revolution would mean a move toward cooperation and equity, away from the zero-sum language, mentality, and culture of money.

No form of money (including the crypto currencies of the electronic age) is revolutionary that doesn't eradicate poverty and change economic/legal infrastructures in the direction of equity and fairness. What Franklin D. Roosevelt said in a 1932 address remains true almost a century later: "No business which depends for existence on paying less than living wages to its workers has any right to continue."

Electronic money is immaterial in some sense, but the meanings and consequences of electronic money are material in every sense. Without a change in consciousness on a global human scale, the new money will remain like the old money, a way to separate the haves from the have-nots, dependent on the buffer of a "middle class." That the middle class is said to be disappearing, or to have already disappeared, is a necessary consequence of any systematized inequity, and constitutes a problem for all classes, not just the one on the bottom rung. Inequity and injustice really do rebound to affect all classes, the envied rich as much as the discounted poor and the so-called middle-class majority. How could it be otherwise? When there is only a one-per-cent of "haves" as against the ninety-nine-per-cent mass of others, any system of stratification must begin to break down. Although generally speaking, most people most of the time are inclined to obey orders and respect hierarchies, there are limits. People who feel they have little to lose also have a tendency to risk more in the way of disobedience. Conversely, "rulers" maintain or seek to maintain social control against popular uprising by the threat, and finally by the use, of violent armed suppression.

Perhaps it's true, as a nice liberal sentiment has it, that "we cannot legislate intelligence, morality, or loyalty," that "these must be inspired, not compelled."[57] On the other hand, it's clearly true that while legislation can't enforce humane practice, it can enforce consequences for lack thereof. (It wasn't until March of 2022, despite many attempts since the first in 1918, that the U.S. government finally passed into law a bill that outlaws lynching. Consider that as of June 2021, despite the "discovery" of hundreds of unmarked graves of indigenous children at residential schools across Canada, this country's government has yet to enforce legal accountability.)

The ubiquitous reality of political power disguises its most pornographic aspects as it seeks to hide the potentials of political action. The purpose of pornographic power is to keep people passive or incite them to violence. In both cases, like subconscious intents, the truth about power must remain invisible for the sake of minority rule.

What hasn't changed through the theorized stages of literacy and money is the persistence of inequity within countries and between them, in fact within and between any grouping of people (including circles as small as that of one's family and friends). What persists are widely unacknowledged (unconsciously held) social assumptions about hierarchies of "value," which in turn account, presumably, for the brutal facts and persistence of pernicious inequity: some people can afford to waste food while others only to die for lack of it. Some can afford shelter and others only to live outside, in full and plain view (but as though invisible) of the homed.

In an equitable society, in a society where the basics of survival (food and shelter) were considered rights and treated as rights, there would be no need for stealing. Rulers who failed to uphold these rights would cease to rule. There would still be jockeying for position in the ego-and-status-award sweepstakes, but sociopaths (estimated at one in four by some counts)[58] would be less numerous and far less likely to ascend to high office, where in fact they are more commonly found. If you're looking to identify sociopaths, stop searching the metaphorical gutters and check out the corner offices of the most powerful CEOs and governing elites. And if you want to distinguish the habitual cheaters from the rest, look up, way up.

In his book *The Power Paradox*, American psychology professor Dacher Keltner distinguished between two kinds of power: legitimate power, which is bestowed by other people, and illegitimate power, which is seized.[59] In Keltner's reasoning, true power is given to leaders in any field by other people who feel their own interests are served by that leader. The other kind of power is opposed or indifferent to the best interests of the people and must be secured by force or coercion—the kind of power we usually interpret *as* power. Like an empire, such brute power is bound to end. It is only the power that is given or bestowed that has lasting influence; the illegitimate kind sooner or later comes tumbling down in an ego-infested conflagration.

Complicating matters in Keltner's thesis is that even bestowed power motivated by good intentions may work against the interests of those doing the purported bestowing.

It seems to me plainer to simply distinguish kinds of power in terms of intention: *power to* as opposed to *power over*—rather than to try to distinguish the virtuous power holders from the vicious ones. By "power to," I mean the ability to accomplish; by "power over," the ability to dominate. Since both are at play in real life and politics, the kind of power with the greatest potential for social good must be power that is widely shared. For individuals, too, the most effective power is that which emphasizes power to (accomplish) rather than power over (others). While power and wealth do not necessarily entail or indicate merit, neither do powerlessness and poverty necessarily encourage, much less ensure, ethical thought or behaviour. "Climbing out of poverty by your own efforts—that is something on which to pride yourself," J. K. Rowling said at a 2008 Harvard Commencement address,

> "... but poverty itself is romanticized only by fools. ... Poverty is not an ennobling experience. Poverty entails fear, and stress, and sometimes depression. It means a thousand petty humiliations and hardships."[60]

Yet studies belie the idea (associated with the nineteenth century but still popular today) that the so-called lower classes are lower in character; studies show instead that it is the rich and powerful who are more inclined than "ordinary" people to break the rules.

> "In the early 2000s, U.S. shoplifters took about $13 billion in goods from retailers each year, and 11 percent of Americans confessed to the act. Themes of power were present in the data: whites were more likely to shoplift than Asians, Latinos, and African Americans. And yes, the wealthy were more likely to shoplift that the poor."[61]

The monetary "revolutions" already cited did not eliminate (or initiate) inequity any more than the language revolutions of literacy eliminated (or initiated) lies. If this latest electronic monetary system actually has the revolutionary implications and powers claimed for it, let it be for the common good, for greater equality, less life-destroying inequity, for greater compassion, instead of just a new system to distinguish rich from poor and all the ladder-imprisoned and ladder-climbing others of the hierarchy in between. Money is power only if backed by armed force against the great unwashed and unarmed. In recorded history, as a friend once countered in discussion of social inequity and a widening gap between rich and poor within countries and between countries, "But Max, there have always been castles and dungeons." I get that. But I also get that there is a big difference between what is and what ought to be, between what is and what might be. And in this, I am far from alone. Across the globe, humans of conscience stand to be counted and work to right wrongs even when they don't make the perpetual 24-hour news cycle.

As noted, both literacy and monetary systems are representational technologies based on a code of symbols. But literacy does not guarantee raised consciousness, and monetary systems don't prevent famines. Though literacy spurred the advance of other technologies, people still die of starvation in famines in the modern world, not for a lack of food production, not because there isn't enough food to go around, but because they lack the money ("currency," hard or electronic) to buy food (or for that matter, to grow their own). While this might strike the general reader as a nonsensical idea, it is not new to economic theory.

Nobel Prize laureate Amartya Sen is called a "humanist" economist because he wrote about the economy of the underclass. He wrote that the cause of famines is not food shortages but a lack of sharing based on a money economy, on a kind of "differential neglect." The contemporary money system equates food with money. Sen himself noted that this idea is not new, citing the nineteenth-century Irish economist David Ricardo, who wrote in similar terms about the Irish potato famines of 1825 and 1840. Sen recognized and theorized about:

> "… why it's perfectly possible that if people don't have money to buy food, they will die. It has nothing to do with the food supply. … even reasonably high-brow economic theory, like equilibrium theory, is perfectly consistent with people dying of hunger in large numbers."[62]

The threat of losing access to the basic necessities of life (food and shelter) are functions of the money system, and the threat, as always in times of crisis, disproportionately affects the overlapping categories of the poor and the systemically disadvantaged "minorities."

If we are to learn anything from the persistence of injustice (I mean all forms, from institutionalized racism and structural inequity to corruption and lack of accountability in places high and low, but especially high), it is that we are inextricably bound up in each other; that sooner or later (sooner in the case of social crises), injustice for one is injustice for all.

"Until we are all free, we are none of us free," said Emma Lazarus, who wrote the famous sonnet "The New Colossus," from which are taken the words that adorn America's Statue of Liberty ("Give me your tired, your poor / Your huddled masses yearning to breathe free"). These words "have become a rallying cry to protect the human rights of immigrants and refugees, and to protest discrimination on the basis of religion and nationality," wrote Esther Schor in her biography of Lazarus, a poet and activist who was born in 1849 and died in 1887).[63] They are words newly relevant to a free-world promise yet unfulfilled.

Human compassion survives the travesties of business as usual and the blinders of going along to get along—and so it must if we are to revise any of the worst and retain any of the best of what it "means to be human" (how quaint the phrase). Creativity and agency are birthrights, and they flower in all groups of people who suffered—and continue to suffer—from historical suppression of their creativity and agency once the knee comes off their necks.

I remember the day when I was a six-year-old child, as we sat around the dinner table and my mother admonished us kids to clean our plates: "Eat your food," she said. "It's a sin to waste food. There are children starving in Africa." I'll never forget the suddenly alarmed look on the face of my twin sister, Frannie, as she answered immediately, with all the innocent sincerity we too soon outgrow: "Well *send* it to them, I don't need it." With her dying breath, Frannie believed what she always had: that any truly intelligent person is kind.

That children and other living things still express this kind of understanding about fairness shows that it's still in us, somewhere, curled up hiding behind a great deal of pain, behind years of experienced unfairness. While those at the pinnacle of the money system seek (successfully) to profit from social crises, others, far more numerous, come out of hiding to object to systemic unfairness, taking to the streets—and more recently, the legislatures—to demand change. And true to their times, these latest makers of good trouble employ electronic communications (*inter alia* and with savvy) to organize mass protest. It was native Canadians themselves, using the technology of ground-penetrating radar, who sought and found the unmarked gravesites of their murdered children. Those seeking redress can use high technologies to great effect. But so too, of course, can the organizers of hatred.

Crucibles of Individuality

It's the way we live and the consciousness underlying our social systems that make us sick, that speak incessantly the lie that as individuals we don't matter. And yet isn't it true, what Mahatma Gandhi said? "The difference between what we do and what we are capable of doing would suffice to solve most of the world's problems."

That individuals of all kinds can act is the salient fact: as individuals, we matter—not because as individuals we are necessarily such great shakes (with many notable and noted exceptions), but because it's as embodied individuals that we may act, and because our actions have consequences inextricably tied to others. As there is no immunity from danger or death, there is no immunity from these others.

> "You can live as a particle crashing about and colliding in a welter of materials with God, or you can live as a particle crashing about and

> colliding in a welter of materials without God. But you cannot live outside the welter of colliding materials."[64]

The power of unquestioned authority—what I think of as addiction to authority—is also the power of its counterpart: the power of individuals to question and defy illegitimate authority. History is replete with examples of such individuals and how they made a difference. And behind both kinds of agency: the power of belief.

> "Belief is both prize & battlefield, within the mind & in the mind's mirror, the world. If we believe humanity is a ladder of tribes, a coliseum of confrontation, exploitation & bestiality, such a humanity is surely brought into being … the moneyed, the privileged, the fortunate, shall not fare so badly in this world, provided our luck holds. What of it if our consciences itch?"[65]

In his novel *Cloud Atlas*, David Mitchell considered the place of the self in society; he concluded that selfishness in an individual "uglifies the soul." But for the species, selfishness is extinction."

> "If we believe that humanity may transcend tooth & claw, if we believe divers races & creeds can share this world as peaceably as the orphans share their candlenut tree, if we believe leaders must be just, violence muzzled, power accountable & the riches of the Earth & its Oceans shared equitably, such a world will come to pass. I am not deceived. It is the hardest of worlds to make real. Torturous advances won over generations can be lost by a single stroke of a myopic president's pen or a vainglorious general's sword."[65]

It takes courage to exercise conscience in matters both large and small. And doesn't that figure? Individuality can cost, big time.

> "[Whoever] would do battle with the many-headed hydra of human nature must pay a world of pain & his family must pay it along with him! & only as you gasp your dying breath shall you understand, your life amounted to no more than one drop in a limitless ocean! / Yet what is any ocean but a multitude of drops?"[66]

The whole point of rank and power for those "in power" is to convince the rest of us that we don't have any, that as individuals we don't matter and can do nothing to effect change. The truth is rather as Margaret Mead put it:

"Never doubt that a small group of thoughtful, committed citizens can change the world; indeed, it's the only thing that ever has."

When John Stuart Mill said that "Whatever crushes individuality is despotism, by whatever name it may be called," he wasn't glorifying selfishness or trying to absolve people of individual responsibility. The famous line was immediately followed by this (much less quoted) one: "Collective rights that contravene human rights are wrongs."[67]

Not authenticity but agency is the point of individuality. Authenticity is not the thing that distinguishes bad from good: consequences are. We matter as individuals because we can act with loving intent—or not. Years ago, I had a friend who in her darker moments, when it seemed the worst of humanity was all there was of humanity, would say only half-jokingly that she was rooting for the bacteria. These days, microbial pathogens are doing just fine on their own. "By sheer force of numbers, they overwhelm us."

> "We, as individuals, can't see them, or sense their presence in any useful manner. The most sophisticated of their species have the ability to outwit or manipulate the one microbial sensing system *Homo sapiens* possess: our immune systems."[68]

If the nineteenth-century historian Jules Michelet had difficulty finding " 'the people,' in its highest ideal, in the people," those of this century seem to be finding each other as they take to streets and legislatures around the globe to fight the decades of corporate power and greed that threaten human life on earth.

I'm still rooting for the humans. This much I've come to understand: if I matter as an individual because I can act for the greater good, then I ought to act as if I matter.

Chapter 9

Before Words

Orality precedes literacy, but what precedes orality? What must come before signs and signals of all sorts: before gestures, before vocalizations, before words? What moves an animal, including the human animal, to communicate anything at all by any means at all, if not the body's own primary language of emotion? And what more compelling emotion than love—the subject of so much imaginative literature in story and song.

"A bird does not sing because it has an answer," says a Chinese proverb. "It sings because it has a song." Perhaps a similar truth holds for our own human species; maybe it's true, as a great singer-songwriter of the sixties generation once said, that "Love is what we are, not what we're looking for."[1]

For the sake of love, it is said, humans may lose themselves in complete identification with someone or something else, an identification that dissolves even as it once defined the arch boundaries of the lonely self. Humans in love find this release from self in the self of the beloved; artists find it in the act of creation. When love is lost or the muse turns her back, the attending anguish is emotional; the pain is as great as any physical pain and is experienced as such—by and in the body as a whole (and not in that part of the body called the brain, that master of ceremonies supposed to house thought).

Love and Loss, Memory and Forgetting

I had a twin sister named Frannie. She was a poet, a dancer, a choreographer, and a social activist. She was brave and kind and at least as stubborn as I. When she danced, I thought Wow, F has discovered a secret of space, how to carve it, with the most minute co-ordinations of spoken poetry and bodily movement.

When she passed in June of 2012, I was inconsolable; I could not accept that I would never see her again, that we would never more argue and make up, that we would never again share tears or laughter, that I would never again rush to her aid nor she to mine. Alone after the shiva, I wandered the house, speaking to no one in particular and the universe as a whole, beseeching, repeating out loud the single word, the question without answer: Never? Never? When I finally left the house in the days following, I simply couldn't grasp that the sun shone, that the light shimmered with the joy it always had. There's nothing like losing someone close to manifest and make brutally clear the difference between *my* world and *the* world.

The art and practice of remembrance is important, but so too, as a close friend once counselled, is that of forgetting. It took about eighteenth months after Frannie passed before I could remember her without tears. In my mind, I still argue with her on the issues over which in life we disagreed, except that now I must play both parts. It's never the love I regret, it's the store of anger and resentments that still fire but find no target. Still, I refuse in my soul to deify the one and repress the other. For there's a difference between ordinary forgetting and the forgetting based on repression.

Ordinary forgetting is so ordinary, it doesn't tend to pack much emotional punch. It might even be enabling and allow us, for instance, to heal from the grief that threatens to overwhelm, or to refuse to dwell on what cannot be changed or helped, or more prosaically, to allow us to get out of bed on an ordinary workday morning; even to approach a task that might otherwise seem impossibly ambitious.

I remember that after my book *Practical Grammar* was published, Frannie said to me: "Wow, you finally did it."

"Did what?

"You wrote the grammar book you always said you would."

"Whaddaya mean?"

"Don't you remember how you used to say, 'When I write my grammar book …' "[2]

This declaration, I now recalled, would be followed by variations on the theme of clarity. My grammar book would clarify, not complicate; mine would treat grammar as the substantive study that from an early age had delighted me and that I hoped would delight others.

As identical twins, F and I had always shared a kind of shorthand language, understanding one another with minimal help from words. The thing is, I hadn't remembered that at all until F spoke the words. Here, I marvelled, was an intention so long buried in my subconscious mind and yet so strongly rooted, that the intention had borne fruit despite my having (not quite completely, it turned out) forgotten all about it.

There was another time that F restored a memory I had not only forgotten, but had actively repressed. I was 21 years old, the year I gave birth to my daughter, the lovely Lienne. The baby was finally asleep; F and I were sitting in the living room talking and drinking tea.

"Remember the dwarf you told me about?" she said.

"Whaddaya mean? Like in a novel or something?"

"No, the dwarf you met in Izmir [Turkey]."

"What are you talking about, Fritzie? I've never seen a dwarf in real life, let alone met one."

"Yes, you did, when you were travelling home from the kibbutz in Israel, with your friends Doug and Sandy, and they took you to visit friends of theirs [a prominent city official and his wife, who was a dwarf]. You were really upset, you told me all about it."

"You're nuts, F. That can't be right, I would have remembered that."

And then, just like the proverbial light going on, I did remember that incident—it was in 1969, only several years before this conversation ensued. I remembered especially the pictures on the mantelpiece, feigning normalcy though the woman's stature among her family members was in the photos and in the flesh clearly different from "normal." I remembered most especially her hands, with the large ostentatious rings on most of her fingers, which were fewer than the standard four and one opposable thumb on each. I don't remember exactly what was so upsetting, but I do remember being fascinated and repulsed at the same time, wanting to study those hands but not wanting to be rude, and maybe even being afraid to look. When I thought about it later, and for years after recovering the memory, I thought it bothered me because it was a metaphor for human relations generally, for the falsity, the posturing, that so often passes for genuine communication among humans in society, and even one on one. I had often felt, and sometimes still feel, as if the whole world shares in a common knowledge that eludes me, alone.

In my senior years, my heart tells me otherwise, tells me that all of us share somehow in this loneliness of individuality (perhaps twins more or less than singletons), but also that language (in the service of meaning) can help us close the gap and assuage the pain of knowing and accepting that we are, actually and after all, each quite alone. Even twins are born and die one at a time.

How many times can a heart break? How much time have you got?

The Primordial Language of the Body

Face-to-face (body-to-body) communication entails a kind of emotional commitment. Even if you harbour no sense of responsibility toward another or to others generally, it's still hard to ignore the emotional impact of someone weeping in your presence (or for that matter, someone approaching you with a scowl). Written works can reach us emotionally and intellectually, but they don't entail emotional commitment beyond the time it takes to read them. Contemporary forms of writing by electronic means, such as emailing or texting, can evade emotion most radically. Telephone talk is a touch more committal, because raw emotion is harder to hide in voice than in text. Face-to-face communications provide real-time clues to underlying emotions; but electronic communications may reveal few or none (I don't count emoticons). Participants in email exchanges don't have to respond to emotional tones or undertones. Meanings in electronic messages are emotionally delimited.

Of course, people in face-to-face communication may also be evasive and try to hide their feelings. (In fact, we consider this a mark of civilized behaviour and teach our children how to do it, and we call it socialization). People may also, face to face, put over lies that are only discovered to be lies at a later date, on the basis of other evidence. We are most outraged when they lie in person and we say they did it "straight to my face." There is, then, no special advantage or guarantee of honesty or sincerity or honorable intent in any form of communication—oral, literate, or electronic. You can rob a person with a metaphorical pen online, but also by picking his real-world pockets. You can lie even without words, if by to lie is meant to attempt to deceive or mislead. Just as people can lie with words spoken or written, they can lie by feigning emotions that they don't actually feel.

In fact, well practised liars become masters of the form precisely by lying in the first instance to themselves. Thus it can be difficult to "really know the sign, the tell of an honest man."

> "In the smile of a self-conscious liar certain muscle groups in the face are not activated. They only come to life as the expression of genuine feeling. The smile of a deceiver is flawed, insufficient. But can we see these muscles resting there inert when there's so much local variation in faces, pads of fat, odd concavities, differences of bone structure? Especially difficult when the first and best unconscious move of a dedicated liar is to persuade himself he's sincere. And once he's sincere, all deception vanishes."[3]

Or as Shakespeare put it in Hamlet: "One may smile, and smile, and be a villain."

If you think of meaning as based in the unconscious, then words can be a kind of map to and model of both inner and outer realms. "Where id was, there shall ego be," said my uncle, the late Dr. Henry Kravitz, thus summarizing in seven words the central insight of Sigmund Freud's psychoanalytic theory.[4] Uncle Henry was a man who smiled easily, who was so full of self-awareness and compassion that he seemed to emit light. And he was eminently quotable. He once described phobic fear as "an externalization of an internal fear."

> "It's easier to be afraid of being alone than to deal with your own aggressions; easier to be afraid of the dark than to face your anxiety over your sexual conflicts, and easier to be terrified of elevators than to recognize your own mounting tensions."[5]

I made him laugh once, at the wedding of a cousin, when he took my hand and led me to the dance floor. "Oy, Mackie, relax," he said after a few moments. "I'm trying, I'm trying," I said.

Bringing up to consciousness meanings from the unconscious is the key method not only of Freud's psychoanalysis, but also of writers and artists and virtually anyone who seeks self-knowledge beyond the conventional. In everyday life, when a neurotic pattern becomes conscious—when you hear yourself and become aware of the pattern—it dissipates, loses its hold, because once the pattern is made conscious, the sequence is broken, and the habit of shadow boxing ceases to reliably oblige. The meaning of the pattern has to remain unconscious in order to work. The neurotic strategy depends on the masking of its underlying motive or intent.

I've read somewhere that the unconscious mind doesn't compute negatives. It doesn't understand "no" (and variations such as "do not"). That's why rigid self-control doesn't attain its desired end. For example, if you go on a diet to lose weight, but there's an almond croissant, your favourite, staring you in the face from behind the glass at the patisserie, you can't resist the goodie by telling yourself: "Do not buy that croissant and do not eat it." All your unconscious hears is: BUY that croissant, EAT it. The conscious negotiations meant to dispel the desire instead augment its unconscious power. The only way to resist is to "dis-identify" with the urge to negotiate as soon as it arises. Once you are negotiating, you're well on your way to wolfing it down; the negotiations are rationalizations in advance. If you remain unaware of unconscious "instructions" you will have to wonder why the diet isn't working, and never graduate to the understanding that all strategies work (maybe not equally well)—if you work them.

Words amount to interpretations by the conscious mind of impulses that arise in the unconscious mind. If you identify with these unconscious interpretations, you re-enact a primal feud, unaware that you've set yourself up for a fight, with the outcome unwittingly assured. You've constructed an arena in which:

> "… the communication between the conscious understanding and the unconscious intent is at variance. … If you take sides, you are going to lose—unless you take sides with the unconscious, because the unconscious always wins."[6]

The unconscious mind understands words, even though it doesn't speak them, because both (conscious and unconscious experience) are based in the same body.

> "… all of these processes—emotion, feeling, and consciousness—depend for their execution on representations of the organism. Their shared essence is the body."[7]

The mind—conscious or unconscious—is no more separable from emotion than the brain is from the body.

In common parlance, the words "emotion" and "feeling" are assigned a common, more or less equivalent meaning. But science distinguishes the two, because while it can measure the physiological signs of emotion, it can't touch feeling. For neuroscientists, it is thus necessary to distinguish "that which is external, such as an emotion, from that which is internal, such as a feeling."[8] Here, I don't distinguish between emotion and feeling; I distinguish instead between emotion and sensation, seeing sensation as bodily response that precedes words and has no need of them. Complicating emotion in humans is that they, unlike other animals, can use words to develop defence mechanisms against emotional experience, and these defences blunt consciousness.

One of the most common defence mechanisms is projection, designed to keep unconscious what is unacceptable to the ego, to fortify the guardian at the gate to awareness by assigning to another or others feelings or motives you yourself harbour but are loath to own. Of course, anger is sometimes righteous and blame is sometimes appropriately placed—these are not invariably instruments of projection or false feeling. But where genuine projection is involved, and despite that we develop defences because we feel we need them, the mechanism itself works counterproductively, shoring up grievances and blinding us to our own deepest feelings and to those of others. Robert Coles wrote that his mother wanted her children to be polite, not because of "some smug superficial rote resort to manners … but out of a genuine desire on her part that we learn to break the hold of the holy self, so insistent on its own gratification, in favor of a turn, a bow, to others." She said she wanted them to know, in moments of frustration or disappointment, how to overcome "the old sequence of turning on others when faced with one's own limitations."[9]

This search for someone or something else to blame strikes me as a veritable staple of human behaviour. I gained some insight into how it works, and how early it takes hold, one summer day with Clementine, when she was almost five years old, as we made our way home from the ice-cream parlour.

We were walking along Montreal's Sherbrooke Street and stopped at the corner of Victoria. I was holding Clem's hand as we waited there for the light to turn green, when she suddenly whipped round and collided into the back of my knees as I held on tight to her hand at the busy intersection. My knees buckled and I fell, using my arms to break the fall and avoid falling on top of Clem. Immediately, before I could say a single word, Clem shouted, "It's your fault!" I instinctively understood that she was projecting, that she expected me to blame her for making me fall, and that she protected herself in advance by blaming me first. Going, as my mother would have said, by the seat of my pants, I began to apologize profusely.

"I'm so sorry, I wasn't paying attention. I'll have to learn to be more careful in future. Do you forgive me?"

When Clem didn't answer right away, I repeated the entreaty: "Do you forgive me?" She said that yes, she did, but I could tell she was still trying to figure out what it meant to forgive. Now, as I remember the incident, I think about the effect that my seat-of-the-pants philosophizing (my "gut" reaction) had on Clem. The walk up the hill on Victoria Street, from Sherbrooke to The Boulevard, is a steep mini-marathon, a twenty-minute climb. Though I make it at least several times a week, these days I need to stop at least once along the way to catch my breath. At the time, I didn't think about how arduous a climb that must have been for Clem's small self, trooper though she is, until she stopped once, about half way up, on the pretext of investigating something on the ground. She didn't complain that she was tired, didn't ask me to carry her (as she sometimes used to do). She had figured out "forgiving"—and she was forgiving me!

You cannot say a single new word to Clem without having to engage in extensive explanation, until she understands the word and makes it her own. This is one of the loveliest things about small children, this insistence on understanding words, on acquiring and then exercising the powers of speech. Their progress in this task, the rate of their learning, is nothing short of phenomenal. (I can even remember my own earliest revelation about language, when in a sudden flash, grown-ups in conversation stopped seeming to me like little more than talking knees, when their talk suddenly acquired meaning: so that's what they're doing! I realized that by talking they were acting, that the talk as it droned on, meant something.)

I think now that Clem braved the hill without objection to show me she had forgiven me. I understand that by asking her to forgive me, I was teaching her how to forgive herself, and helping myself to do the same. Why am I surprised that in this rampant, run-wild, mental phenomenon of projection, there is potential for genuine understanding? Of course there is! Where else could genuine understanding begin if not in the human capacity for self-awareness and self-reflection, in the capacity to notice oneself, as it's said, in the act?

A year or so later, Clem's understanding of forgiveness came to even fuller fruition. I was in Toronto looking after her, and it was the night her parents would be returning from a conference in Miami, after a five-day absence. Clem refused to go to sleep, in fact did an astoundingly competent job of forcing herself stay up. She had a score to settle: she was going to let her parents have it but good for leaving her in the first place; in preparation, she was test-driving her original anger with them and rehearsing her response—I just happened to be there. After she hurled a couple of nasty comments in my direction, I said to her: "The way you are speaking to me now makes me think you don't want me to be here with you."

"I don't!" she screamed.

"Fine, Clem, then I'm going downstairs to the kitchen to wash the dinner dishes and that's where I'll be if you need me. And one more thing, Clem, just so you know, you're not the only person in the world with feelings. For example, I, your Bubby, I have feelings. And when you speak to me like this, you hurt my feelings."

Some ten minutes later, Clem entered the kitchen, her eyes red from crying and tears still streaming down her beautiful face. "I'm sorry I hurt your feelings, Bubby," she said through her sobs. It was so heartfelt, her intent so immediately clear, that I was moved in kind. I fell to my knees, hands still sudsy with dishwater, and held her close and murmured words of endearment and told her I knew she didn't mean to hurt my feelings. I thought about this incident for months afterward, and the memory retains its vividness even now. I thought that if grownups could somehow maintain this connection to their own feelings, surely the world would become that stubbornly elusive dream of a common humanity, that better place.

Animal Communication and Human Exceptionalism

The language of words is supposed by many to be at the root of an assumed superiority of humans over other animals, what makes human nature "exceptional"—what distinguishes the human species from the whole rest of the animal kingdom, endowing it with unique and nearly divine abilities. I concede that humans are the only animals that have over eons developed a complex language of words, the only animals that write and publish the books I so cherish, but that's no reason to believe that the other animals cannot in their own ways laugh or weep, in their own vernaculars tell stories, and by their own means engage in purposeful or intentional communication.

Once, in discussion with Clementine about the superpowers of various super-heroes and how she wished to acquire these powers, I said to her: "You know, love is the greatest superpower of all." She tossed that one off right quick. "No," she said, "I mean *real* superpowers like jumping over tall buildings." (I stand corrected.)

Nevertheless, many animals evince abilities at least as impressive as, and even far superior to, those of our own species, abilities that would qualify even according to Clementine as super.

> "For millennia, biologists have discovered to their astonishment and delight the ingenious contrivances of the living world: the biomechanical perfection of cheetahs, the infrared pinhole cameras of snakes, the sonar of bats, the superglue of barnacles, the steel-strong silk of spiders, the dozens of grips of the human hand, the DNA repair machinery in all complex organisms. After all, entropy and more malevolent forces like predators and parasites are constantly gnawing at an organism's right to life and do not forgive slapdash engineering."[10]

In terms of speed and raw physical prowess, there are among the other animals many much faster than we, and better by far at running and jumping. The cheetah, earth's fastest animal, can run 70 miles per hour (for ten to twenty seconds at a stretch), and the puma can leap as high as 40 feet; some species of hummingbird can beat their wings up to 80 times a second.

Some animals can see way better than humans can. Eagles, with a high concentration of cone cells and other visual advantages, can see about four times as much detail with their eyes as we can with ours. Sharks don't need to rely on eyes to track and consume their prey with lightning precision: they pick up the electrical impulses of movement with unerring accuracy.

Bats are the only mammals that can fly, and they use echolocation, emitting high pitched sound waves and using the echoes to "see" even in the dark. Bloodhounds have much greater ability to smell than humans: with noses that contain some 200 million cells, they can track the scent of another animal days after it has left an area. There is even a lizard, the plumed basilisk, that Christ-like can stand on its hind legs and walk on water.[11]

In his book *The Corfu Trilogy*, Gerald Durrell tells of the rotifer (a microscopic animal commonly found in ditches, puddles, and ponds). Rotifers appear to die when their watery habitats dry up, only to come alive again with replenishing rains. Without the water that sustains their life, rotifers become like dust particles blown around by wind, but unlike dust particles they retain the seed of life.

> "If it is a hot summer ... and the pond is liable to dry up, they go down to the bottom and form a sort of hard shell round themselves. It's a sort of suspended animation, for the pond can dry up for ... seven or eight years, and they will just lie there in the dust. But as soon as the first rain falls and fills the pond, they come to life again."[12]

Some would say, yes, but humans are the only animals aware of their own mortality. I don't think that's true either: we may be the only animals who think we understand death because we can talk about it, but human talk, Lord and Evolution know, is not necessarily evidence of understanding. I think of this intent to live, and the sheer force of it, a force shared by all forms of life and life itself, as the ultimate meaning of evolution.

Only humans use words, but all animals communicate (often more succinctly and more sincerely than humans)—by means of vocalizations, visual cues, gestures, and scents. The more social a species, the more it communicates.

> "Communication and cognition are intertwined. Powers of thought shape the ability to communicate which in turn influences the social arrangements in which animals live, which further fuel cognition and

> communication—and so on across evolutionary time, in multiple feedback loops that have helped shape animal societies. ... That parrots live in treetops and dolphins live underwater is secondary to the social forces that shaped them."[13]

All languages—bodily and linguistic—serve to communicate, and communication is essential to all species, especially social species.

Cases in point: Elephants can stamp their feet to produce vibrations so strong they can travel for miles to other elephants, who receive these messages with their feet. In the desert, kangaroo rats (relatives of pocket gophers) dig burrows and from the safety of home drum with their feet to communicate underground with others of their species. Insects like crickets and grasshoppers stridulate (produce sound by rubbing body parts together), and so do some insect-eating mammals, such as tenrecs (of the same family as hedgehogs). To alert others in their hive to a nearby bounty of pollen bearing flowers, honey bees perform intricate dances that spell it out. Even the skin of a whale shark transmits meaning. The patterns on its skin "can be understood as an evolutionary adaptation for conveying information—not intentionally, but instead passively, by blending with the patterns of sun-dappled water."[14]

All of these body languages evolve, just as human languages do. Evolution may not intend, but living creatures do. However stark the differences between species, all appear to share one common rock-bottom intent: to go on living as individuals. Despite the fact that what is born must die, all creatures are equipped at birth with built-in abilities and automatic responses (call them instincts) that serve this common goal and delay the inevitable.

Without some form of communication, social life would be impossible for the human species as for all other social species, for whom communal decision making is a necessary fact of life. Without the ability to communicate, it would be impossible to maintain social relationships—and so, species survival. We are not the only animals that "vote." We think of decision-making systems as the exclusive preserve of humans, but such systems, though they don't involve ballot boxes (or removal of ballot boxes), exist throughout the animal kingdom, where they rely not on political hierarchies but rather on a kind of group cohesion, on community.

> "Consensus decision-making systems are found throughout the animal kingdom, from honeybees to swans to elephants. Rarely does one dominant individual decide where everyone else will go."[15]

African wild dogs are thought to indicate their preferences with sneezing; whooper swans signal theirs through a quorum of head movements; ant colonies do it with chemical signals. "For mated red-crowned cranes, ritual dances help nourish a lifelong relationship."

> "The diversity of biological communication systems isn't just a wonderful chapter of natural history. It's the foundation of social life. … The study of animal communication isn't just about how animals exchange messages. It's about what these messages make possible."[16]

From simple greetings to mating rituals, the principle that communication shapes social intelligence operates in all species. Hermit crabs, when they outgrow their native shells, negotiate exchanges of shells with others of their kind. The complex social life of American crows (sometimes described as feathered apes) is said to explain their cognitive abilities. As intelligence shapes social life, social life in turn shapes intelligence.

Although humans may deem animal communications "merely" biological, in fact human communication also relies on body language and not alone—and not primarily—on the complex language of words.

Jane Goodall tells the wonderful story of an experience she had while studying chimpanzees in Tanzania's Gombe Reserve. Among her favourite chimps was one she named David. She'd been following him for a while, and when she found him sitting by a stream, as if, she says, he were waiting for her, she held out to him in her hand a palm nut, a favourite food. David didn't seem to want the goodie:

> "… he reached out, he took the nut and with one movement dropped it, but at the same time he held my hand with a very gentle pressure. That's how chimpanzees reassure each other and calm each other down. So it was like a communication that didn't need words, which we both inherited from a very ancient primate past. It was as if he were saying, 'I'm not spurning you; I just don't want the nut.' "[17]

Systems of wordless communication abound:

> "All animals have systems of communication based on songs, in the case of birds, or displays or smells. Proto-humans had their own systems of communication, as do modern chimpanzees and gorillas, involving grunting and displays. … Humans are not the first of the three million species now alive that communicate by voice. Vervet monkeys,

> for example, have a proto-language that has at least nine different words. … there's a grunt that means 'leopard' and a different grunt that means 'snake' and another grunt that means 'eagle' and one that means 'strange monkey.' What vervets lack is grammar, the ability to combine words in particular ways to generate new meanings. Monkeys don't have that. Chimpanzees don't have it."[18]

It seems clear nevertheless that some animals do indeed possess languages that in fundamental ways work very much like word-based human languages, complete with vocabularies, names, and even syntax. Other animals (not only vervet monkeys) employ different kinds of vocalizations to warn about the different kinds of predators (one for aerial threats that says "head for ground" and another for terrestrial enemies that says "climb that tree for all you're worth"). The Australian magpie is vocally prolific; its vocabularies contain hundreds of syllables. Many animals, without benefit of names, use the sense of smell to recognize each other as individuals (sockeye salmon, for instance, recognize their siblings by scent) or by unique calls that function as names (sperm whales recognize other individuals as members of their family and of their clan). "It's recently been shown that even wasps can recognize the faces of other wasps."[19]

> "… many other creatures recognize individuals by the sound of their clicks, howls, trumpets, and songs—their voices. Because voice represents the individual, voices are symbols of identity. … For a symbol to work, one must have a concept of what the symbol represents."[20]

The differences between the way humans communicate with words and the way other animals communicate (without them) is finally a difference of degree, not kind.

> "Prairie dogs have communication systems so rich that they've been compared to human language. … It's not only overtly brainy animals like primates and elephants who have language-like communication systems. Japanese tit songbirds arrange their calls syntactically. Meaning changes with sound order. Coral trout were among the first fish to demonstrate referential communication."[21]

Various birds employ syntax—the critical element in human language—by arranging sounds in different order for different meanings.

> "Syntax has been described in the calls of Japanese tits, small songbirds related to chickadees, and in Carolina chickadees as well. These

> birds produce many fewer sounds than we do, but simple syntax helps make the most of what they have. And although more complex forms of grammar—such as embedding messages within other messages, as demonstrated in this sentence—are exceptionally developed in human language, European starling calls also appear to contain nested grammatical forms."[22]

Our human language is (justly) prized, but there's a difference between pride and arrogance. Pride can inspire and empower; arrogance is often destructive and at best misleading to the point of blindness.

> "… many people still talk of the 'lower' animals. This despite the certainty, based on the sheer numbers of species, that God clearly has what the great British biologist J. B. S. Haldane called 'an inordinate fondness for beetles.' "[23]

Humans see themselves as the top-ranking species, but if numbers of individuals in a given species counted for much, it would be the invertebrates most likely to succeed and inherit the earth; they comprise the vast majority—a whopping 97 per cent—of all species alive today.

In terms of understanding the other animals and the toll our human ways have taken on so many species of flora and fauna, we do well to remember the wisdom inherent in these supposedly lower life forms and life styles. The other animals, after all, do not foul their own nests, and they affirm life, the mother of all. Notes one contemporary writer: "A century ago, people laughed at the notion that we were descended from monkeys. Today, the individuals most offended by that claim are the monkeys."[24]

Even plants dig deep for water and reach relentlessly for the life-giving sun. In recent decades, biologists are coming to understand what indigenous cultures have always known: "that the plants and animals have their own councils, and a common language."[25]

Of course, it's not all sweetness and light in the "natural world"; it's more complex than my preceding homilies would suggest. Microscopic pathogens gather in algae with as much determination as pretty plants reach for the sun. There is aggression in the rest of the animal kingdom too. Hyena pups are born ready to go for each others' throats. Jackals hunt and scavenge for food in packs, calculating how best to isolate and surround their chosen prey. Vultures feed mainly on carrion and will gather with others of their kind in anticipation of a death before convening on the corpse to dine.

There's a famous photograph taken during the 1993 famine in Sudan by former South African photojournalist Kevin Carter. It depicts a child struggling against the final stages of starvation, while about five feet away sits a vulture, waiting patiently. According to some accounts, Carter chased the vulture away and the child "recovered enough to resume her trek" to a UN food station. The photo ran first in the *New York Times* on 26 March 1993, before being picked up worldwide. Carter, who received a Pulitzer Prize for this photograph, died by suicide on 27 July 1994. He was 33 years old and flat broke. According to Wikipedia, he left a suicide note that read in part:

> "The pain of life overrides the joy to the point that joy does not exist. ... depressed ... without phone ... money for rent ... money for child support ... money for debts ... money!!! ... I am haunted by the vivid memories of killings & corpses & anger & pain ... of starving or wounded children, of trigger-happy madmen, often police, of killer executioners."

In creature struggles for survival, even my treasured birds are not immune. One writer noted that the Galápagos is home to "the vampire finch, an affable little bird that nests in cacti, has elaborate and entirely different songs for different islands, and feeds on blood."[26] There are indeed aspects of nature red in tooth and claw, but that's not all there is (and perhaps more to the point, humans are hardly immune from or above the bloody fray). While competition and rivalry exist in the nonhuman world just as they do in the human world, such competition in the former is for actual resources such as food, not for the shoring up of self-narratives. Among the other animals, it's hunger and not anger that drives predation.

Here again, the other animals have something important to teach us about non-violence, for even though carnivorous animals hunt others for food, they also know something about how to avert unnecessary conflict and settle disputes when conflicts do occur. The other animals may behave in violent ways, but for the sake of survival, not for that of bottled rage.

> "Male elephant seals can easily weigh several tons. Their battles are commensurately ferocious. Most disputes are settled without coming to blows, though, with males instead posturing and trumpeting and slapping the ground to convey their strength. ... Ultraviolet markings on Augrabies flat lizards signify an aggressive temperament, giving other lizards the chance to make an informed decision about whether they really want to fight."[27]

As in the rest of the animal kingdom, communication among people is an exchange not of information but of meaning:

> "Human communication is not just a transfer of information like two fax machines connected with a wire; it is a series of alternating displays of behavior by sensitive, scheming, second-guessing, social animals."[28]

The exchange may be facilitated by a common language but it doesn't absolutely require words or other tools beyond body language. People who speak different languages and people who can't read can still "read strangers' eyes."

> "They understand that grand coincidence brings us together, upright and within earshot, in this flickering generation of human life on this durable planet—common language or not."[29]

The power of communication exceeds the power of words. Our own human fixation on words as the primary means of communicating may blind us to this fact and to our own assumptions.

***

Scientists used to believe (and some still do believe) that the other animals can communicate only "emotionally," that they are incapable of reference to objects or events other than experienced emotional states (such as alarm), and most important, that they do not communicate with intent. Such views regard animal communication as a product of the involuntary autonomic nervous system—as if built-in meanings of body language were self-explanatory.

> "Homeostatic regulation is accomplished by the development of special nerve cells and nerve nets (or plexuses) scattered throughout our bodies, as well as by direct chemical means (hormones, for example). These scattered nerve cells and plexuses become organized into a system or confederation that is largely autonomous in its functioning—hence its name, the autonomic nervous system. The autonomic nervous system was only recognized and explored in the early part of the twentieth country, whereas many of the functions of the central nervous system, especially the brain, had already been mapped in detail in the nineteenth century. This is something of a paradox, for the autonomic nervous system evolved long before the central nervous system."[30]

I do not agree with the common assumption that animals don't vocalize with intent or meaning; neither that they need a "theory of mind" in order to intend or to mean what they communicate. In fact, I think what does distinguish our language from that of the other animals is that the others don't speak *without* meaning or intent; neither do they consider why they vocalize and thus they cannot forget what they are "speaking" about. They certainly don't ask themselves such questions. An animal calling out danger to its group may be doing so unconsciously (instinctively, as an older scientific era would have it), without pre-thought or planning—true. But that animal is clearly communicating in response to environmental conditions, that is to say for a reason, and that communication is understood by others of the species.

We impose a human-centric lens when it comes to communication among the other animals, and then, in a major disconnect, we imagine that their languages—the essence or meaning of their communications—are quintessentially different from our own. The truth is they are quintessentially the same.

Do the other animals, then, possess language?

> "I do think animals have languages, but they are entirely truthful languages. It seems that we are the only animals who can lie—who can think and say what is not so and never was so, or what has never been yet might be. We can invent; we can suppose; we can imagine. All that gets mixed in with memory. And so we're the only animals who can tell stories."[31]

I don't agree with this idea of the "entirely truthful" nature of animal language, nor that humans are the only animals that can and do lie. Mammals other than humans (and perhaps other animals) can and do practice deception, as for example when a monkey hides food, looking around to ensure the act of hiding and the hiding place itself haven't been witnessed by other hungry members of its group. Maybe what's true is not that humans are the only animals that lie, but that humans are the only animals that can and do lie *to themselves*. Neither is storytelling unique to humans. Some animals can tell stories with pantomime (what else to call the "mapping" dances of bees?).

Of course there is a difference between the abstract thought that literacy enabled in humans and the more concrete thinking and languages of other animals. Yet regardless of the kind of languages used to communicate, the fact remains that everything that lives communicates. Even plants:

> "That plants could be likened to animals seems a contradiction in terms. Yet in recent years, scientists have described many animal-like patterns of botanical behavior. Plants can share nutrients with needy neighbors,

> react differently to related plants than they do to those unrelated, and even learn by association. … Lacking central nervous systems, plants are supposed to be incapable of [cognition]—yet when a leaf is damaged, it releases chemical signals that alert other leaves, in a manner not unlike the cells in an animal's body. Plants may even communicate with one another, perhaps using sound and even magnetic fields as well as chemicals."[32]

Even the supposedly inanimate:

> "Before the aurora borealis appears, the sensitive needles of compasses all over the world are restless for hours, agitating on their pins in airplanes and ships, trembling in desk drawers, in attics, in boxes on shelves."[33]

In the sense of responding to an environment, not only living creatures but all things communicate, because everything's connected. As one indigenous biologist put it: "The land knows you, even when you are lost.[34]

And again, not all sweetness and light: even a deadly virus communicates in the unfortunate sense that it makes contact, though uninvited and unwelcome. (In April of 2020, when she was three years old, my friend Zoë Macdonald understood the essence of a viral threat even though she mixed up the words in voicing her unique appreciation for the powers of the corona virus to cause disease and death: "We can't go to the park," she said, "because of the corona pirates.")

Ultimately, animal communication, at least among mammals, is very much like our own. Qualities and abilities once thought of as uniquely human (not only language and tool making but also thought and empathy) turn out not to be such marks of distinction after all. The other animals fashion tools to accomplish goals and communicate a wide range of emotion.

Animals tell their own stories in their own ways; they love and hate, forge and shift allegiances depending on changing circumstances; they even get humour. There is something like laughter that has been described in kea parrots, and in rats, who apparently "laugh while playing and when they're tickled" (even though without amplifying technology, we cannot hear their high-pitched voices).[35]

The emotions we think of as especially human, are not unique to humans; they are in fact widespread in other life forms, and not just in our primate cousins, whose expression we easily recognize because it most resembles our own.

We may describe emotion in the rest of the animal kingdom with adjectives different from those we reserve for ourselves (not heartfelt or heroic or brave, for instance, but instead: instinctual, automatic, unconscious). It used to be supposed that the other animals are incapable of the emotions we consider strictly human, such as altruism. More recent science says animals are not invariably selfish or amoral; ethics are after all evolutionary adaptations in the service of survival.

> "Psychologically speaking, animals can therefore be perfectly unselfish. If we scratch Washoe, the ape who rescued a drowning female, or Mae Perm, the elephant who guided her blind buddy, it is unlikely that we'll see bleeding hypocrites. Rather, we'll discover two kind souls, highly sensitive to the predicament of others."[36]

Jaak Panksepp, who founded the field of "affective neuroscience," saw his work ignored and even ridiculed for years before it was accepted and began to influence scientific thinking. He "placed human and animal emotions on a continuum":

> "His work situated the emotions in ancient subcortical brain areas shared across all vertebrates rather than in the recently expanded cerebral cortex. His 1998 magnum opus, *Affective Neuroscience: The Foundations of Human and Animal Emotions*, became a best seller by academic standards."[37]

Even the much cited "theory of mind" (the ability to divine, to anticipate and interpret, the intentions of others) doesn't fit the "only humans" bill. In some respects, the other animals are actually better at this than humans in terms of consequences (perhaps because the other animals aren't so easily misled by self-images). No animal in the wild has to say "Hey, watch out! There's a cheetah nearby, intent on making you lunch!" but it's still the last of the herd to notice the fierce predator that *becomes* the cheetah's lunch. Both animals, hunter and hunted, understand the situation and the signals (that's why stealth is of the essence in predators that hunt singly and why sharp senses are critical for their chosen prey).

I once watched, entranced for hours, a BBC series called *Serengeti* that told stories of the animal kingdom by personalizing specific animals as dramatis personae. In one scene, I couldn't help but think of Donald Trump (thoughts about whom I normally do my best to avoid). In this scene, a particularly nasty baboon leader is foraging next to a waterway, some distance away from the plebeians of his herd, who are used to keeping their distance from their temperamental chief. Baboons are supposed to have each other's backs under normal circumstances. In this instance, all the other baboons watch silently as a crocodile with culinary intent creeps closer and closer to their oblivious leader. Not a single member of the watchful tribe warns him. He escapes with barely a second to spare, but I am pleased to report that in a later episode, this Trumpish baboon leader does finally meet his just deserts at the hands of another male baboon, one lowly in status but noble in mien, as the latter rises to the occasion in a successful attempt to protect an orphaned baby.

What has the preceding to do with words? Perhaps only this: that we humans are ferocious in our attempts to establish our identities in terms of relative status, and especially by means of label-words (unlike the great apes, for instance, who stick with such nonverbal cues as chest-thumping). The other animals don't need to pay so much attention to badges of identity: instead of "having" identities, they are, to invent a word: id-entities. But what most distinguishes us and our identities from the "natural" world is what we imagine to be our god-sanctioned or socially-sanctioned dominion over the realm.

You might expect animal scientists at least to understand that the other animals, without words, are nevertheless sensate: that they feel pain and pleasure, just as humans do. That is sadly not the case. In the age before anesthetics, scientists conducted experiments on live dogs. The venerated Descartes saw the practice as justified in the pursuit of knowledge. The countercultural Voltaire wrote in passionate objection:

> "Barbarians seize this dog, which in friendship surpasses man so prodigiously; they nail it on a table, and they dissect it alive in order to show the mesenteric veins. You discover in it all the same organs of feeling that are in yourself. Answer me, machinist, has nature arranged all the means of feeling in this animal, so that it may not feel? Has it nerves in order to be impassible?"[38]

In his book *The Tale of the Dueling Neurosurgeons*, Sam Kean wrote about "a series of diabolical experiments" conducted in 1941 on rats by the famous neuroscientist Roger Sperry, who wanted to test his idea that neurons are interchangeable and brain circuits can be rewired. The experiments involved:

> "... opening up the rats' two back legs, finding the nerves that carried pain signals to the brain, and switching them, so that the left pain nerve

> was now located in the right leg, and vice versa. / Once a rat recovered from surgery, Sperry placed it on an electrified grille where, if it stepped on a certain spot, it got a shock. The result was a black comedy. … The rat's neurons never learned better … Month after month passed, but no matter how many times the poor booby shocked one leg, it always hiked the other one up."[39]

Poor booby, indeed. And what of the neurosurgeon? Was it really necessary to torture a helpless animal to understand that all creatures are sensate and that it is this sensate creature, not its butchered neurons, that learns? Contemporary studies have shown "identical opiate receptors" in the brains of all vertebrates as well as in insects and other invertebrates.[40] Such understanding is apparently more amenable to compassionate novelists than to emotion-blind scientists.

> "It was once convenient to think biblically, to believe we're surrounded for our benefit by edible automata on land and sea. Now it turns out that even fish feel pain. This is the growing complication of the modern condition, the expanding circle of moral sympathy. Not only distant people are our brothers and sisters, but foxes too, and laboratory mice, and now the fish."[41]

Studies with the anti-depressant drug diazepam showed the drug "helps both fish and humans [and] hints at profound neurological similarities. … the consensus view is now that fish do feel pain." But "a parallel case is even more baffling." For decades, scientists believed that human infants were "subhuman organisms" whose vocalizations were random, who could feel neither pleasure (their smiles were deemed the result of gas) nor, more gruesomely, pain.

> "Serious scientists conducted torturous experiments on human infants with needle pricks, hot and cold water, and head restraints, to make the point that they feel nothing. The babies' reactions were considered emotion-free reflexes. … Only in the 1980s did medical procedures change, when it was revealed that babies have a full-blown pain response with grimacing and crying. Today we read about these experiments with disbelief. One wonders if their pain response couldn't have been noticed earlier!"[42]

***

Bob Dylan, bard of an American generation, was right to sing: "It's all just a dream, babe, a vacuum, a scheme, babe, that sucks you into feeling like thi-i-i-is." But he was counseling self-awareness, not avoidance, of feelings. Emotion reflected upon has greater potential to raise consciousness than the secondary phenomenon of words has ever been or perhaps ever will be. The words we best remember (or miss-remember) are inevitably those that evoked strong feeling in their moment.

Many of the problems of individuals in human society are based on simple human stupidity; but many others are based on miscommunication. Take for instance variations on the themes and manoeuvres of passive aggression. Active or outright aggression is more dangerous, at least theoretically, but it doesn't take fifty years to figure out, and response in the interest of self-defence is immediate. Passive aggression is different: it uses words and deeds not readily identifiable as hostile to express hostility against a chosen target, to "gaslight" the target and simultaneously avoid responsibility. It's a cowardly mechanism, often used by those lacking awareness of their own unconscious hostility, who would likely describe their behaviour as friendly concern or "honesty"—the kind that cuts like a hot knife. (Tony Morrison wrote somewhere that she learned to discount as potential partners men who said "honest" things like "You're wearing that?!" immediately on hearing them voiced.)

Emotion cannot exist without the apparently perturbing fact of individual bodies, bounded, we suppose, by skin. And like emotion itself, individuality is hardly a foregone good, hardly unassailable: individuals may behave in ways compassionate but also in ways (quite consciously) unconscionable.

> "One night in a Quito hotel room, I read the Gideon Bible, an edition with facing columns in English and Spanish. I read for twenty minutes before a double-edged razor blade fell from its pages."[43]

Even empathy cuts both ways.

> "The typical definition of empathy—sensitivity to another's emotions, understanding another's situation—says nothing about being nice. Like intelligence or physical strength, it is a neutral capacity. It can be used for good or evil, depending on one's intentions. … Despite the rosy-colored assumptions surrounding the term, empathy is an all-purpose capacity."[44]

Feelings don't operate on a binary footing. Feeling involves gradations of suffering and pain as well as of pleasure and joy; it involves rivalry as well as mutual aid. You cannot attenuate the ability to feel in only one direction. For example, young males are expected to act like big boys, who as Everyone knows, don't cry. On the other hand, as my mother used to say: "A man who cannot cry is a man not to be trusted."

In pursuit of objective knowledge, science tends to ignore the import of emotion. On the other hand, to glorify or privilege emotion won't do either. Emotion is not like magic fairy dust, that puts an end to all struggle and misery among humans. Feelings are not uniformly positive, they can also be destructive, even when they make us feel good, maybe even especially when they make us feel good: "The illusion that exalts us," said Pushkin, "is dearer to us than ten thousand truths."[45] Not invariably, though; there are notable exceptions to Pushkin's general rule: "I no longer need to take part in the competition of the big brains," said Einstein nearly a century ago. "Participating [in the process] has always seemed to me to be an awful type of slavery no less evil than the passion for money or power."[46]

Whether you believe in God or in Evolution (or more rarely in both), nothing protects the individual from the time and chance that happens to them all. Life is not a protection racket; there is no deal.

Still, I cannot help but think that if humans were not so fiercely self-conceived as utterly separate from each other, bolstered in this conception by psychological mechanisms for displacing emotion, and if they could retain their feeling connection to their emotions instead of "outgrowing" them, learning to suppress emotion per se—if this, then wouldn't a better world be closer to hand? Wouldn't there arise new paths to this better world, along with the will and the means to achieve it? Given greater emotional self-awareness on a wide scale, wouldn't humans move to alleviate unnecessary suffering and eliminate routine and systemic injustice? Wouldn't we humans, with all our fancy talk and technology, be more likely to act in concert to achieve such ends?

I look back at the record of the years and marvel: all that's happened in these many years really has happened, though it seems hardly possible. And what I most long to feel is the exaltation of which the late great Leonard Cohen sang, about "the minor fall, the major lift," and nothing on my lips but "hallelujah."

The Old Mind/Body Problem

Charles Darwin long ago wrote: "The fact that the lower animals are excited by the same emotions as ourselves is so well established, that it will not be necessary to weary the reader by many details."[47]

At the risk of wearying the reader, I note that old ideas may persist, long outliving their best-before dates, and common practice has a way of lining up with vested interests and established biases. "In every argument, there are hidden assumptions," Neil Turok wrote. "The more deeply they are buried, the longer it takes to reveal them."[48]

That the other animals have emotions and a mental life similar to those of humans was an idea dismissed by the sociobiology of the 1970s and 1980s, despite decades of experiments that failed to find a defining difference. Not tool use, not symbolic communication, not mirrors neurons, not theory of mind—none clearly distinguishes the human animal from the others. Not even the mapped human genome sets humans apart. Genes by themselves are basically inert: they don't determine anything on their own, distinct from their environment and circumstances. "Wondering which gene is responsible for a trait such as intelligence is like wondering which piano key is responsible for a symphony."[49]

Human emotions and human communications are utterly comparable to those of the other animals, because human bodies are equally so.

> "If you look at side-by-side drawings of human, elephant, and dolphin brains, the similarities overwhelm the differences. We are essentially the same, merely molded by long experience into different outer shapes for coping with different outer surroundings … But beneath the skin, kin."[50]

Contemporary studies negate the idea of humans as separate and quintessentially different from the whole animal kingdom. Mammalian bodies especially, including mammalian brains, are more similar than different.

> "… all mammalian brains including ours operate largely on the same principles with much of the same equipment. They all have nerve cells (neurons made of the same stuff and in the same way), and hormones that stimulate the brain and such organs as the pituitary and thyroid glands."[51]

In the organism, emotion is primary; privileging thought over emotion is a relatively recent notion: "For most of recorded history, human beings situated the mind—and by extension the soul—not within the brain but within the heart."[52]

Albert Einstein, one the most celebrated intellects of the twentieth century, also saw emotion as the prime mover: "Feeling and longing are the motive force behind all human endeavour and human creation, in however exalted a guise the latter may present themselves to us."[53]

Because emotion is identical with its expression, it surpasses words. Emotion is hardwired, as it would have to be. Essential bodily functions are too essential to be left to the vagaries of what we call thought or reason. No humans would last long if they had to depend on reasoning to keep their lungs breathing or their hearts beating, or to respond appropriately to basic needs and environmental threats. If they did have to depend on reasoning, humans would long ago have forgotten how to breathe (*pace* Bob Dylan).

Whether you call it emotion or feeling or sensation, body language—this primal resource of the living—unlike the language of words, does not require sequencing to make "sense."

> "The difference between a thought and a raw feeling is that every and any thought, be it a fantasy, a theory, a memory, has the defining feature of having a beginning, a middle and an end—an ordered temporal sequence that a pure emotion does not require."[54]

The biological substrate of language is not a brain hemisphere or a "module" in the brain; it's not a collection of neurons or the synapses where they fire. It's emotions that move bodies.

> "Life and the life urge inside the boundary that circumscribes an organism preceded the appearance of nervous systems, of brains."[55]

Emotion is not dependent on language, and neither is thought, because thought is not synonymous with words. Albert Einstein famously said that words, spoken or written, played only a secondary role in his thought process.

> "The psychical entities which seem to serve as elements in thought are certain signs and more or less clear images which can be 'voluntarily' reproduced and combined. … This combinatory play seems to be the essential feature in productive thought—before there is any connection with logical construction in words or other kinds of signs which can be communicated to others. The above-mentioned elements are, in my case, of visual and some muscular type. Conventional words or other signs have to be sought for laboriously only in a secondary state, when the mentioned associative play is sufficiently established and can be reproduced at will."[56]

On the other hand, without words, thought cannot be communicated to others, as Einstein also noted: "Describing the physical laws without reference to geometry is similar to describing our thoughts without words."[57] Thought is not separable from emotion.

> "Emotions are an essential part of our intellect. The idea that they are separate remains so ingrained, however, that it survives in full force in many circles."[58]

Both emotion and thought require homes in living bodies. Like emotion, thought is a body language. Yet despite overwhelming evidence to the contrary, the human brain is still widely supposed to be different not only from the brains of all other creatures, but more strangely, separate as well from the human body. Though it is the source of both emotion and thought, the body gets little respect compared to the famed life of the mind.

> "The mind wants to live forever, or to learn a very good reason why not. The mind wants the world to return its love, or its awareness; the mind wants to know all the world, and all eternity, and God. The mind's sidekick, however, will settle for two eggs over easy."[59]

Thus the old and tired mind/body debate (aka the "problem" of consciousness) persists; it begins with the buried assumption that the body is somehow separate from the brain and even more removed from the mind. Neuroscientists explain how the brain communicates with the body by reference to special brain cells called neurons. Only neurons aren't that special, not the exclusive property of the brain, and not the exclusive property of humans or mammals or primates. Even invertebrates have neurons.

> "A person's individual brain neurons are basically indistinguishable from those of a killer whale, elephant, or mouse—or fly. The synapses, various nerve-cell types, connections, even the genes creating those neurons: essentially identical across species."[60]

What does make human neurons different from the neurons of other organisms is their much greater number and organization.

> "Although neurons may differ in shape and size, they are essentially the same from the most primitive animal life to the most advanced. It is their number and organization that differ: we have a hundred billion nerve cells, while a jelly fish has a thousand. But their status as cells capable of rapid and repetitive firing is essentially the same."[61]

Much ado is made of the human prefrontal cortex, but as with other aspects of animal/human dualism, the difference is one of degree and not kind. Our primate cousins also sport a prefrontal cortex, but in humans that equipment is "in evolutionary and developmental terms very sophisticated, occupying as it does 33 per cent of the human brain but only 17 per cent of the brains of our nearest relatives, the chimps."[62]

Perhaps, though, space occupied and complexity of organization are not necessarily or invariably species advantages. Translated from a wider than human-centric perspective: humans are mammals with overdeveloped brains—and underdeveloped emotions.

According only secondary status to the body feeds the persistence of the debate over the "problem" of consciousness. "How a conscious mind emerges from a physical brain is still the central paradox of neuroscience."[63] Yet even in science, the emotions of the body remain more powerful than the conjectures of the supposedly separate mind.

> "Our ability to do science is rooted in our relationship with the universe, our nature as living beings. Our feelings and instincts are far more profound than our ideas. Our ideas allow us to imagine many things, but they can be unreliable, misguided, or misleading. It is the real world that keeps us honest."[64]

Then again, what's real and what's not are often enough in doubt. When Clem was about six years old, we were watching together a video with cartoon characters, when she suddenly turned to me and asked: "We're in reality, right?" And then, pointing to the screen, she said: "But they're not." When she looked to me again for confirmation (I had to bite my tongue to abstain from debate), I said: "Uh, right." When she's older, I'll direct her to mathematics, the language of science, as described in Neil Turok's fine book, *The Universe Within*:

> "Mathematics is our 'third eye,' allowing us to see and understand how things work in realms so remote from our experience that they cannot be visualized. Mathematicians are often viewed as unworldly, working in a dreamed up, artificial setting. But quantum physics teaches us that, in a very real sense, we all live in an imaginary reality."[65]

The trouble with words is also the promise of words. What does distinguish human emotion and human thought from that of the other animals is the kind of relationship forged by words:

> "... the way in which emotions have become connected to the complex ideas, values, principles, and judgments that only humans can have, and in that connection lies our legitimate sense that human emotion is special. Human emotion is not just about sexual pleasure or fear of snakes. It is also about the horror of witnessing suffering and about the satisfaction of seeing justice served."[66]

Science favours information over emotion, numbers over anecdote, and logic over intuition. We are right to second-guess our subjective emotional reactions, but we are wrong to rule them out. Greater self-awareness, especially of feelings, is not opposed to knowledge, but one of its most powerful vectors. The intelligence of the mind is none other than the intelligence of body. Emotion is the prototypical form of information. Raised consciousness profits the soul and the social peace.

Dean Burnett, a neuroscientist and stand-up comedian, asked the crucial question: What determines how human attention is directed? "If the brain is constantly being bombarded with sensory information, what is it about certain stimuli or input that prioritises it over other things?"[67]

What else but intent?

> "Choice of attention—to pay attention to this and ignore that—is to the inner life what choice of action is to the outer."[68]

What if there is an energy beyond the electromagnetic spectrum and its name is intent? Then it matters to become aware of the intent at the base of the words we employ.

Linguistic Theory Closer to Home

Domesticated animals clearly get human meanings, and not just, as is usually maintained, merely by tone of voice. Cats in the wild don't meow: meowing is a language that evolved in domesticated cats, one they use to communicate with their human caretakers. As for dogs, it's uncanny how much they seem to understand about human language. Say "Wanna go for a walk?" to the family dog and then tell me the dog doesn't "understand" the words. No good saying that with dogs, it's just conditioning to tone of voice; if that's true, it's conditioning for us too. One zoologist:

> "... went so far as to say that anyone who has lived with a dog and is unconvinced that dogs have feelings like us is psychologically deranged,

> dangerous even … Hence my simple and unscientific recommendation that any academic who doubts the depth of animal emotions ought to get a dog."[69]

It's the idea that our dogs don't understand us (because they don't speak words) that's suspect and downright unscientific. "As my dogs are constantly explaining," wrote Carl Safina, "many of the most important things are said without words."[70]

That line always reminds me of Kali, a large and lovely dog who lives nearby. When she's out in the yard and wants to alert her people to something going on in the neighbourhood, she barks insistently. Her people invariably yell at her to stop: Kali, stop it! This tactic only encourages Kali to increase the volume. When she hears her people doing what amounts to barking of their own, she assumes quite logically that whatever she's barking at is well worthy of attention and concerted vocal response. All that barking must be appropriate if her own people are chiming in! The funniest part is how her humans never seem to notice that their verbal remonstrations—Stop it, Kali! Kali, Stop it! Stop it!—never get Kali to stop barking and only encourage her to keep sounding the alarm. The humans don't get it because they believe in language; the dog believes in raw reality—and in barking.

When I lived in B.C. and taught at a small university there, I had a wolf dog named Shawnee, who had been raised by native Canadians. His mother, I was told, was a wolf, and his father, a black lab. With his thick black coat, his high haunches, and his gorgeous amber eyes, Shawnee resembled more his mother. One day, I was in the kitchen with two of my sisters, Frannie and Psyche.[71] I had just begun unpacking the groceries. There was a block of cheese wrapped in plastic sitting at the edge of the kitchen table. Shawnee had managed to take hold of the cheese without anyone noticing. Then he headed, very quietly, out of the kitchen. I noticed him, just in time, with the block of cheese sticking out of either side of his mouth. I said to Frannie, who was closer to the doorway, "Block his way, don't let him leave the kitchen," and she obliged, barring his exit. Then I turned to Shawnee for a heart to heart (such a pity, I used to think about him, that he was the wrong species, since otherwise he was the perfect male for me).

My sister Psyche was sitting in a chair at the kitchen table, just behind Shawnee and a little to his left. I said to Shawnee: "I don't care how long it takes or what you have to say about it, you are not having that cheese. Now drop it." He growled (the terrifying, low in the throat growl, close-to-inaudible one he used only when he meant serious business, when he meant: Don't even think about it). I kept insisting that whatever it took, he was not leaving the kitchen with that cheese. Then I got a better idea than direct confrontation with this powerful creature. I said to him: "All right, you cannot have that cheese, but you can have a cookie."

Another growl, but less committed. Finally I said, brandishing said cookie, the rock-hard "milkbone" that would break the teeth of any human who tried to bite into it: "Okay, Shawnee, if you don't want this cookie, I'm going to give it to Psyche, and turning my attention and my gaze toward her, said: "Psyche, would you like this cookie?"

Shawnee looked over his shoulder at Psyche, whereupon he got the joke: his tail wagged, he dropped the cheese, and I relinquished the cookie. Talk about successful negotiations.

Another episode in my travels with Shawnee indicates the depth and power of his wordless comprehension. I had read a book by a dog specialist who suggested that the way to discipline a dog without violence was to show the dog you could reach him even though he was out of arm's length, by throwing something light, like a bunched-up page of newspaper.

I was amazed to find that this strategy worked. Each time I wanted Shawnee to stop doing what it was he was doing (usually chewing something inedible), I would throw the newspaper wad at him; he would stop immediately, look at me, study me, as if he were impressed that I wasn't quite as stupid as I appeared, as if he'd gained a new respect for me as a related mammal that though clearly lacking his strength still possessed special powers of my own.

Several days after I began the treatment, Shawnee came into the house (he'd been out in the back yard, practising I guess). He looked straight at me as if to get my attention (Hey Mom, check this out), and with his chewie gripped between his jaws, he began to lob his head back and forth in my direction. Once he'd thus gained momentum, he let the thing fly right at me (missing me by a hair). As if to say: I figured out how you do that. I was duly impressed, though the disciplinary technique never worked as well afterward.

Now tell me that dogs understand only tone of voice.

I had a similar experience with Frannie's cat, Bootsie.

Frannie had gone home to Montreal, and left Bootsie with me. Bootsie didn't seem to miss her; he resorted to sleeping in my bed with me whereas before he had slept in Frannie's bed with her. I guess he figured it was close enough.

A year or two went by before Frannie returned.

We were standing side by side near the kitchen sink, when Bootsie seemed to notice for the first time that there were two of us. He looked from my feet to my head, then to F's feet and up to her head, then repeated the procedure, before apparently satisfying himself that he had sussed out the truth.

Birdsong

I practise the classical guitar in a corner of my bedroom. There's a balcony off this bedroom and when I moved to this apartment, I set up my music stand and other paraphernalia there, near the balcony, where I keep several bird feeders. I've always loved birds, especially ones that sing.

The first day I played in this new corner, I had the balcony door open, to let in the sweet late summer air. When I heard birdsong, I looked up to see a gorgeous male cardinal with his stark black and red coloring and his distinctive feather cap, staring right at me. (Wow, that's one strange big bird, I imagined him thinking.) Then he sang back.

Years later, several varieties of birds still come for the seed, and the cardinals still come for the music. The other day, I heard one clearly imitating the rhythm of a piece I play that uses a tremolo technique (Francisco Tarrega's "Recuerdos de la Alhambra"). The cardinal didn't get the melody, but the rhythmic intonation was right on. I've heard other birds who sing with more melody respond while I'm playing (one the other day that stunned me with its whistling musicality, a species I have yet to identify). I fantasize that the bird minions will learn my language, and I theirs, and that one day, we will all make beautiful music together. That idea may not be as preposterous as it sounds. I read recently that Mozart went beyond fantasy with regard to European starlings, who are excellent vocal mimics.

> "... any given starling can imitate about twenty other birds' sounds. They make good pets when raised from chicks, as their imprinting instinct is strong. Mozart kept a starling for three years and taught it to sing bars of his music. When his bird died, the composer buried it in his backyard and wrote a commemorative poem."[72]

Crows are also considered songbirds, though their cawing is not melodic as we understand melody. (All they ever say is Caw, Caw, Caw, but I've noticed even in crows different intonations depending on what I take to be their intended meanings.) Not talented singers, crows are, on the other hand, fantastically smart and expressive in their own way. It took me weeks to hit on a workable method for how to feed the crows peanuts while keeping them away from the smaller birds at the balcony feeders: I put a container of peanuts closer to the ground attached to a wire fence some distance from the balcony. I worried for a while about the competition for peanuts between the crows and the squirrels, but in the end, they resolved the matter for themselves. It was a crow that led the way to a truce of sorts, and I'll never forget the deciding incident, the day that a determined crow faced off with an insistent squirrel, both after the same peanut. The crow won, but instead of flying off with the peanut as usual, he taunted his rival, broadcasting victory. Back and forth, back and forth he strutted, displaying the peanut clenched in his beak to the now-cowering squirrel, as much as if to say: Who's the chump now, eh? It was so obvious, I laughed out loud. Whenever I hear the phrase "something to crow about," I'll remember that scene.

Magpies, of the same family as crows, are also "well-known for taunting larger animals, especially pets."[73] Before Frannie's cat Bootsie would descend the side-door stairs to make his daily neighbourhood rounds, he'd check, very cautiously, for the magpies, who took every opportunity to dive-bomb him on sight. Once assured that the magpies were otherwise engaged, Bootsie would resume his out-of-the-way-you-others-the-king-approaches stance and continue nonchalantly, as if never at all concerned, to saunter on to his usual routes.

Less romantic notions than my own about birds are somewhat reinforced by more stalwart, scientific reasoning.

> "Lots of us are fascinated by birds because, for one thing, they can be identified. There are eight thousand species of them, and for those of us who like pigeonholing, birds can be pigeonholed. They're pretty. They sing and they can be recognized by sight. They're not like rats or bacteria, which distinguish each other by smell, a sense that we humans are hopeless at. Instead, birds recognize each other in the same way that we recognize each other, by sight and sound. Birds are the best understood of all animals, so in fact much of what we know about behaviour and evolutionary biology and biogeography has been learned from birds."[74]

More moving than the above explication of bird love is Loren Eiseley's rumination on why birds sing, even and maybe especially, when times are hard. Eiseley was describing something he saw: the murder of a smaller bird by a raven who after the murder sat "glistening in the common light, formidable, unmoving, unperturbed, untouchable," and how after the murder, witnessed by other small birds, these latter sang:

> "The sighing died. It was then I saw the judgment. It was the judgment of life against death. I will never see it again so forcefully presented. I will never hear it again in notes so tragically prolonged. For in the midst of protest, they forgot the violence. There, in that clearing, the crystal note of a song sparrow lifted hesitantly in the hush. And finally, after painful fluttering, another took the song, and then another, the song passing from one bird to another, doubtfully at first, as though some evil thing was being slowly forgotten. Till suddenly they took heart and sang from many throats joyously together as birds are known to sing. They sang because life is sweet and sunlight beautiful. They sang under the brooding shadow of the raven. In simple truth they had forgotten the raven, for they were the singers of life, and not of death."[75]

As primates go, we humans are pretty confused. We seem so often to be looking for some kind of meaning we can't quite name. But we're good at names (and at name-calling). And we're good at using words to distinguish one thing from another. So good, in fact, that we often search within ourselves for what takes shape only in interaction with others, or travel wide for what turns out to emerge only within, with reflection, stark and solitary. The minor miracle of this meaning we cannot name isn't just that we keep trying to name it, but that every once in a while, we come to understand that without words, before and beyond words, yes—but especially with the help of words—we stumble on to something that matters. Fame may be where you find it, but meaning is what you make it.

For decades I had a recurring dream that I came to call "the lost dream." It was a nightmare really, and in it I would be trying to get to home or to work or to school—and never succeeding. The dream would seem to go on forever, with complex scenarios (mostly dark and threatening), over vast distances involving a huge cast (of mostly disinterested strangers)—but it never resolved with my reaching the supposed, or any, destination.

I would struggle to extricate myself and wake in the midst of a scene, in a cold sweat. In the early decades of this recurring dream, I figured it was about finding home, finding something familiar, or maybe about high anxiety over successfully completing some task. With the passage of years, I began to understand that the dream wasn't at all about finding something familiar, it was about fleeing something unacknowledged, some unnamed demon.

Then one night, about fifteen years ago, I heard a commanding voice; it sounded like my own, only at once more distant and more authoritative, almost impatient. It said: "If you want to know where you are, open your eyes." Since then, the dream recurs every once in a while. But when it does, I wake unafraid and unperturbed and ask myself immediately: "What am I being blind to? What would I see if I opened my eyes?"

Chapter 10

How to Keep a Commonplace Book

When I began commonplacing, I read hard copy and wrote longhand. When necessary, I used a clunky manual typewriter to transcribe handwritten notes. (These long-gone typewriters required the writer to pound the individual letter keys to produce the individual letters and to use a manual "carriage return" lever to begin each new line.) Later, I graduated to an IBM Selectric, once all the rage in high technology. (Introduced in 1961 and discontinued a quarter century later, the Selectric sold millions of copies worldwide.) Personal computers came out in 1981, and although I used one at work, I initially resisted the technology for home use. Looking back, I can't imagine why. By now, I'm entirely comfortable composing at the keyboard (much faster at capturing words as they, like deadlines, whizz by), and I'm as dependent on my computer for all kinds of purposes (including basic research) as any whippersnapper. But I still prefer reading hard copy and I still take notes by hand. While I recognize that this preference dates me and may constitute merely a generational bias, I do believe that keeping a commonplace book is best done by copying out your chosen quotations by hand, and only then using a computer to transcribe your handwritten notes and fast-write further responses.

The ability to write longhand is disappearing (many of my students knew only printing by hand and generally avoided any kind of handwriting, using instead their computers and their high-tech phones for recording words and numbers and more rarely, passing thoughts). I'm far from alone in regarding this development—loss of the ability to write longhand and of its practice—as retrogressive. As study after study reiterates the advantages of note-taking by longhand, many schools are rethinking—and reversing—the move to dispense with teaching cursive. (For example, while many of my university students twenty-five years ago could neither write nor read cursive, my granddaughter, nearing nine-years-old in 2022, is proficient at both.)

So here follow some words about technology over the ages.

Every new technology, from papyri to parchment and quill pen to computer keyboard, inspires hopes and fears. Classical scholars worried about the potential for writing to injure the power of memory. Some believed the spread of literacy would lead to a lessened capacity for independent thought. Renaissance thinkers looked instead to writing as a powerful tool to retrieve the rhetorical arts of classical Greece. The coming of print was criticized by many as regressive, as was the advent of the typewriter. Romantic scholars challenged the authority of the word and worried that industrialization would enforce conformity and interfere with the power to create. Educators of the late modern era began to agonize over what they saw as steady deterioration in intellectual ability and general knowledge, blaming computers for the assumed decline, thus engaging the tendency, surely eternal, of an older generation to look askance at a younger one.

The fact is that all generations inherit the good and the bad, all evince strengths and weaknesses, and all deal with the challenges of their time. What matters here, in terms of learning to commonplace (or for that matter, learning per se), is not so much the bells and whistles of technology, but the technology of thought. Even the most nihilistic of postmodernists still uses something to record his or her thoughts (from pen on paper to the latest computer application).

The most important lesson learned from the practice of commonplacing is that good reading and good writing are allies and that both depend finally on a kind of internalization: the capacity to read with an open mind and through a process of mental paraphrasing to render meaning in words of your own. Such internalizing provides an antidote to spectator culture, for in order to recall ideas thus internalized, one must consult one's otherwise silent self.

Try reading a chapter of a book or several pages or even a single paragraph; then look away from the text and ask yourself to recall what you've just read. I've tried it with my former students, and with myself, and the truth is stunning: very little to not much. Yet in surveys of how they study, most students say they rely on the same strategy: they re-read.[1] But you can read without focused attention and you can also write without paying close attention. Re-reading doesn't help learning or retention unless it's coupled with testing recall (that is, pausing periodically to ask yourself if you've understood what you've just read). The trouble is that because material becomes more familiar with re-reading, the strategy of merely reading and re-reading fools you into believing you have understood when you really haven't. In order to understand reading material, to learn and ultimately to make the object of study your own, you have to internalize (by paraphrasing) and recall your understanding from within. It is these processes of internalization, recall, and self-expression (and not a blind insistence on "time-saving" or instant certainty over a tolerance for ambiguity) that make the difference in genuine literacy.

***

E. M. Forster stopped writing fiction in midlife (his last novel was the 1924 *A Passage to India*). In 1926, at age 47, he began keeping a commonplace book, a practice he maintained to the end of his life. Though he had quit fiction, he continued to publish essays and reviews, and some critics suggest his commonplace book served as a kind of template for his nonfiction book *Aspects of the Novel*, published in 1927.

Forster died in 1970, and his commonplace book was published posthumously, first in 1978 in a limited facsimile edition of 350 copies, and again in 1985, edited and with an introduction by Philip Gardner. The book opens with hopeful commentary on the prospects of the practice:

> "Commonplaces: My difficulty in making them is that I shall not know what they are about until they are finished. […] I must know what is inside me before I can tell what I am after. Perhaps, if I get through a dozen pages of this book, I shall tell, and my New Ethic result. Each commonplace will be very short: how pleasant it would be to feel copious as well as fluid! the modern mind takes such small flights."

Decades later, on 31 January 1961, in a gloomier mood, Forster wrote this:

> "Going to Bits: This phrase describes me today and is indeed the one I have been looking for; not tragic, not mortal disintegration; only a central weakness which prevents me from concentrating or settling down. … I have so wanted to write and write ahead. The phrase 'obligatory creation' has haunted me. I have so wanted to get out of my morning bath promptly: have decided to do so beforehand, and have then lain in it as usual and watched myself not getting out. It looks as if there is a physical as well as a moral break in the orders I send out. I have plenty of interesting thoughts but keep losing them like the post cards I have written, or like my cap. I can't clear anything up yet interrupt a 'good read' in order to clear up. I hope tomorrow to copy out a piece

> of someone else's prose: it is the best device known to me for taking one out of oneself, plunge into another's minutiae."[2]

That later entry may not strike you as a rousing inducement to take up the practice, but if you're game, here follow my top tips on how to keep a commonplace book.

1. When you copy out quotations, copy analytically rather than mechanically; from memory rather than from text. Instead of fixing your eyes on the text and copying word-for-word, write only as many words at a time as you can remember (usually between five and seven). When you've done that, return to the text and repeat the process with the next chunk, again writing down only as many words at a time as you are able to fix in mind. This process ensures that you are internalizing the words, since it requires you to consult your short-term memory.

2. Like the writer I cite here I believe copying by hand is preferable to typing notes into an electronic file:

> "It can be hard to slow ourselves down and really contemplate a piece of text. That's probably always been true, but for me, at least, typing has made it more difficult; when most of my writing is done with my fingers flying over a keyboard, I can transcribe an author's words faster than my brain can properly take them in. If I really want to discipline myself and look closely at a writer's style, I still copy out sections of that author's work by hand, pen on paper. I'm a firm believer that this is the best and most reliable way to learn to be a better stylist, not just when it comes to punctuation but for the other elements of style as well. I believe this because I've seen it work, over and over, throughout the years."[3]

As noted, such preference may reflect only a generational bias, gleaned from habits of learning formed in a pre-computer age. For younger people, longhand writing may not even be an option (my daughter, a professional script writer, says it hurts her hands). No matter: the important thing is still to copy from memory and not from text (that is, typing instead of writing, but still only as many words at a time as can be remembered, recalled from within, without looking back at the text). Most distinctly inadvisable is to cut and paste from one electronic screen to another, a process worse than useless because it entirely bypasses the need for internalization. What finds no home within can never find expression without.

3. Once you've copied the excerpt, paraphrase it (composing directly at your computer keyboard if this suits your preference). Put the gist of the passage in your own words (don't just replace the words of the original with synonymous words). To paraphrase involves a kind of self-talk, the very essence of learning and of writing—not a secondary or nonessential step in the process. The paraphrase may not come easily, but it will come if you keep at it and if you let it. The greater the difficulty in paraphrasing a chosen excerpt, the more likely it is that you didn't fully understand its meaning in the first place. Yet that you chose to copy the words to begin with indicates there's gold beyond the resistance.

4. Respond. Once you're satisfied that your paraphrase adequately represents the original quotation, respond at whatever length and in whatever manner suits your purpose. Do you agree? Disagree? Does it answer a question for you? Does it raise one? Does it remind you of something? Even if it seems it's only the music in the words that grabs you, respond. The fear that you have nothing to say tends to vanish as soon as you say something. (One of the most enduring lessons I've learned from my commonplacing habit is how apt I am to respond precipitously to some statements, especially ones with which I heartily disagree. From teaching, I learned how common is this tendency.)

5. How to organize your commonplace book depends on what you hope to do with it or get out of it. For this book, I organized my commonplace notes on the subject of language and under anticipated chapter headings, but any method that's consistent will work. Whatever your goal, and whether your commonplace book is meant for private purposes or for publication, date every entry, every time. To imagine you'll remember when you'd read or taken notes from a given source, without writing it down, is a fool's errand—like the unforgettably vivid dream that somehow manages to evaporate with morning light.

I was glad to finish this book so I could get back to commonplacing freely, without thought of publication; glad also to put to bed, at least for a while, my obsession with language, and to move on to other greener concerns. (I still fantasize, though, about a commoners' commonplace book, one that would combine the commonplacing notes of numbers of writers on various topics, like a new kind of textbook.)

Another important insight gleaned from my commonplacing habit is one often before noted: the high level of intellect and emotion involved in humour. There are some words you feel compelled to preserve in a commonplace notebook that don't require much if any response. They are those that leave you laughing out loud. Here are a few of my favourites.

In his massive work about the brain and human behaviour, Robert Sapolsky combines erudition with a friendly (human) voice, one that erupts full-blown in the many asides to the otherwise dense text, replete with polysyllabic words from the often arcane world of neuroscience. One of those asides follows several paragraphs in which Sapolsky briefly relays the history of a famous late-19th-century disagreement among scientists. One group believed in the neuron doctrine (that each neuron is a separate entity); another stuck to the idea of the "synctitium" (that there's one boss super neuron). Following this exposition, the author comments:

> "Ironic footnote: [Santiago Ramón y] Cajal was the chief exponent of the neuron doctrine. And the leading voice in favor of synctitiums? [Camillo] Golgi; the technique he invented showed that he was wrong. He apparently moped the entire way to Stockholm to receive his Nobel Prize in 1906—shared with Cajal. The two loathed each other, didn't even speak. In his Nobel address, Cajal managed to muster the good manners to praise Golgi. Golgi, in his, attacked Cajal and the neuron doctrine. Jerk."[4]

Then there's the incomparable Lily Tomlin: "When we speak to God we are said to be praying, but when God speaks to us, we are said to be schizophrenic."[5] And that great line from *Little Big Man*: "Sometimes the magic works."[6]

My current all-time favourite laugh-out-loud quote comes from the irresistible Louise Penny, in the "Acknowledgments" section at the end of her 2021 novel *The Madness of Crowds*. The section proceeds as per usual, thanking various individuals involved in the editing and production of the book. In the last paragraph, Penny offers special thanks to several close friends. "I feel their presence every day," she writes. "Guiding me along as I navigate life. Helping me as I write." And then this, the single line that constitutes the very last paragraph: "All this to say, if you didn't like the book, it's their fault."[7]

What she said.

***

BIBLIOGRAPHY

Auden, W. H. *A Certain World.* New York: Viking, 1970.

Birkerts, Sven. *The Gutenberg Elegies: The Fate of Reading in an Electronic Age.* New York: Fawcett Columbine, 1994.

Boswell, James. *The Life of Samuel Johnson.* New York: Everyman's Library, 1993.

Bridle, James. *New Dark Age: Technology and the End of the Future.* London: Verso, 2018.

Bronowski, J., and Bruce Mazlish. *The Western Intellectual Tradition: From Leonardo to Hegel.* New York: Harper & Brothers, 1960. (Published in 1986 by Dorset Press).

Broussard, Meredith. *Artificial Unintelligence: How Computers Misunderstand the World.* Cambridge, Mass.: MIT Press, 2018.

Bruce, Harry. *Page Fright: Foibles and Fetishes of Famous Writers.* Toronto: McClelland & Stewart, 2010.

Burnett, Dean. *The Idiot Brain: A Neuroscientist Explains What Your Head Is Really Up To.* Harper Collins, 2016.

Caro, Robert A. *Working: Researching, Interviewing, Writing.* New York: Alfred A. Knopf, 2019.

Carr, Nicholas. *The Shallows: What the Internet Is Doing to Our Brains.* New York: Norton, 2011.

Charlton, James, and Bill Henderson, eds. *Book Love: A Celebration of Writers, Readers, and the Printed and Bound Book.* New York: Pushcart Press, 2017.

Clark, Roy Peter. *Writing Tools: 50 Essential Strategies for Every Writer.* New York: Little, Brown and Company, 2006.

Cole, K. C. *The Universe and the Teacup: The Mathematics of Truth and Beauty.* New York: Houghton Mifflin Harcourt, 1997.

Cormack, Bradin, and Carla Mazzio. *Book Use, Book Theory: 1500-1700.* Chicago: University of Chicago Press, 2005.

Crystal, David. *The Cambridge Encyclopedia of Language.* New York: Cambridge University Press, 1987.

Damasio, Antonio. *The Feeling of What Happens: Body and Emotion in the Making of Consciousness.* New York: Harcourt, 1999.

Darnton, Robert. "Extraordinary Commonplaces." *The New York Review of Books*, 21 December 2000.

Darwin, Charles. *On the Origin of Species by Means of Natural Selection; or, The Preservation of Favoured Races in the Struggle for Life*. London: John Murray, 1859.

Darwin, Charles. *The Descent of Man*. London: John Murray, 1871.

De Waal, Frans. *Mama's Last Hug: Animal Emotions and What They Tell Us About Ourselves*. New York: W. W. Norton & Company, 2019.

Dennett, Daniel C. *From Bacteria to Bach and Back: The Evolution of Minds*. New York: W. W. Norton & Company, 2017.

Diamond, Jared. *Guns, Germs, and Steel: The Fates of Human Societies*. New York: W. W. Norton & Company, 1997, 1999.

Dillard, Annie. *For the Time Being*. New York: Viking/Penguin, 1999.

Dillard, Annie. *Teaching a Stone to Talk: Expeditions and Encounters*. New York: Harper Perennial, 1982.

Dossey, Larry. *Space, Time, and Medicine*. Boulder, Colorado: Shambhala, 1982).

Durrell, Gerald. *The Corfu Trilogy: Three Classic Tales of Childhood on an Island Paradise*. New York: Penguin, 2006. First published in Great Britain, 1956.

Eiseley, Loren. *Collected Essays on Evolution, Nature, and the Cosmos*. Vol. 1. New York: The Library of America, 2016.

Gardner, Philip, ed. *E. M. Forster Commonplace Book*. Stanford: Stanford University Press, 1985.

Gnanadesikan, Amalia E. *The Writing Revolution: From Cuneiform to the Internet*. UK: Wiley-Blackwell, 2009.

Goldman, Emma. *The Traffic in Women and Other Essays on Feminism*. Washington: Times Change Press, 1970.

Gordon, Cyrus H. *The Common Background of Greek and Hebrew Civilizations*. New York: W. W. Norton & Company, 1965.

Gottschall, Jonathan. *The Storytelling Animal: How Stories Make Us Human*. New York: Houghton Mifflin Harcourt, 2012.

Gruber Garvey, Ellen. *Writing with Scissors: American Scrapbooks from the Civil War to the Harlem Renaissance*. New York: Oxford University Press, 2012.

Havens, Earle. *Commonplace Books: A History of Manuscripts and Printed Books from Antiquity to the Twentieth Century*. New Haven, CT: University Press of New England, 2001.

Hess, Jillian Marissa. "Commonplace-Book Stylistics: Romantic and Victorian Technologies of Reading and Writing." PhD dissertation. December 2012, Stanford University (online at http://purl.standford.edu/ct368gf9765).

Hurford, James R. *The Origins of Language: A Slim Guide*. Oxford: Oxford University Press, 2014.

Illich, Ivan, and Barry Sanders. *ABC: The Alphabetization of the Popular Mind*. New York: Vintage, 1988.

Jackendoff, Ray. *A User's Guide to Thought and Meaning.* New York: Oxford University Press, 2012.

Jacobs, Alan. *The Pleasures of Reading in an Age of Distraction.* New York: Oxford University Press, 2011.

Jacobs, Jane. *Dark Age Ahead.* Toronto: Random House Canada, 2004.

James, William. *Principles of Psychology.* New York: Henry Holt, 1901.

James, William. *Selected Papers on Philosophy.* London: J. M. Dent & Sons Ltd., 1917. New York: E. P. Dutton & Co. Inc., 1961.

Jaynes, Julian. *The Origin of Consciousness in the Breakdown of the Bicameral Mind.* Boston: Houghton Mifflin, 1976.

Karr, Mary. *The Art of Memoir.* New York: HarperCollins, 2015.

Katzev, Richard. *In the Country of Books: Commonplace Books and Other Readings.* Leicester, UK: Matador, 2009.

Kean, Sam. *The Tale of the Dueling Neurosurgeons: The History of the Human Brain as Revealed by True Stories of Trauma, Madness, and Recovery.* New York: Little, Brown and Company, 2014.

Keim, Brandon. "Secrets of Animal Communication." Special Issue. Washington, D.C.: *National Geographic.* November 2019.)

Keltner, Dacher. *The Power Paradox: How We Gain and Lose Influence.* New York: Penguin, 2016.

Kenneally, Christine. *The First Word: The Search for the Origins of Language.* New York: Penguin, 2007.

Kidder, Tracy, and Richard Todd. *Good Prose: The Art of Nonfiction.* New York: Random House, 2013.

Kimmerer, Robin Wall. *Braiding Sweetgrass: Indigenous Wisdom, Scientific Knowledge, and the Teachings of Plants.* Minneapolis, Minn.: Milkweed Editions, 2013.

King, Thomas. *The Truth About Stories: A Native Narrative.* Toronto: House of Anansi, 2003.

Kurlansky, Mark. *Paper: Paging Through History.* New York: W. W. Norton and Company, 2016.

Kushner, Aviya. *The Grammar of God: A Journey into the Words and Worlds of the Bible.* New York: Spiegel and Grau, 2015).

Landon, Brooks. *Building Great Sentences.* New York: Penguin, 2013.

Le Guin, Ursula K. *Steering the Craft.* Portland, OR: Eighth Mountain Press, 1998.

Le Guin, Ursula K. *Words Are My Matter: Writings About Life and Books.* Easthampton, MA: Small Beer Press, 2016.

Lehmann, Nicholas. "The Reading Wars." *Atlantic Monthly*, November 1997.

Lehrer, Jonah. *Proust Was a Neuroscientist.* New York: Houghton Mifflin, 2007.

Loughery, John, ed. *The Eloquent Essay: An Anthology of Classic and Creative Nonfiction.* New York: Persea Books, 2000.

Lydon, Michael. *Writing and Life.* Hanover and London: University Press of New England, 1990, 1995.

Makari, George. *Soul Machine: The Invention of the Modern Mind.* New York: W. W. Norton & Company, 2015.

Manguel, Alberto. *A History of Reading.* Toronto: Vintage Canada, 1996.

Marzluff, John, and Tony Angell. *Gifts of the Crow: How Perception, Emotion, and Thought Allow Smart Birds to Behave Like Humans.* New York: Free Press, 2012.

McAdam, E. L., and George Milne, eds. *A Johnson Reader.* New York: Pantheon, 1964.

McEwan, Ian. *Saturday.* New York: Alfred A. Knopf Canada, 2015.

Miller, Andy. *The Year of Reading Dangerously: How Fifty Great Books (and Two Not-So-Great Ones) Saved My Life.* London: Fourth Estate/HarperCollins, 2014.

Mitchell, David. *Cloud Atlas.* Toronto: Vintage Canada, 2004.

Moss, Ann. *Printed Commonplace-Books and the Structuring of Renaissance Thought.* Oxford: Oxford University Press, 1966.

Mumford, Lewis. *Technics and Civilization.* New York: Harcourt, Brace and Company, 1934.

Murphy, James J. "Roman Writing Instruction as Described by Quintilian." In James J. Murphy, ed. *A Short History of Writing Instruction: From Ancient Greece to 20th Century America.* Davis: Hermagoras Press, 1990.

Nafisi, Azar. *Reading Lolita in Tehran: A Memoir in Books.* New York: Random House, 2003.

O'Conner, Patricia T. *Woe Is I: The Grammarphobe's Guide to Better English in Plain English.* New York: Riverhead Books, 1996.

O'Toole, Fintan. "Auden: Cranky, Cautious, Brilliant." *New York Review of Books*, Oct. 22, 2015.

Oakley, Barbara. *A Mind for Numbers: How to Excel at Math and Science.* New York: Random House, 2014.

Oates, Joyce Carol, and Robert Atwan, eds. *The Best American Essays of the Century.* New York: Houghton Mifflin, 2000.

Olson, Randy. *Houston, We Have a Narrative: Why Science Needs Story.* Chicago: University of Chicago Press, 2015.

Ong, Walter J. *Orality and Literacy: The Technologizing of the Word.* London and New York: Methuen, 1982.

Orlean, Susan. *The Library Book.* New York: Simon & Schuster, 2018.

Ostler, Nicholas. *Empires of the Word: A Language History of the World.* New York: Harper Collins, 2005.

Page, Jake. *Dogs: A Natural History.* New York: HarperCollins, 2007.

Parks, Tim. *Where I'm Reading From: The Changing World of Books.* New York: Random House, 2015.

Pinker, Steven. *The Language Instinct: How the Mind Creates Language.* New York: HarperCollins, 1994.

Pinker, Steven. *The Sense of Style.* New York: Penguin, 2014.

Postman, Neil. *Technopoly: The Surrender of Culture to Technology.* New York: Vintage, 1992.

Proust, Marcel. *À la recherche du temps perdu.* 1913-1927. Paris: Grasset and Gallimard. Trans. C. K. Scott Moncrieff, *In Search of Lost Time.* New York: Gilmartin, 1992.

Quindlen, Anna. *How Reading Changed My Life.* New York: Random House, 1998.

Raymond, Jon, ed. *The World Split Open: Great Authors on How and Why We Write.* Portland, Oregon, and Brooklyn, New York: Tin House Books, 2014.

Rhodes, Richard. *How to Write: Advice and Reflections.* New York: HarperCollins, 1995.

Roszak, Theodore. *The Cult of Information: The Folklore of Computers and the True Art of Thinking.* New York: Pantheon, 1986.

Rushkoff, Douglas. *Team Human.* New York: W. W. Norton & Company, 2019.

Ruvinsky, Maxine. *Practical Grammar: A Canadian Writer's Resource.* 3rd edition. Don Mills, Ontario: Oxford University Press Canada, 2014.

Rybczynski, Witold. *Taming the Tiger: The Struggle to Control Technology.* New York: Penguin, 1983.

Sacks, Oliver. *The River of Consciousness.* New York: Alfred A. Knopf, 2017.

Safina, Carl. *Beyond Words: What Animals Think and Feel.* New York: Henry Holt and Company, 2015.

Shapiro, James. *Evolution: A View from the 21st Century.* Upper Saddle River, NJ: FT Press Science, 2011.

Shell, Marc. *Money, Language and Thought.* Baltimore and London: Johns Hopkins University Press, 1982.

Sims, Norman, ed. *The Literary Journalists: The New Art of Personal Reportage.* New York: Ballantine, 1984).

Snow, C.P. *The Two Cultures and the Scientific Revolution.* New York: Cambridge University Press, 1959.

Tammet, Daniel. *Every Word Is a Bird We Teach to Sing: Encounters in the Mysteries and Meanings of Language.* New York: Little, Brown and Company, 2017.

The Ultimate Quotable Einstein. Collected and edited by Alice Calaprice. Princeton, NJ: Princeton University Press and Cambridge, MA: Harvard University Press, 2011.

Turkle, Sherry. *Alone Together: Why We Expect More from Technology and Less from Each Other.* New York: Basic Books, 2011.

Turok, Neil. *The Universe Within: From Quantum to Cosmos.* Toronto: House of Anansi, 2012.

Ulin, David L. *The Lost Art of Reading: Why Books Matter in a Distracted Time.* Seattle: Sasquatch Books, 2010.

Van Doren, Charles. *A History of Knowledge.* New York: Random House, 1991.

Wachtel, Eleanor. *Original Minds: In Conversation with CBC Radio's Eleanor Wachtel.* Toronto: HarperCollins, 2003.

Watson, Cecilia. *Semicolon: The Past, Present, and Future of a Misunderstood Mark*. New York: HarperCollins, 2019.

Weatherford, Jack. *The History of Money*. New York: Three Rivers Press, 1997.

White, Fred. *The Daily Reader.* Cincinnati, OH: Writer's Digest Books, 2009.

Wilber, Ken, ed. *Quantum Questions: Mystical Writings of the World's Great Physicists* Boulder, Colo.: Shambhala Publications, 1984.

Wolf, Maryanne. *Proust and the Squid: The Story and Science of the Reading Brain*. New York: Harper, 2007.

Woolf, Virginia. *A Room of One's Own*. 1929. Edited with an introduction by Morag Shiach. Oxford: Oxford University Press, 1992.

Wright, Ronald. *A Short History of Progress*. Toronto: House of Anansi, 2004.

Endnotes

CHAPTER 1 / DISCOVERING THE COMMONPLACE BOOK.

[1] Quoted in Tracy Kidder and Richard Todd, *Good Prose: The Art of Nonfiction* (New York: Random House, 2013), 67.
[2] The idea in so-called discovery writing (that a work of fiction need not be planned), was alluded to by Arthur Koestler (in his 1964 book *The Ghost in the Machine*, pp. 39-40): "When Alice in Wonderland was admonished to think carefully before speaking, she explained: 'How can I know what I think till I see what I say?' " It was also referenced in W. H. Auden's essay in the book Poets at Work (c. 1959).

CHAPTER 2 / WHAT'S A COMMONPLACE BOOK? (AND SOME REASONS TO WRITE YOUR OWN)

[1] Michael Stolberg, "John Locke's 'New Method of Making Common-Place-Books': Tradition, Innovation and Epistemic Effects" (*Early Science and Medicine* 10, 2014), 448-470. Accessed online at Michael.stolberg@uni-wuerzburg.de.
[2] Ann Moss, *Printed Commonplace-Books and the Structuring of Renaissance Thought* (New York: Oxford University Press, 1996).
[3] A. Bronson Alcott, *Table Talk of A. Bronson Alcott* (Boston: Roberts Brothers, 1877), 12.
[4] Charles Van Doren, *A History of Knowledge* (New York: Random House, 1991), 47-48.
[5] *Benét's Reader's Encyclopedia* (5th ed., 2008).
[6] *New Lexicon Webster's Encyclopedic Dictionary of the English Language*, Canadian Edition (New York: Lexicon Publications, Inc., 1988).
[7] *Concise Oxford Dictionary of Current English*, 9th edition (Oxford: Oxford University Press, 1995).
[8] Jillian Marissa Hess, "Commonplace-Book Stylistics: Romantic and Victorian Technologies of Reading and Writing" (Stanford University, 2012). Accessed online in 2015 at ttp://purl.stanford.edu/ct368gf9765.
[9] Ann Moss, *Printed Commonplace-Books.*
[10] David Allan, *Commonplace Books and Reading in Georgian England* (Cambridge, UK: Cambridge University Press, 2010).

11. Bradin Cormack and Carla Mazzio, *Book Use, Book Theory: 1500-1700* (Chicago: University of Chicago Press, 2005). Accessed online at https://www.lib.uchicago.edu/.../commonplacethinking.html.
12. A. Bronson Alcott, *Table-Talk of A. Bronson Alcott*, 12.
13. I refer to The Common Reader series, the essays in *Granite and Rainbow*, and the two books that deal with Woolf's feminist thinking, *A Room of One's Own* and the subsequent *Three Guineas.*
14. First published in 1953, the diary covers the years 1918 to 1941. Woolf appeared to have used it for several purposes: for typical diary entries, recording observations on the people and events in her life; for essays on her writing and her writing practice; and for commonplace-style notes on her reading.
15. Fintan O'Toole, "Auden: Cranky, Cautious, Brilliant," *New York Review of Books* (22 October 2015), 47-48.
16. Robert Darnton, "Extraordinary Commonplaces," *New York Review of Books* (21 December 2000).
17. Much about Shakespeare's personal life is unknown or unverified, including the cause of his death in April 1616, and the date of his birth, which is assumed from baptism records to be 23 April 1564.
18. You can read the full text of Jonson's *Timber* online (https://www.gutenberg.org).
19. Cited by Richard Katzev, *In the Country of Books: Commonplace Books and Other Readings* (Leicester, UK: Matador, 2009), 33.
20. *The Concise Oxford Dictionary of Proverbs* (New York: Oxford University Press, 1993).
21. Accessed online (https://www.goodreads.com/author/quotes/9876.John_Milton).
22. Locke first published "*Méthode nouvelle de dresser des recueils*" in Le Clerc's Bibliothèque universelle II (1685), translated into English in Le Clerc's Observations (London 1697).
23. Stolberg, "John Locke's 'New Method of Making Common-Place-Books': Tradition, Innovation and Epistemic Effects" (*Early Science and Medicine* 10, 2014).
24. Other Enlightenment thinkers of the eighteenth century include famous espousers of a range of views (including David Hume, Jean Jacques Rousseau, Immanuel Kant, and Thomas Jefferson). The very idea of a historical period known as "the Enlightenment," during which humanity is thought to have made unparalleled progress, is however much contested. The controversy is outside the scope of this book, but for interested readers, I quote: "For critics … this period became one of insidious social control, brute prejudice masked as science, bureaucratically normalized terror, and internalized censorship." – George Makari, *Soul Machine: The Invention of the Modern Mind* (New York: W. W. Norton, 2015), xv.
25. Anthony Grafton, "Jumping Through the Computer Screen," *New York Review of Books*, 23 December 2010. Reviewing the book *Reinventing Knowledge: From Alexandria to the Internet*, by Ian F. McNeely and Lisa Wolverton (W. W. Norton, 2009).
26. Grafton, "Jumping Through the Computer Screen," *New York Review of Books*, 23 December 2010.

[27] Oxford: Clarendon Press, 3rd edition, 1973; "with corrections and revised addenda," nine of them, between 1956 and 1973.
[28] Andrew O'Hagan, "Word Wizard," *New York Review of Books* (29 April 2006), on *Defining the World: The Extraordinary Story of Dr. Johnson's Dictionary*, by Henry Hitchings. The famous Oxford English Dictionary began publishing in 1884. See K.M. Elisabeth Murray, *Caught in the Web of Words: James Murray and the Oxford English Dictionary* (Yale University Press, 1977), and Simon Winchester, *The Meaning of Everything: The Story of the Oxford English Dictionary* (Oxford University Press, 2003).
[29] *A Johnson Reader*, eds. E. L. McAdam and George Milne (New York: Pantheon, 1964), 149, 152.
[30] *A Johnson Reader*, 142.
[31] *A Johnson Reader*, 186 (from the Rambler, No. 208, Saturday, March 14, 1752).
[32] Cormack and Mazzio, *Book Use, Book Theory*.
[33] Adam Kirsch, "Giacomo Leopardi's 'Zibaldone,' the Least Known Masterpiece of European Literature," *The New Republic*, November 2013.
[34] Hess, "Commonplace-Book Stylistics," 172.
[35] *Ibid.*
[36] Tim Parks, *Where I'm Reading From: The Changing World of Books* (New York: Random House, 2015).
[37] George Makari, *Soul Machine: The Invention of the Modern Mind* (New York: W. W. Norton, 2015), 421.
[38] See Hess, "Commonplace-Book Stylistics"."
[39] See for example: Gayle B. Price, "A case for a modern commonplace book," in *College Composition and Communication* 31, No. 2 (May 1980), 175-182.
[40] William Roberts, a retired professor of psychology and formerly Editor, *Canadian Journal of Behavioural Science*, 2014-2018, told me that he kept a commonplace book as a student at Reed College. Richard Katzev, a retired sociology professor, taught at Reed for years; in 2009, Katzev published *In the Country of Books: Commonplace Books and Other Readings*. The book now has an online version.
[41] Ian Carr, "William Boyd—The Commonplace and the Books," *Canadian Bulletin of Medical History* (Vol. 10, Issue 1, Spring 1993), 77-86. Published online in 2006 [https://utpjournals.press/doi/abs/10.3138/cbmh.10.1.77].
[42] Declan Kiberd, *The Guardian* (16 June 2009).
[43] John Tytell, *Ezra Pound: The Solitary Volcano* (New York: Anchor Press, 1988), 293, 302–303.
[44] E. Fuller Torrey, *The Roots of Treason and the Secrets of St Elizabeths* (New York: Houghton Mifflin Harcourt, 1984), 200. Torrey was a psychiatrist who worked at St. Elizabeths when Pound was jailed there; he claimed to have been fired for writing the book, which charged that another psychiatrist at the hospital committed perjury to help Pound avoid trial as mentally unfit.
[45] Robert Hillyer, "Treason's Strange Fruit" and "Poetry's New Priesthood," *The Saturday Review of Literature*, 11 and 18 June, 1949.

[46.] James Gifford, "Reading Fletcher's Commonplace Books: The Breadth of Cultural Influences in New Westminster, British Columbia, 1887-1897," (Streetprint.org, c. 2004). Gifford describes Streetprint.org as an attempt to create a user-friendly electronic archive for scholars, run from the Canadian Research Chairs Humanities Computing Studio at the University of Alberta. Accessed June 2017. [https://sites.ualberta.ca/~gifford/fletchers.pdf].
[47.] Sappho was a prominent teacher and poet born circa 630 BCE on the Greek island of Lesbos.
[48.] Deborah Lynn Pfuntner, "Romantic Women Writers and Their Commonplace Books," Texas A & M University, 2016. Accessed online at https://oaktrust.library.tamu.edu. See also two books on which Pfuntner says her own work builds: David Allan, *Commonplace Books and Reading in Georgian England*, and Earle Havens, *Commonplace Books: A History of Manuscripts and Printed Books from Antiquity to the Twentieth Century*.
[49.] Douglas Rushkoff, *Team Human* (New York: W.W. Norton & Company, 2019), 67, 73.
[50.] Tracy Kidder, in Tracy Kidder and Richard Todd, *Good Prose: The Art of Nonfiction* (New York: Random House, 2013), 133.

CHAPTER 3 / LANGUAGE, MEANING, AND THE TROUBLE WITH WORDS

[1.] George Makari, *Soul Machine: The Invention of the Modern Mind* (New York: W. W. Norton, 2015)
[2.] Makari, *Soul Machine*, 218.
[3.] Makari, 407.
[4.] James Hurford, *The Origins of Language: A Slim Guide* (Oxford: Oxford University Press, 2014), 60. Cited in Daniel Dennett, *From Bacteria to Bach and Back: The Evolution of Minds* (New York: W. W. Norton, 2017), 272-273.
[5.] Tracy Kidder and Richard Todd, *Good Prose: The Art of Nonfiction* (New York: Random House, 2013), 84.
[6.] Richard Rodriguez, "Aria: A Memoir of a Bilingual Childhood," *Best American Essays of the Century* (New York: Houghton-Mifflin, 2000).
[7.] Annie Dillard, "Total Eclipse," *Teaching a Stone to Talk* (New York: Harper Perennial, 1983), 19.
[8.] William James, *The Principles of Psychology* (New York: Henry Holt, 1901), 255. Quoted in Richard Katzev, *In the Country of Books: Commonplace Books and Other Readings* (Leicester, UK: Matador, 2009), 47.
[9.] Daniel Tammet, *Every Word Is a Bird We Teach to Sing: Encounters in the Mysteries and Meanings of Language* (New York: Little, Brown and Company, 2017), 257.
[10.] Rachel Carson, "The Marginal World." (New York: Houghton Mifflin, 2000.) First published in 1955 in her book *The Edge of the Sea* and the same year in *The New Yorker*.)
[11.] Iain McGilchrist, *The Master and His Emissary: The Divided Brain and the Making of the Western World* (New Haven and London: Yale University Press, 2009), 192.

[12] Sam Maggs, "New Species of Wacky Monkey-Porcupine Hybrid Discovered in Brazil." Accessed online (https://www.themarysue.com/monkey-porcupine).
[13] Richard Irwin (https://explore.scimednet.org).
[14] William James, "What Pragmatism Means." *Selected Papers on Philosophy* (London: J. M. Dent & Sons, 1917), 204-205.
[15] Marilynne Robinson, "On Beauty," *The World Split Open: Great Authors on How and Why We Write* (New York: Tin House Books, 2014), 133.
[16] Robert Stone, "Morality and Truth in Literature" *The World Split Open: Great Authors on How and Why We Write* (New York: Tin House Books, 2014), 160.
[17] Joshua Rothman, "Same Difference: What the idea of equality can do for us, and what it can't." *The New Yorker*, January 13, 2020 (26-31), 29
[18] Tim Parks, *Teach Us to Sit Still* (London: Harvill Secker, 2010), 208, 3.
[19] Ellen J. Langer, *Counter Clockwise: Mindful Health and the Power of Possibility* (New York: Ballantine, 2009), 97-99.
[20] Ray Jackendoff, *A User's Guide to Thought and Meaning* (New York: Oxford University Press, 2012), 223.
[21] Joshua Rothman, "Same Difference," 31.
[22] Robert Darnton, "How to Read a Book" *New York Review of Books*, 6 June 1996.
[23] William James, "What Pragmatism Means," *Selected Papers*, 199.
[24] William James, "What Pragmatism Means," 218.
[25] Wallace Stegner, "Fiction to Make Sense of Life," in *The World Split Open*, 145.
[26] James R. Hurford, *The Origins of Language: A Slim Guide* (Oxford: Oxford University Press, 2014), 153.
[27] Robert A. Caro, *Working: Researching, Interviewing, Writing* (New York: Alfred A. Knopf, 2019), 112.
[28] Maxine Ruvinsky, *Investigative Reporting in Canada* (Don Mills, Ontario: Oxford University Press Canada, 2008), 195-196, 208.
[29] Maxine Ruvinsky, "Lintroscan" (Canadian Press, Montreal bureau, 15 December 1992). MONTREAL (CP) – An American technology for breast-cancer screening that poses no radiation risk, and doesn't hurt, may soon be available in Canada."
[30] Maxine Ruvinsky, "Bad Medicine, Good Business," *The Hour* (May 23-29, 1996 / Vol. 4, No. 21).
[31] Neil Macdonald, CBC Opinion, 23 October 2019, retrieved online. [https://www.cbc.ca/news/opinion/neil-macdonald-trudeau-opinion.])
[32] Noam Chomsky, in *Original Minds: Conversations with CBC Radio's Eleanor Wachtel* (Toronto: HarperCollins Canada, 2003), 369.
[33] Caro, *Working: Researching, Interviewing, Writing*, 114.
[34] W. H. Auden, *A Certain World: A Commonplace Book* (New York: Viking, 1970), 207.
[35] Auden quoted in Fintan O'Toole, "Auden: Cranky, Cautious, Brilliant," *New York Review of Books*, 22 October 2015, 47-48.
[36] Noam Chomsky, quoted in Wachtel, *Original Minds*, 364-365.

CHAPTER 4 / GRAMMAR: SENSE AND NONSENSE

1. Nicholas Lehmann, "The Reading Wars," *Atlantic Monthly* (November 1997, Vol. 280, No. 5), 128.
2. Siegfried Engelmann, Phyllis Haddox, and Elaine Bruner, *Teach Your Child to Read in 100 Easy Lessons* (New York: Touchstone, 1986).
3. John McWhorter, "How I Taught My Kid to Read," *The Atlantic* (9 June 2019).
4. See also Mark Seidenberg's 2017 book *Language at the Speed of Sight: How We Read, Why So Many Can't, and What Can Be Done About It.*
5. Anna Quindlen, *How Reading Changed My Life* (New York: Random House, 1998), 21.
6. *Ibid.*
7. Steven Pinker, *The Sense of Style: The Thinking Person's Guide to Writing in the 21st Century* (New York: Viking, 2014), 78-79.
8. Steven Pinker, "Oaf of Office," *New York Times*, 22 January 2009. (Cited in Buhner, *Ensouling Language*, 346).
9. Pinker, *Sense of Style*, 195, 261, 218.
10. Pinker, *Sense of Style*, 192.
11. *Paperback Oxford Canadian Dictionary*, 2004.
12. David Crystal, *The Cambridge Encyclopedia of Language* (New York: Cambridge University Press, 1987), 88.
13. Brooks Landon, *Building Great Sentences* (New York: Penguin, 2013), 31.
14. Ursula K. Le Guin, *Steering the Craft: Exercises and Discussions on Story Writing for the Lone Navigator or the Mutinous Crew* (Portland, Oregon: Eighth Mountain Press, 1998), 40-41.
15. Candace Pert, *Molecules of Emotion* (New York: Scribner, 1997).
16. Ursula K. Le Guin, *The Wave in the Mind* (Boston: Shambhala, 2004), 225.
17. Marilynne Robinson, "On Beauty," *The World Split Open* (New York: Tin House Books, 2014), 123.
18. Richard Rhodes, *How to Write: Advice and Reflections* (New York: HarperCollins, 1995), 41.
19. Deborah Eisenberg, "The Genius of Peter Nadas," *New York Times*, 2008.
20. Ben Yagoda, *How to Not Write Bad: The Most Common Writing Problems and the Best Ways to Avoid Them* (New York: Riverhead Books, 2013), 86.
21. Patricia T. O'Conner. *Woe Is I: The Grammarphobe's Guide to Better English in Plain English* (New York: Riverhead Books, 1996), 1.
22. Yagoda, 79.
23. Pinker, *Sense of Style*, 233.
24. For sticklers and on matters of correct usage, it can hardly get more staid than H. W. Fowler. His *A Dictionary of Modern English Usage*, 2nd edition, revised by Sir Ernest Gowers (Oxford: Oxford University Press, 1965), spends four columns of small type on the word "than"; it also notes that the word may be used as a conjunction or as a preposition.
25. Maxine Ruvinsky, *Practical Grammar: A Canadian Writer's Resource* (Don Mills, Ontario: Oxford University Press, 2014), 42.

[26] Ruvinsky, *Practical Grammar*, 43.
[27] Le Guin, *The Wave in the Mind*, 251, 252.
[28] Tracy Kidder and Richard Todd, *Good Prose: The Art of Nonfiction* (New York: Random House, 2013), 122.
[29] Cited in Stephen Harrod Buhner, *Ensouling Language: On the Art of Nonfiction and the Writer's Life* (Rochester, Vermont/Toronto, Canada: Inner Traditions, 2010), 346.
[30] Pico Iyer, "In Praise of the Humble Comma," *The Eloquent Essay: An Anthology of Classic and Creative Nonfiction.* Edited and with an introduction by John Loughery. (New York: Persea Books, 2000), 93-94.
[31] Michael Lydon, *Writing and Life* (Hanover and London: University Press of New England, 1990, 1995), 6.
[32] Annie Dillard, *Teaching a Stone to Talk: Expeditions and Encounters* (New York: Harper Perennial, 1982), 24.
[33] Aviya Kushner, *The Grammar of God: A Journey into the Words and Worlds of the Bible* (New York: Spiegel & Grau/Random House, 2015), xxviii.
[34] Lauren Leibowitz, " 'The Grammarians' Gives Voice to the Laws of Language," 18 October 2019. *The New Yorker.* Accessed online. (https://www.newyorker.com/recommends/read/the-grammarians-gives-voice-to-the-laws-of-language).
[35] Cited in Steven Pinker, *The Language Instinct: How the Mind Creates Language* (New York: Harper Collins, 1994), 93.

CHAPTER 5 / TRUTH IN LITERATURE: FICTION AND NONFICTION

[1] John McPhee, in Norman Sims, ed., *The Literary Journalists: The New Art of Personal Reportage* (New York: Ballantine, 1984), 3.
[2] The venerable *New Yorker*, perhaps the best magazine on the North American continent, is a notable exception; its fact-checking methods are unstinting and legendary.
[3] Ken Auletta, *Backstory: Inside the Business of News* (New York: Penguin, 2003), xx.
[4] Kristina Borjesson, ed. Into the Buzzsaw: Leading Journalists Expose the Myth of a Free Press (Amherst, NY: Prometheus Books, 2002).
[5] Ursula K. Le Guin, *The Wave in the Mind* (Boston: Shambhala, 2004), 140.
[6] E. L. Doctorow, "Childhood of a Writer," *The World Split Open: Great Authors on How and Why We Write* (New York: Tin House Books, 2014), 66-67.
[7] James J. Murphy, "Rhetorical History as a Guide to the Salvation of American Reading and Writing: A Plea for Curricular Courage" in James J. Murphy, Ed. *The Rhetorical Tradition and Modern Writing* (New York: Modern Language Association of America, 1982), 3-12.
[8] Harry Bruce, *Page Fright: Foibles and Fetishes of Famous Writers* (Toronto: McClelland & Stewart, 2010), 310.
[9] Richard Rhodes, *How to Write: Advice and Reflections* (New York: Quill/Harper Collins, 1995), 37.
[10] Rhodes, 35-36.

[11] Rhodes, 47.
[12] Marilynne Robinson, "On Beauty," *The World Split Open: Great Writers on How and Why We Write* (New York: Tin House Books, 2014), 131.
[13] Azar Nafisi, *Reading Lolita in Tehran: A Memoir in Books* (New York: Random House, 2003), 268.
[14] Roger Sales, "Wrestling with Fiction," *New York Review of Books* (21 March 1974), quoting from Alfred Kazin's *Bright Book of Life: American Novelists from Hemingway to Mailer.*
[15] Alan Jacobs, *The Pleasures of Reading in an Age of Distraction* (New York: Oxford University Press, 2011), 130. In a footnote on Walter Benjamin's essay "The Storyteller."
[16] Morrie Ruvinsky, "Bess Anderson: First Female Messiah," *The Heart and Other Strangers* (Santa Monica, CA: Story Thread Press, 2018), 129-130.
[17] Eudora Welty, "Writing and Analyzing a Story," *The Eloquent Essay: An Anthology of Classic and Creative Nonfiction.* Edited by John Loughery (New York: Persea Books, 2000), 33.
[18] Randy Olson, *Houston, We Have a Narrative: Why Science Needs Story* (Chicago: University of Chicago Press, 2015).
[19] Umberto Eco, in Eleanor Wachtel, *Original Minds: Conversations with CBC Radio's Eleanor Wachtel* (Toronto: HarperCollins Canada, 2003), 297.
[20] According to the online site (https://quora.com) the honorary doctorate was awarded in 2002.
[21] https://simanaitissays.com/2015/07/14/the-bookshelves-at-221b/.
[22] Jonathan Gottschall, *The Storytelling Animal: How Stories Make Us Human* (New York: Houghton Mifflin Harcourt, 2012), 152.
[23] Roy Peter Clark, "The Line between Fact and Fiction," 30 July 2002. Archived and accessed online at (https://www.poynter.org/archive/2002/the-line-between-fact-and-fiction/).
[24] Virginia Woolf, reviewing Harold Nicholson's book *Some People.* Woolf used the same analogy in her novel *Orlando*, writing that nature "has played so many queer tricks upon us, making us so unequally of clay and diamonds, of rainbow and granite, and stuffed them into a case." (https://www.sparknotes.com/lit/orlando/themes).
[25] Gottschall, *The Storytelling Animal*, 186.
[26] Ursula K. Le Guin, *Words Are My Matter: Writings about Life and Books 2000 -2016* (Easthampton, MA: Small Beer Press, 2016), 113.
[27] Robert Stone, "Morality and Truth in Literature," *The World Split Open* (New York: Tin House Books, 2014), 166.
[28] Rhodes, *How to Write*, 47.
[29] E. L. Doctorow, "Childhood of a Writer," *The World Split Open* (New York: Tin House Books, 2014), 66.
[30] E. L. Doctorow, "Childhood of a Writer,"67.
[31] Marilynne Robinson, "On Beauty," *The World Split Open*, 138.

[32] A. S. Byatt, "Narrate or Die," *New York Times Magazine* (18 April 1999). Quoted in Steven Pinker, *The Blank Slate: The Modern Denial of Human Nature* (New York: Viking, 2002), 419.
[33] Gottschall, *The Storytelling Animal*, 56.
[34] Umberto Eco, in Eleanor Wachtel, *Original Minds: Conversations with CBC Radio's Eleanor Wachtel* (Toronto: HarperCollins Canada, 2003), 297.
[35] Tim Parks, *Where I'm Reading From: The Changing World of Books* (New York: Random House, 2015), 109.
[36] Mary Karr, *The Art of Memoir* (New York: Harper Collins, 2015), 84.
[37] Wallace Stegner, "Fiction to Make Sense of Life," *World Split Open* (New York: Tin House Books, 2014), 158.
[38] Lewis Carroll, *Through the Looking Glass* (London: Macmillan, 1871). Accessed online at gutenberg.org. The book was a sequel to Carroll's *Alice's Adventures in Wonderland* (first published in 1865). The name Lewis Carroll is a pen name for Charles Lutwidge Dodgson (1832-1898), who was also a mathematician, an inventor, and an Anglican deacon. I've read online that this English writer of children's fiction also wrote eleven books on mathematics and twelve of literary nonfiction.
[39] Walter J. Ong, *Orality and Literacy: The Technologizing of the Word*, (London/ New York: Methuen, 1982) 139-140.
[40] Carl Sagan, "The Fine Art of Baloney Detection," in *The Eloquent Essay: An Anthology of Classic and Creative Nonfiction* (New York: Persea Books, 2000), 155-156.
[41] Robert Stone, "Morality and Truth in Literature" in *The World Split Open*, 160. From a talk that Stone gave in April of 1988.
[42] Antinomian: "of or related to the view that Christians are released from the obligation of observing the moral law" (Concise Oxford Dictionary, 1995). An adjective referring to the doctrine in theology "that faith frees the Christian from the obligations of the moral law" (Funk & Wagnalls Standard Dictionary, 1974).
[43] Stone, 164.
[44] Gottschall, *The Storytelling Animal*, 153.
[45] Edmund White, "The House of Edith," a review of Hermione Lee's book *Edith Wharton*. The review appeared in the *New York Review of Books*, 26 April 2007.
[46] Quoted in Benjamin Taylor, *Proust: The Search* (New Haven, CT: Yale University Press, 2015), 79.
[47] George Steiner in Eleanor Wachtel, *Original Minds: Conversations with CBC Radio's Eleanor Wachtel* (Toronto: Harper Collins Canada, 2003), 119.
[48] Benjamin Taylor, *Proust: The Search*, 113.
[49] Taylor, *Proust: The Search*, 152.
[50] Quoted in Taylor, *Proust: The Search*, 114.
[51] Marcel Proust, *In Search of Lost Time* (New York: Modern Library/Random House, 1992), 606. À la recherche du temps perdu was originally translated into English with the ill-conceived title "Remembrance of Things Past."
[52] Taylor, Proust: *The Search*, 115.

[53.] See Louis Peitzman's Buzzfeed article, "14 Authors You Might Not Know Had Bigoted Views," July 1, 2013. (https://www.buzzfeed.com/louispeitzman/authors-you-might-not-know-had-bigoted-views).
[54.] Robert Stone, "Morality and Truth in Literature," *The World Split Open*, 161-162.
[55.] Susan Orlean, *The Library Book* (New York: Simon & Schuster, 2018), 96.
[56.] *Ibid.*
[57.] Orlean, 97.
[58.] Jeanette Winterson, "What Is Art For?" in *The World Split Open*, 176. The essay is from a talk the English writer, broadcaster, and professor of creative writing gave on 9 November 2000.
[59.] Quoted in Harry Bruce, *Page Fright: Foibles and Fetishes of Famous Writers* (Toronto: McClelland & Stewart, 2009), 185.
[60.] Mary Oliver, "The Perfect Days," quoted in *Lapham's Quarterly/ Happiness* (Volume XII, Number 3, Summer 2019), 170.
[61.] Jon Raymond, "Introduction," *The World Split Open*, 3-4.
[62.] Tracy Kidder, *Good Prose*, 123-124.
[63.] With thanks to my good friend Grant Fleming, who taught sports writing for a couple of years in the Journalism Department where I taught from 1999 until 2015. I once said to him: "Life promises us nothing but our first breath." Some years later, Grant corrected me: "Remember when you said that? You were wrong: it also promises us our last."
[64.] Thomas King, *The Truth About Stories: A Native Narrative* (Toronto: House of Anansi, 2003), 167.
[65.] Le Guin, *Words Are My Matter*, 113.

CHAPTER 6 / LANGUAGE ORIGINS AND EVOLUTION

[1.] "Rethinking Neanderthals," *Smithsonian Magazine* online: www.smithsonianmag.com.
[2.] "How the Hyoid Bone Changed History," *Live Science* online: www.livescience.com.
[3.] Roger Lewin, *The Origin of Modern Humans*, quoted in Fred White, ed., *The Daily Reader* (Cincinnati, Ohio: Writer's Digest Books), 34.
[4.] Christine Kenneally, *The First Word: The Search for the Origins of Language* (New York: Penguin, 2007), 216.
[5.] James Kingsland, *Siddhartha's Brain: Unlocking the Ancient Science of Enlightenment* (New York: William Morrow/HarperCollins, 2016), 208.
[6.] Charles Darwin, quoted in Daniel C. Dennett, *From Bacteria to Bach and Back: The Evolution of Minds* (New York: W.W. Norton & Company, 2017), 251.
[7.] Erwin Schroedinger, "The Mystic Vision," in *Quantum Questions: Mystical Writings of the World's Great Physicists*. Ken Wilbur, ed. (Boulder, Colorado: Shambhala Publications, 1984), 97.
[8.] St. Augustine, quoted in Fred White, ed., *The Daily Reader* (Cincinnati, Ohio: Writer's Digest Books), 58.

[9] Clive Barker, *Weaveworld*, cited in Bauer, ed. *In the Beginning*, 180.
[10] Aviya Kushner, *The Grammar of God* (New York: Spiegel and Grau, 2015), 11.
[11] Kushner, *The Grammar of God*, 19.
[12] Kenneally, *The First Word*, 10.
[13] Kenneally, 201.
[14] Kenneally, 194.
[15] Kenneally, 7.
[16] Steven Pinker, *Enlightenment Now: The Case for Reason, Science, Humanism, and Progress* (New York: Viking / Penguin Random House, LLC, 2018), 356.
[17] Edward O. Wilson, "The Forces of Evolution" from *The Diversity of Life*. In Fred White, *The Daily Reader* (Cincinnati, Ohio: Writer's Digest Books, 2009), 6.
[18] Steven Pinker, *How the Mind Works* (New York: W.W. Norton & Company, 1997), 167.
[19] Unlike the widely recognized Darwin (1809-1882), whose name has become synonymous with the theory, Wallace (1823-1913) is lesser known, though he independently conceived the theory of evolution through natural selection; his paper on the subject was jointly published with some of Darwin's writings in 1858.
[20] Carl Safina, *Becoming Wild: How Animal Cultures Raise Families, Create Beauty, and Achieve Peace* (New York: Henry Holt, 2020), 212.
[21] " 'First Human' Discovered in Ethiopia," British Broadcasting Corporation online, 4 March 2015.
[22] See Aida Gómez-Robles, "Science Advances," in *Proceedings of the National Academy of Sciences*, 15 May 2019. Accessed online at https://advances.sciencemag.org.
[23] A supporting theory for evolution was espoused about the same time by the Austrian monk Gregor Mendel (1822-1884), considered the father of modern genetics. Mendel's experiments showed that in plants, some characteristics are indeed passed on from one generation to another, and thus these characteristics can be used to trace ancestry.
[24] The two-volume *Shorter Oxford English Dictionary* (3rd edition 1973; with first and second editions in 1933 and 1939).
[25] Darwin quoted in White, *The Daily Reader*, 94.
[26] James Shapiro, *Evolution: A View from the 21st Century* (Upper Saddle River, NJ: FT Press Science, 2011), 143.
[27] See the website and an article by Stephen L. Talbott: (www.natureinstitute.org/article/stephen-l-talbott/evolution-a-third-way).
[28] Stephen Talbott, "Evolution: A Third Way?" From *In Context* #33 (Spring, 2015). Accessed online.
[29] Arthur Koestler, *The Ghost in the Machine* (Arthur Koestler, 1967. First published by Hutchinson & Co., 1967 / Reprint edition by Last Century Media), xii.
[30] See this online site: https://www.newscientist.com/article/mg24432601-100-were-beginning-to-question-the-idea-of-species-including-our-own/. December 11, 2019.
[31] Frans de Waal, *Mama's Last Hug: Animal Emotions and What They Tell Us about Ourselves* (New York: W. W. Norton & Company, 2019), 45.
[32] James Shapiro, "The significance of bacterial colony patterns," *BioEssays* (Vol. 17, No. 7, 1995), 597-607.

33. Jake Page, *Dogs: A Natural History* (New York: HarperCollins, 2007), 3-4.
34. Frans de Waal, *Mama's Last Hug*, 18.
35. Thomas H. Huxley; quotation accessed online at http://www.quotationspage.com.
36. Kenneally, *The First Word*, 285-286.
37. Marilynne Robinson, in *The World Split Open: Great Authors on How and Why We Write* (New York: Tin House Books, 2014), 132.
38. Kenneally, *The First Word*, 287-288.
39. James Hurford, *The Origins of Language: A Slim Guide* (Oxford University Press, 2014), 153.
40. Kenneally, *The First Word*, 197.
41. Kenneally, 269.
42. Paul Davies, *Are We Alone? Philosophical Implications of the Discovery of Extraterrestrial Life*. Quoted in White, *The Daily Reader*, 187.
43. Smithsonian Institute, online at https://humanorigins.si.edu/education/introduction-human-evolution. Other estimates say anatomically modern humans arose in Africa about 135,000 years ago. See Jake Page, *Dogs: A Natural History* (New York: HarperCollins, 2007).
44. Frans de Waal, *Mama's Last Hug*, 242.
45. *New York Times* (online) 18 January 2017.
46. Loren Eiseley, "The Cosmic Orphan," reprinted in *The Treasury of the Encyclopedia Britannica*. 15th edition. Clifton Fadiman, ed. (New York: Viking/Penguin, 1992), 391.
47. Loren Eiseley, "The Cosmic Orphan" reprinted in *The Treasury of the Encyclopedia Britannica*. Clifton Fadiman, ed. (New York: Viking/Penguin, 1992), 384-392.
48. This and subsequent quotations from "The Cosmic Orphan" are taken from its reprint in *The Treasury of the Encyclopedia Britannica*, cited above, unless otherwise indicated.
49. Kenneally, *The First Word*, 13.
50. Shimon Edelman, *The Happiness of Pursuit: What Neuroscience Can Teach Us About the Good Life* (New York: Basic Books, 2012), 102-103.
51. Ivan Illich and Barry Sanders, *ABC: The Alphabetization of the Popular Mind* (New York: Random House, 1988), 87.
52. Amalia E. Gnanadesikan, *The Writing Revolution: Cuneiform to the Internet* (UK: Wiley-Blackwell, 2009), 2.
53. Maryanne Wolf, *Proust and the Squid: The Story and Science of the Reading Brain* (New York: Harper Perennial, 2008), 24.
54. Anna Quindlen, *How Reading Changed My Life* (New York: Ballantine/Random House, 1998), 17.
55. Jared Diamond, quoted in Eleanor Wachtel, *Original Minds* (Toronto: Harper Collins, 2003), 241-242.
56. Brandon Keim, "Secrets of Animal Communication" in *National Geographic* November 2019 (Washington, D.C.: National Geographic), 43.
57. Wikipedia: "In the narrow sense, Mesopotamia is the area between the Euphrates and Tigris rivers, north or northwest of the bottleneck at Baghdad, in modern Iraq; it is Al-Jazīrah ("The Island") of the Arabs." Accessed 09 December 2020.

[58.] *Benét's Reader's Encyclopedia*, 4th edition (New York: HarperCollins, 1996).
[59.] Walter J. Ong, *Orality and Literacy: The Technologizing of the Word* (London/ New York: Methuen, 1982), 99.
[60.] Jared Diamond, *Guns, Germs, and Steel: The Fates of Human Societies* (New York: W. W. Norton & Company, 1999), 235.
[61.] Ivan Illich and Barry Sanders, *ABC: The Alphabetization of the Popular Mind* (New York: Vintage Books / Random House, 1988), 10-11.
[62.] Cyrus H. Gordon, *The Common Background of Greek and Hebrew Civilizations* (New York: W. W. Norton & Company, 1965, 1962), 9-10.
[63.] Illich, *ABC*, 9.
[64.] Wolf, *Proust and the Squid*, 94.
[65.] Wolf, 99.
[66.] Ong, *Orality and Literacy*, 28.
[67.] Wolf, 59-60.
[68.] Robert Darnton, "How to Read a Book," in *New York Review of Books* (6 June, 1996). Reviewing Roger Chartier's *Forms and Meanings: Texts, Performances, and Audiences from Codex to Computer*. Accessed online.
[69.] Illich, 46-49.
[70.] Illich, 45.
[71.] Illich, 31.
[72.] Ong, 118.
[73.] Ong, 118-119.
[74.] Illich, 31.
[75.] Ong, 127.
[76.] Illich, 94.
[77.] Anthony Grafton, "Jumping Through the Computer Screen," *New York Review of Books* (Dec. 23, 2010). A review of the book *Reinventing Knowledge: From Alexandria to the Internet*, by Ian F. McNeely and Lisa Wolverton.
[78.] Ronald Wright, *A Short History of Progress* (Toronto: House of Anansi Press, 2004), 19, 118.
[79.] Fred White, *The Daily Reader*, 336. Quoting Frederick Ferré, *Philosophy of Technology*.
[80.] Ong, 97.
[81.] Roger Penrose, *The Emperor's New Mind: Concerning Computers, Minds, and the Laws of Physics*. Quoted in White, *The Daily Reader*, 114.
[82.] Lewis Mumford, "The Monastery and the Clock," *Technics and Civilization* (New York: Harcourt, Brace and Company, Inc., 1934). In *Exploring the Ways of Mankind*, Walter Goldschmidt, ed. (New York: Holt, Rinehart and Winston, 1960), 156-157.
[83.] Ong, *Orality and Literacy*, 82.
[84.] James Bridle, *New Dark Age: Technology and the End of the Future* (London: Verso, 2018), 63.
[85.] Some complex societies, including one of the world's largest empires in the early 16th century, the Inca of South America, proceeded without benefit of writing. See Jared Diamond's *Guns, Germs, and Steel: The Fates of Human Societies*, 237.

86. See Nicholas Ostler, *Empires of the Word: A Language History of the World* (New York: Harper Collins, 2005).
87. Jared Diamond, in Eleanor Wachtel, *Original Minds: Conversations with CBC Radio's Eleanor Wachtel* (Toronto: Harper Flamingo Canada, 2003), 244.
88. Ong, 154, 178-179.
89. Ritchie Calder, "Saddlebag Drugs" in *Medicine and Man: The Story of the Art and Science of Healing*. Quoted in *The Daily Reader* (Cincinnati, Ohio: Writer's Digest Books/ F & W Media, 2009), 292.
90. Candace Pert, *Molecules of Emotion* (New York: Simon & Schuster), 223.
91. *Ibid.*
92. https://www.aljazeera.com/news/2017/5/21/global-shortage-of-penicillin-reasons-and-consequences.
93. Ong, *Orality and Literacy*, 136.

CHAPTER 7 / LITERACY AND ITS DISCONTENTS

1. Walter J. Ong, *Orality and Literacy: The Technologizing of the Word* (London: Methuen & Co. Ltd., 1982), 9.
2. Fred White, ed. *The Daily Reader* (Cincinnati, OH: Writer's Digest Books, 2009), 63. Quoting from David Abram, *The Spell of the Sensuous: Perception and Language in a More-Than-Human World.*
3. Jake Page, *Dogs: A Natural History* (New York: HarperCollins, 2007), 117.
4. Paul Kalanithi, *When Breath Becomes Air* (New York: Random House, 2016), 109.
5. Kalanithi, 112.
6. Ong, *Orality and Literacy*, 72.
7. Annie Dillard, *Pilgrim at Tinker Creek* (New York: Harper& Row, 1974), 30-31.
8. Ong, 75, 162.
9. Ong, 178.
10. Defoe is better known for his novel *Robinson Crusoe*, published in 1719.
11. Ivan Illich and Barry Sanders, *ABC: The Alphabetization of the Popular Mind* (New York: Random House, 1988), 93. Considered England's first novel, Defoe's *Journal* was long preceded by the first novel in Spanish (*Don Quixote*, by Miguel de Cervantes, published in two parts in 1605 and 1615).
12. Illich and Sanders, *ABC*, 97.
13. Ong, *Orality and Literacy*,79.
14. Illich and Sanders, *ABC*, 10.
15. Amalia E. Gnanadesikan, *The Writing Revolution: Cuneiform to the Internet* (UK: Wiley-Blackwell, 2009), 4-5.
16. Illich and Sanders, 65. Among the first grammar books in English was Robert Lowth's *A Short Introduction to English Grammar*, published in 1758.
17. Illich and Sanders, *ABC*, 66-67.
18. Illich and Sanders, 69.

[19]. Jane Jacobs, *Dark Age Ahead* (Toronto: Random House Canada, 2004), 5.
[20]. Brian Christian and Tom Griffiths, *Algorithms to Live By: The Computer Science of Human Decisions* (Toronto: Penguin/Random House Canada, 2016), 220-221.
[21]. Steven Pinker, *The Language Instinct* (New York: HarperCollins, 1994), 28.
[22]. Illich and Sanders, *ABC*, 32-34.
[23]. Bruce Chatwin, *The Songlines* (New York: Viking, 1987), 269.
[24]. Chatwin, 189.
[25]. Ong, *Orality and Literacy*, 115.
[26]. Ong, 96.
[27]. Ong, 119.
[28]. Ong, 113.
[29]. Richard Powers, in Harry Bruce, *Page Fright* (Toronto: McClelland & Stewart Ltd., 2009), 105.
[30]. Bruce, *Page Fright*,105.
[31]. With apologies to Ada Lovelace. "As with the invention of paper, it is not really possible to say who invented the computer or when, despite this being recent history. Lately, it has become popular to attribute the invention—as Walter Isaacson suggests in *The Innovators* and James Essinger affirms in *Ada's Algorithm*—to Ada Lovelace, poet Lord Byron's neglected and brilliant daughter. In the early nineteenth century, she wrote the first algorithm intended to be carried out by a machine." – Mark Kurlansky, *Paper*, 325.
[32]. Rebecca Solnit, quoted in Cecilia Watson, *Semicolon: The Past, Present, and Future of a Misunderstood Mark* (New York: HarperCollins, 2019), 122.
[33]. Illich and Sanders, 105.
[34]. Theodore Roszak, *The Cult of Information: The Folklore of Computers and the True Art of Thinking* (New York: Pantheon, 1986), 70.
[35]. Illich and Sanders, 107.
[36]. White, *The Daily Reader*, 24. Quoting from Susan Jacoby's *The Age of American Unreason.*
[37]. Nicholas Carr, *The Shallows: What the Internet Is Doing to Our Brains* (New York: W. W. Norton, 2011, 2010), 118.
[38]. Jon Raymond, ed. "Introduction," *The World Split Open*, 2.
[39]. Anna Quindlen, *How Reading Changed My Life* (New York: Ballantine Books, 1998), 65.
[40]. Alberto Manguel, *A History of Reading* (Toronto: Vintage Canada, 1996), 135.
[41]. Sven Birkerts, *The Gutenberg Elegies: The Fate of Reading in an Electronic* Age (New York: Ballantine Books, 1994), 32.
[42]. Alan Jacobs, *The Pleasures of Reading in an Age of Distraction* (New York: Oxford University Press, 2011), 142.
[43]. Sherry Turkle, *Alone Together: Why We Expect More from Technology and Less from Each Other* (New York: Basic Books, 2011), 1.
[44]. Carr, *The Shallows*, 178-179.
[45]. Carr, 179.
[46]. Maryanne Wolf, *Proust and the Squid: The Story and Science of the Reading Brain* (New York: HarperCollins, 2007), 74. Quoting from Plato's *Phaedrus.*

[47.] Illich and Sanders, *ABC*, 26. Quoting from Plato's *Symposium*.
[48.] Wolf, *Proust and the Squid*, 69. Quoting from Plato's *Phaedrus*.
[49.] *Ibid.* Quoting Sir Frederic Kenyon.
[50.] Dorothy Sayers, *The Lost Tools of Learning* (London: Methuen, 1948), 2. An address first delivered at Oxford University in 1947. Transcript accessed online at (http://www.gbt.org/text/sayers.html).
[51.] Students first had to master the trivium, or three core subjects, of rhetoric, grammar, and dialectic (logic). If they succeeded, they could progress to the quadrivium, consisting of geometry, arithmetic, astronomy, and music. Together, the trivium and quadrivium formed the seven subjects of what today we call the liberal arts tradition.
[52.] W. H. Auden, *A Certain World: A Commonplace Book* (New York: Viking, 1970), 237.
[53.] Illich and Sanders, *ABC*, ix.
[54.] Wolf, *Proust and the Squid*, 226.
[55.] Robert Darnton, "How to Read a Book," *The New York Review of Books*, 6 June 1996.
[56.] Neil Postman, *Technopoly*, quoted in White, *The Daily Reader*, 152.
[57.] Mark Kurlansky, *Paper: Paging Through History*, 334.
[58.] Meredith Broussard, *Artificial Unintelligence: How Computers Misunderstand the World* (Cambridge, MA: MIT Press, 2018), 154.
[59.] Broussard, *Artificial Unintelligence*, 194.
[60.] Witold Rybczynski, *Taming the Tiger: The Struggle to Control Technology* (New York: Penguin, 1983), 223, 227.
[61.] James Bridle, *New Dark Age: Technology and the End of the Future* (London: Verso, 2018), 186.
[62.] Broussard, 115.
[63.] *Ibid.* Here, Broussard quotes from Frank Pasquale, *The Black Box Society: The Secret Algorithms That Control Money and Information* (Cambridge, MA: Harvard University Press, 2015).
[64.] Illich and Sanders, *ABC*, ix.
[65.] David L. Ulin, *The Lost Art of Reading: Why Books Matter in a Distracted Time* (Seattle: Sasquatch Books, 2010), 4-5.
[66.] Ursula M. Franklin, *The Real World of Technology* (Toronto: House of Anansi, 1992, 1999), 59.
[67.] Andy Miller, *The Year of Reading Dangerously: How Fifty Great Books (and Two Not-So-Great Ones) Saved My Life* (London: Fourth Estate/HarperCollins, 2014), 276.
[68.] Illich and Sanders, *ABC*, 84-85.
[69.] Mark Kurlansky, *Paper: Paging Through History*, 230-231.
[70.] Kurlansky, 162.
[71.] Kurlansky, 237.
[72.] Frederick Douglass (1817-1895), in a famous speech, April 1886.
[73.] David L. Ulin, *The Lost Art of Reading*, 84. Quoting from an article written by Rich Cohen and originally published in the *Los Angeles Times*.

[74.] David Shields, *Reality Hunger*, quoted in David L. Ulin, *The Lost Art of Reading*, 43.
[75.] Robert Graves (1895-1985), in a 1962 interview on BBC-TV. See the site (http://www.quotationspage.com).
[76.] Kurlansky, *Paper*, 204, 230.
[77.] Kurlansky, 238.
[78.] Quindlen, *How Reading Changed My Life* (New York: Random House, 1998),19.
[79.] Susan Orlean, *The Library Book* (New York: Simon & Schuster, 2018), 98.
[80.] Gerald Early, "Life with Daughters: Watching the Miss America Pageant" *Kenyon Review*, 1990. Selected by Joyce Carol Oates for *The Best American Essays 1991*), 545.
[81.] Neil Postman, *Building a Bridge to the 18th Century: How the Past Can Improve Our Future* (New York: Alfred A. Knopf, 1999), cited in Roy Peter Clark, *Writing Tools: 50 Essential Strategies for Every Writer* (New York: Little, Brown and Company, 2006), 42.
[82.] Ray Jackendoff, *A User's Guide to Thought and Meaning* (New York: Oxford University Press, 2012), 90-91.
[83.] Julian Jaynes, *The Origin of Consciousness in the Breakdown of the Bicameral Mind* (Boston: Houghton Mifflin, 1976), 26-27.
[84.] Ong, 179.
[85.] Accessed online at www.writersdigest.com/writing-quotes.
[86.] Wolf, *Proust and the Squid*, 65-66.
[87.] Wolf, 212. Quoting James Carroll, "America's Bookstores: Shrines to the Truth." *Boston Globe*, 30 Jan., 2001.
[88.] Orlean, *The Library Book*, 309-310.
[89.] Miller, *The Year of Reading Dangerously*, 295.
[90.] Kurlansky, *Paper*, 336.
[91.] David Marchese, "Jon Stewart Is Back to Weigh In," *New York Times*, 15 June 2020.
[92.] William James, *Selected Papers on Philosophy*. 1917 (London: J. M. Dent & Sons Ltd., and New York: E. P. Dutton & Co. Inc., 1961), 141.
[93.] Steven Pinker, *Enlightenment Now: The Case for Reason, Science, Humanism, and Progress* (New York: Viking/Penguin Random House, 2018), 406.
[94.] Ian McEwan, *Saturday* (New York: Alfred A. Knopf, 2005), 77. Quoting biologist Sir Peter Brian Medawar (1915-1987).
[95.] Sir Ernest Shackleton, quoted in Wachtel, "Introduction," *Original Minds* (Toronto: HarperCollins, 2003), 5.

CHAPTER 8 / NAMING, IDENTITY, AND CRUCIBLES OF INDIVIDUALITY

[1.] Andy Miller, *The Year of Reading Dangerously: How Fifty Great Books (and Two Not-So-Great Ones) Saved My Life* (London: Fourth Estate/HarperCollins, 2014), 162.
[2.] Antonin Artaud, *The Theater and Its Double*. Quoted in White, *The Daily Reader* (Cincinnati, OH: Writer's Digest Books), 306.
[3.] Andy Miller, *The Year of Reading Dangerously*, 194.

[4] Neil Postman, "Invisible Technologies," in *Science and Technology Today: Readings for Writers*, Nancy R. MacKenzie, ed. (New York: St. Martin's Press, 1995), 128. Excerpted from Neil Postman, *Technopoly: The Surrender of Culture to Technology* (New York: Vintage, 1992).
[5] Cyrus H. Gordon, *The Common Backgrounds of Greek and Hebrew Civilizations* (New York: Norton & Company, 1965), 11.
[6] Loren Eiseley, "The Cosmic Orphan," reprinted as "Human Life," in *The Treasury of the Encyclopedia Britannica*, 15th edition. Clifton Fadiman, ed. (New York: Viking/Penguin, 1992), 389-390.
[7] E. L. Doctorow: "Childhood of a Writer," *The World Split Open,* 58.
[8] See Edwin Black, *IBM and the Holocaust: The Strategic Alliance Between Nazi Germany and America's Most Powerful Corporation* (New York: Crown Publishers, 2001).
[9] Robin Wall Kimmerer, *Braiding Sweetgrass: Indigenous Wisdom, Scientific Knowledge, and the Teachings of Plants* (Minneapolis: Milkweed Editions/Green Press Initiative, 2013), 15-16.
[10] Oliver Sacks, in Eleanor Wachtel, *Original Minds: In Conversation with CBC Radio's Eleanor Wachtel* (Toronto: Harper Collins, 2003), 259.
[11] Mary Beard, *Women and Power* (New York: W. W. Norton, 2017), 62.
[12] Beard, *Women and Power*, 58.
[13] White, *The Daily Reader*, 345.
[14] Emma Goldman, *The Traffic in Women and Other Essays on Feminism* (Washington: Times Change Press, 1970), 46.
[15] J. Bronowski and Bruce Mazlish. *The Western Intellectual Tradition: From Leonardo to Hegel* (New York: Harper & Brothers, 1960. Published in 1986 by Dorset, by arrangement with Harper & Row), 130.
[16] *Ibid.*
[17] *Ibid.*
[18] Bronowski and Mazlish, *The Western Intellectual Tradition*, 426.
[19] Steven Pinker, *Enlightenment Now: The Case for Reason, Science, Humanism, and Progress* (New York: Viking, 2018), 297.
[20] Steven Rose, "Darwin, Race and Gender" in *EMBO Reports*, 2009 April 10(4), 297-298. Accessed online at https://www.ncbi.nlm.nih.gov/pmc/articles/PMC2672903/
[21] *Ibid.*
[22] Steven Pinker, *The Language Instinct: How the Mind Creates Language* (New York: HarperCollins, 1994), 430.
[23] Called *nu shu*, this language is depicted in Lisa See's novel *Snow Flower and the Secret Fan.* The last speaker of *nu shu* died in the early 21st century, according to Maryanne Wolf in her book *Proust and the Squid: The Story and Science of the Reading Brain* (New York: Harper, 2007), 49.
[24] See Wolf, *Proust and the Squid*, 39-40.
[25] Walter J. Ong, *Orality and Literacy: The Technologizing of the Word.* (London and New York: Methuen, 1982),113.

[26] Ong, 113-114.
[27] James Bridle, *New Dark Age: Technology and the End of the Future* (London: Verso, 2018), 86.
[28] Bridle, *New Dark Age*, 89.
[29] Bridle, *New Dark Age*, 91. See John P. A. Ioannidis, "Why Most Published Research Findings Are False," *PLOS ONE*, August 2005.
[30] C. P. Snow. *The Two Cultures and the Scientific Revolution* (New York: Cambridge University Press, 1959), 15-16.
[31] John von Neumann, *The Computer and the Brain*, 2nd ed. (New Haven, CT: Yale University Press, 2000), 82.
[32] Gerald Durrell, *The Corfu Trilogy: Three Classic Tales of Childhood on an Island Paradise* (New York: Penguin Books, 2006), 393-394.
[33] Ken Wilber, ed. *Quantum Questions: Mystical Writings of the World's Great Physicists* (Boulder, Colorado: Shambhala Publications, 1984), 33.
[34] Neil Turok, *The Universe Within* (Toronto: House of Anansi Press, 2012), 93.
[35] Turok, *The Universe Within*, 111.
[36] K. C. Cole, *The Universe and the Teacup: The Mathematics of Truth and Beauty*. Quoted in White, *The Daily Reader*, 83.
[37] Larry Dossey, *Space, Time, and Medicine* (Boulder, Colorado: Shambhala, 1982), 113.
[38] Candace B. Pert, *Molecules of Emotion: Why You Feel the Way You Feel* (New York: Simon & Schuster, 1997), 260.
[39] W. H. Auden, *A Certain World* (New York: Viking, 1970), 92.
[40] William James, *Selected Papers on Philosophy*, (London: J. M. Dent & Sons Ltd., 1917 / New York: E. P. Dutton & Co. Inc., 1961), 151-152.
[41] Dean Rusk, accessed online at https://www.brainyquote.com.
[42] Shimon Edelman, *The Happiness of Pursuit: What Neuroscience Can Teach us About the Good Life* (New York: Basic Books, 2012), ix.
[43] William James, *Selected Papers*, 93-94.
[44] Carl Safina, *Beyond Words: What Animals Think and Feel* (New York: Henry Holt, 2015), 140.
[45] Alice Calaprice, ed. *The Ultimate Quotable Einstein* (Princeton, NJ: Princeton University Press / Cambridge, MA: Harvard University Press, 2011), 371.
[46] Neil Turok, *The Universe Within: From Quantum to Cosmos* (Toronto: House of Anansi Press, 2012), 167-168.
[47] Julian Jaynes, *The Origins of Consciousness in the Breakdown of the Bicameral Mind* (Boston: Houghton Mifflin, 1976), 12.
[48] White, *The Daily Reader*, 205. Quoting from Sylvia Nasar, *A Beautiful Mind: A Biography of John Forbes, Nash, Jr.* (Nash won the 1994 Nobel Prize in Economics.)
[49] Marc Shell, *Money, Language and Thought* (Baltimore: Johns Hopkins University Press, 1982), 1-2.
[50] Shell, *Money, Language and Thought*, 2.

[51] The Chinese were first to use paper bills, "folding money," during the Tang Dynasty, 618-907 CE. It would take hundreds more years for paper money to spread to Europe in the seventeenth century.
[52] Jack Weatherford, *The History of Money* (New York: Three Rivers Press, 1997), xiii.
[53] Weatherford, xi.
[54] Weatherford, xii.
[55] *Ibid.*
[56] A. Whitney Griswold, *Vital Speeches 19* (15 July 1953), 588. Also in his book *Liberal Education and the Democratic Ideal and Other Essays* (1959). Accessed online at https://www.brainyquote.com.
[57] Martha Stout, *The Sociopath Next Door* (New York: Three Rivers Press, 2005).
[58] Dacher Keltner, *The Power Paradox: How We Gain and Lose Influence* (New York: Penguin, 2016).
[59] The text of J. K. Rowling's speech is available online and in her book *Very Good Lives: The Fringe Benefits of Failure and the Importance of Imagination.* (Little, Brown and Company, 2015).
[60] Dacher Keltner, *The Power Paradox*, 127. "In one study, more than 27,000 working adults in twenty-seven different countries were asked how often it's justified to: 1) claim government benefits to which you are not entitled; 2) avoid paying a fare on public transportation; 3) cheat on taxes; and 4) accept a bribe. The participants also rated their income on a ten-point scale. Wealthier participants were more likely to say it's okay to engage in the four unethical acts."
[61] Amartya Sen quoted in Eleanor Wachtel, *Original Minds*, 180.
[62] Esther Schor, *Emma Lazarus* (New York: Schocken Books / Penguin Random House LLC, 2006, 2017), ix, 156.
[63] Annie Dillard, *For the Time Being* (New York: Viking/Penguin, 1999), 118.
[64] David Mitchell, *Cloud Atlas* (Toronto: Vintage Canada, 2014), 508.
[65] *Ibid.*
[66] Mitchell, *Cloud Atlas*, 509.
[67] John Stuart Mill, *On Liberty*. Accessed online at https://www.brainyquote.com.
[68] Laurie Garrett, *The Coming Plague: Newly Emerging Diseases in a World Out of Balance* (New York: Penguin Books, 1994), 618.

CHAPTER 9 / BEFORE WORDS

[1] Ritchie Pierce Havens (January 21, 1941 – April 22, 2013) was an American singer-songwriter and guitarist whose music fused elements of folk, soul, and R&B. His hands were large and amazing. To play bar chords, he'd use the thumb of his left hand, over the top of the guitar's fret board.
[2] Maxine Ruvinsky, *Practical Grammar: A Canadian Writer's Resource* (Don Mills, Ontario: Oxford University Press, 3rd edition, 2014).
[3] Ian McEwan, *Saturday* (New York: Alfred A. Knopf Canada, 2005), 141.

[4] Dr. Henry Kravitz died on 13 March 2000. He had worked in the Department of Psychiatry at Montreal's Jewish General Hospital and often led it, more than nominally. According to a journal article, while he was still in training as a psychoanalyst, he implemented "what may have been the first psychodynamically-oriented group therapy in Montreal." See John J. Sigal, "The contribution of the Department of Psychiatry of the Jewish General Hospital to the development of psychoanalysis in Quebec" (*Filigrane*, volume 10, numéro 1, printemps 2001), 60.
[5] Quoted in Catherine Jones, "How Phobic Fear Makes Monsters Out of Molehills" (*Maclean's* magazine, 21 April 1962), 25.
[6] Richard Bandler and John Grinder, *Frogs into Princes: Neuro-Linguistic Programming* (Moab, Utah: Real People Press, 1979), 170-171.
[7] Antonio Damasio, *The Feeling of What Happens: Body and Emotion in the Making of Consciousness* (New York: Harcourt, 1999), 284.
[8] Damasio, 291.
[9] Robert Coles, *The Moral Intelligence of Children* (New York: Random House, 1997), 185.
[10] Steven Pinker, *How the Mind Works* (New York: W. W. Norton, 1997), 167.
[11] See the following blog entry: https://www.mahlatini.com/blog/2012/10/amazing-animal-abilities.
[12] Gerald Durrell, *The Corfu Trilogy: Three Classic Tales of Childhood on an Island Paradise* (New York: Penguin, 2006), 393. Rotifers come in many different shapes; they are not protozoans (they consist of many cells), and they can reproduce sexually or by parthenogenesis.
[13] Brandon Keim, "Secrets of Animal Communication," (Washington, D.C.: *National Geographic*, Special Issue, November 2019), 72, 74.
[14] Brandon Keim, "Secrets of Animal Communication," 9.
[15] Keim, 76.
[16] Keim, 45.
[17] Jane Goodall, quoted in Eleanor Wachtel, *Original Minds (*Toronto: HarperCollins Canada, 2003), 63.
[18] Jared Diamond, quoted in *Original Minds*, 228-229.
[19] Oliver Sacks, *The River of Consciousness* (New York: Alfred A. Knopf, 2017), 75.
[20] Carl Safina, *Becoming Wild: How Cultures Raise Families, Create Beauty, and Achieve Peace* (New York: Henry Holt and Company, 2020), 24.
[21] Keim, "Secrets," 41.
[22] Keim, 39-41.
[23] Jake Page, *Dogs: A Natural History* (New York: HarperCollins, 2007), 136.
[24] Jacob M. Appel, *Scouting for the Reaper* (New York: Black Lawrence Press, 2014). Accessed online at: https://untamedscience.com/order/primates.
[25] Robin Wall Kimmerer, *Braiding Sweetgrass: Indigenous Wisdom, Scientific Knowledge, and the Teachings of Plants* (Minneapolis: Milkweed Editions/Green Press Initiative, 2013), 18.
[26] Christian Wiman, "The Cancer Chair: Is Suffering Meaningless?" *Harper's Magazine* (Feb. 2020), 57.

[27.] Keim, "Secrets of Animal Communication," 61.
[28.] Steven Pinker, *The Language Instinct*, 230.
[29.] Annie Dillard, *For the Time Being* (New York: Viking/Penguin, 1999), 162-163.
[30.] Oliver Sacks, *The River of Consciousness* (New York: Alfred A. Knopf, 2017), 149-150.
[31.] Ursula K. Le Guin in Jon Raymond, ed. *The World Split Open* (New York: Tin House Books, 2014), 101.
[32.] Keim, "Secrets," 109.
[33.] Annie Dillard, *Pilgrim at Tinker Creek* (New York: Harper & Row, 1974), 257.
[34.] Robin Wall Kimmerer, *Braiding Sweetgrass*, 36.
[35.] Keim, 46.
[36.] Frans de Waal, *Mama's Last Hug They Tell Us about Ourselves* (New York: W. W. Norton, 2019), 119.
[37.] Frans de Waal, *Mama's Last Hug*, 256.
[38.] Voltaire quoted in Carl Safina, *Beyond Words*, 80.
[39.] Sam Kean, *The Tale of the Dueling Neurosurgeons: The History of the Human Brain as Revealed by True Stories of Trauma, Madness, and Recovery* (New York: Little, Brown and Company, 2014), 315-316.
[40.] Candace Pert, *Molecules of Emotion*, 134.
[41.] Ian McEwan, *Saturday* (New York: Alfred A. Knopf Canada, 2015), 127.
[42.] Frans de Waal, *Mama's Last Hug*, 268-269.
[43.] Annie Dillard, *For the Time Being* (New York: Viking/Penguin, 1999), 138.
[44.] De Waal, *Mama's Last Hug*, 103.
[45.] Quoted in *Lapham's Quarterly* (Volume 12, Number 3, Summer 2019), 33.
[46.] *The Ultimate Quotable Einstein*. Alice Calaprice, ed. (Princeton, NJ: Princeton University Press / Cambridge, MA: Harvard University Press, 2011), 422-423
[47.] Carl Safina, *Becoming Wild*, 174. Quoting from Charles Darwin, *The Descent of Man*, 39.
[48.] Neil Turok, *The Universe Within*, 111-112.
[49.] Dean Burnett, *The Idiot Brain* (New York: HarperCollins, 2016), 146.
[50.] Carl Safina, *Beyond Words: What Animals Think and Feel* (New York: Henry Holt, 2015), 324.
[51.] Jake Page, Dogs: *A Natural History* (New York: HarperCollins, 2007), 149.
[52.] Sam Kean, *The Tale of the Dueling Neurosurgeons*, 224.
[53.] Einstein, in Ken Wilber, ed. *Quantum Questions: Mystical Writings of the World's Great Physicists* (Boulder, Colorado: Shambhala, 1984), 101. Original source: Einstein's *Ideas and Opinions* (New York: Crown Publishers, 1954).
[54.] Susan Greenfield, *You and Me: The Neuroscience of Identity* (London: Notting Hill Editions Ltd., 2011), 131-132.
[55.] Antonio Damasio, *The Feeling of What Happens* (New York: Harcourt, 1999), 139.
[56.] One of the earliest references to this famous quote is in Jacques Hadamard's book *Psychology of Invention in the Mathematical Field* (published in the late 1930s). For a recent reference, see Paul Ellis, "Muscular Thinking, *New Scientist* online, 14 April 2020.
[57.] *The Ultimate Quotable Einstein*, 377.

[58] De Waal, *Mama's Last Hug*, 205.
[59] Annie Dillard, *Teaching a Stone to Talk*, 486.
[60] Carl Safina, *Beyond Words: What Animals Think and Feel* (New York: Henry Holt, 2015), 344.
[61] Oliver Sacks, *The River of Consciousness* (New York: Alfred A. Knopf, 2017), 65.
[62] Susan Greenfield, *You and Me*, 123.
[63] Sam Kean, *The Tale of the Dueling Neurosurgeons*, 15.
[64] Neil Turok, *The Universe Within*, 14.
[65] Turok, 95.
[66] Damasio, *The Feeling of What Happens*, 35.
[67] Dean Burnett, *The Idiot Brain: A Neuroscientist Explains What Your Head Is Really Up To* (Toronto: HarperCollins, 2016), 177-178.
[68] W. H. Auden, *A Certain World*, 306.
[69] Frans de Waal, *Mama's Last Hug*, 50, 107.
[70] Carl Safina, *Beyond Words: What Animals Think and Feel* (New York: Henry Holt, 2015), 316.
[71] Psyche's Hebrew name was "Chaika," but brother Morrie, at age two, couldn't pronounce the name correctly, instead calling her Sighkee. The name, written as "Psyche," stuck, though long ago, a school teacher of Psyche's struggled to pronounce it, deciding finally, believe it or not, on "Pasichey."
[72] Noah Strycker, *The Thing with Feathers* (New York: Riverhead Books, 2014), 41.
[73] Strycker, 193.
[74] Jared Diamond, quoted in Eleanor Wachtel, *Original Minds*, 226-227.
[75] Loren Eiseley, "The Judgment of the Birds," *Eiseley: Collected Essays on Evolution, Nature, and the Cosmos* (New York: Literary Classics of the United States, 2016), 110.

CHAPTER 10 / HOW TO KEEP A COMMONPLACE BOOK

[1] See Barbara Oakley, *A Mind for Numbers: How to Excel at Math and Science* (New York: Random House, 2014).
[2] *E. M. Forster Commonplace Book*. Philip Gardner, ed. (Stanford, CA: Stanford University Press, 1985), 224.
[3] Cecilia Watson, *Semicolon: The Past, Present, and Future of a Misunderstood Mark* (New York: HarperCollins, 2019), 103.
[4] Robert M. Sapolsky, *Behave: The Biology of Humans at Our Best and Worst* (New York: Penguin, 2017), 688.
[5] Quoted by Joan Borysenko in her book *Fire in the Soul: A New Psychology of Spiritual Optimism* (New York: Warner Books, 1993), 38.
[6] 1970s American film by Arthur Penn; based on the 1964 novel *Little Big Man* by Thomas Berger.
[7] Louise Penny, *The Madness of Crowds* (Three Pines Creations / New York: St. Martin's Press, 2021), 436.

***

CPSIA information can be obtained
at www.ICGtesting.com
Printed in the USA
BVHW050930120822
644443BV00007B/163

9 781778 224904